JOURNEY INTO JOY

Also available by Brendan Kennelly

The Penguin Book of Irish Verse (Penguin, 1970; 2nd edition 1981)
The Boats Are Home (Gallery Press, 1980)
Cromwell (Beaver Row, 1983; Bloodaxe Books, 1987)
Moloney Up and At It (Mercier Press, 1984)
Mary (Aisling Press, 1987)
Landmarks of Irish Drama (Methuen, 1988)
Love of Ireland: Poems from the Irish (Mercier Press, 1989)
A Time for Voices: Selected Poems 1960-1990 (Bloodaxe Books, 1990)
The Book of Judas (Bloodaxe Books, 1991)
Medea (Bloodaxe Books, 1992)
Breathing Spaces: Early Poems (Bloodaxe Books, 1992)
Between Innocence and Peace: Favourite Poems of Ireland
    (Mercier Press, 1993)
The Trojan Women (Bloodaxe Books, 1993)

AS CO-EDITOR

*Ireland's Women: Writing Past and Present,*with Katie Donovan
    & A. Norman Jeffares (Kyle Cathie/Gill & Macmillan, 1994)
Dublines, with Katie Donovan (Bloodaxe Books, 1994)

ESSAYS ON BRENDAN KENNELLY

Dark Fathers into Light: Brendan Kennelly, edited by Richard Pine
    Bloodaxe Critical Anthologies: 2 (Bloodaxe Books, 1994)

BRENDAN KENNELLY

Journey into Joy

SELECTED PROSE

EDITED BY ÅKE PERSSON

BLOODAXE BOOKS

Essays & selection copyright © Brendan Kennelly 1994
Introduction copyright © Åke Persson 1994
Notes copyright © Brendan Kennelly & Åke Persson 1994

ISBN: 1 85224 209 4 hardback edition
1 85224 210 8 paperback edition

First published 1994 by
Bloodaxe Books Ltd,
P.O. Box 1SN,
Newcastle upon Tyne NE99 1SN.

Bloodaxe Books Ltd acknowledges
the financial assistance of Northern Arts.

Cover printing by J. Thomson Colour Printers Ltd, Glasgow.

Printed in Great Britain by
Bell & Bain Limited, Glasgow, Scotland.

For Derry & Jeanne Jeffares

Contents

PREFACE

Looking at these essays written over a period of some thirty years I'm inclined to smile at the cocky quality of some of them, especially the early pieces. Some, not all. Wanting to persuade someone of something is, I think, a reason for this. There are also these curious moments when whole-hearted enthusiasm boils over into a clumsy, urgent, unintended arrogance. On the other hand, better to annoy, even enrage, than to make yawn. The burning convictions of youth are perhaps the raw material of the sceptical uncertainties, not without their own intensity, of later years. These two kinds of mental and emotional life make for different kinds of criticism which are, nevertheless, intricately connected. It's not a matter of diminished passion for writing of various kinds, it's rather a sense that a deepening experience of this battered, cruel, stupid, fascinating world makes writing itself at once more hypnotic and impoverished than before, more striking now for the sad honesty of its inadequacy than for its world-changing potential. Why should one presume to expect so much of it? Why is one so slow to admit its intrinsic poverty (no matter how clever or 'stimulating' people are in talking or writing about it), its abiding limitations, within which generations of youngsters are 'educated'? Why can I only grudgingly concede that what is considered by many of the most articulate members of our society to be 'moving', 'beautiful', 'skilled', 'profound', 'important', 'accomplished', 'ultimately affirmative' is, in fact, pretty impotent, useless, an elegant, feeble straw in the wind? The sneer on a terrorist's face may be an answer. One sufficiently destructive moment can wipe out a century's devoted effort. And violence works. Murder works. Terrorism works. Let's clarify that. Then why do we continue to dare presume to expect so much of literature? I don't ask this out of disappointment or sadness but out of a recognition that literature plays little or no part in planting compassion where it is most needed, has little or no effect on people who set out to destroy other people. It may chronicle them but it won't change them. This leads me to ask: what effect does it have on oneself, after several decades' immersion in it? Not a great deal, I suspect. (But this tendency not to lie automatically to oneself may well be one of its deepest consequences.) Reading and re-reading writers one admires tends to make one bored with one's own dishonesty, a dishonesty that is often deepened and polished by education. It is possible that the study of accuracy may lead one to wish to be more accurate with oneself in matters of, for example, self-knowledge, an effective measure against the dominance of fear in the heart and in a society where fear shapes more policies, ambitions and structures than we care to recognise. Part of the journey into joy is in witnessing the accuracy and courage with which other people reveal their experiences of this world. The push of a writer's whole being towards candid precision rooted, perhaps, in an impulse to celebrate the scattered bits and pieces that constitute all our lives, may well be an answer to the sneer on a terrorist's face. Better still, perhaps, to immortalise the sneer itself.

The criticism I would like to write now would be rooted in this attentive witnessing of the efforts of others to mould something new and shapely out of days and nights of casually battered consciousness. The violence we do to ourselves, frequently under the name of 'responsibility', leads inevitably to the violence we inflict on others and on the world. The worst violence, perhaps, is lies. Literature, so often accredited with being concerned with truth, is fascinated by lies and remains faithful to its compulsion to explore their workings, their universality, their necessity and their style. Criticism is the anatomy of that fascination and that faithfulness. I believe that the fascinated wonder out of which literature is born, which haunts its making and pervades its finished state, necessitates the detachment that makes possible the sense of justice in the act of criticism. People who are capable of being fair-minded are usually cool customers.

I wish to thank Åke Persson for his scholarship, care and industry in producing this book. It wouldn't have existed without him.

BRENDAN KENNELLY

INTRODUCTION

1

It is tempting to say that, in Ireland, Brendan Kennelly does not need any introduction, as he is known far beyond the academic and literary institutions. People know that he is a poet, and he is recognised from his numerous appearances in the media, since he is a frequent guest on arts shows, chat-shows and debates on current affairs. He is a regular contributor to the Irish national newspapers, and more recently he has done TV and radio commercials.

Brendan Kennelly has, then, a high profile in contemporary Irish society, and together with fellow-poet Paul Durcan, he is arguably the most popular reciter of poetry in Ireland, firmly believing that the study of literature is far too important to be taken over by the academic élite alone. Furthermore, his poetry is written in an accessible language, not embarrassed to deal with apparently small, trivial and everyday matters, yet simultaneously addressing large and urgent issues, both private and public, thus speaking to a broad spectrum of the Irish public.

The fact that he is able to attract large crowds to readings and lectures is evidence of his popularity, but despite this popularity he has, until quite recently, received relatively little recognition by the literary establishment. This non-recognition could perhaps be *because* of his popularity, since Kennelly in the late 1970s and early 1980s created a popular personal myth of flamboyance and decadence, which has possibly helped to obscure his importance as a writer. As a poet, he has frequently (before *Cromwell*) been dismissed with assessments such as 'one comes away from much of Kennelly's poetry with a feeling that its air of passionate engagement is largely a matter of rhetoric'.[1] Similarly, he is often praised in empty phrases like 'one of the leading contemporary poets in Ireland'. Even less attention has been paid to his critical writings. Therefore, it is the purpose of this introduction to highlight some of the most prominent ideas on which Brendan Kennelly's creative and critical writing is founded.

2

When a poet publishes a work of criticism, for example, a collection of essays on other writers, it is often pointed out that one of the main interests of the work lies in the opportunity it gives the

reader to get inside that particular poet's mind in order to reach a
closer understanding of his/her creative achievements and, similarly,
to move towards an understanding of how the processes of his/her
creative imagination work. When making critical statements, the
writer consciously or unconsciously makes statements on his/her
own works and artistic position. There is little doubt that Kennelly's
critical writing sheds light on his own creative writing, and not
seldom do we get the feeling that Kennelly the poet-critic is reflecting on his own artistic concerns. At the same time, it could be
argued that his creative writing illuminates his critical writing; they
go together, and *should* go together if his views are to be taken
seriously. The result of the two activities is a consistent and coherent
view of literature, its function and principal aims. However, although
the poet Kennelly is always present in the essays, always sensitive
to other writers' attempt to come to terms with various kinds of
suffering and their attempts to express them, Kennelly's critical
voice remains in the foreground.

Kennelly's early essay 'The Heroic Ideal in Yeats's Cuchulain
Plays',[2] which is in fact based on part of his extensive chapter on
Yeats in his first major critical undertaking, his Ph.D. thesis *Modern
Irish Poets and the Irish Epic* (1966),[3] hints at the conviction that
literature is essentially a struggle with the self, a conflict between
voices and forces, which becomes the written work. Later, in his
crucial essay, 'Poetry and Violence', Kennelly re-emphasises that
view, stating that 'The light of poetry often finds its origins in the
darkness of our natures' (36).[4] The constant quest for light and
joy, he argues, must begin with a genuine, often ruthless, dialogue
with the self; and in the act of reading and writing poetry, that
dialogue takes place. 'When we read poetry,' he writes in the same
essay, '*really* read it, we are putting ourselves on trial' (36). The
honest writer, in Kennelly's view, does just that; nothing is sacred
in that kind of self-scrutiny.

As particularly Kavanagh, Yeats and Joyce, but also O'Casey,
are regularly referred to in the essays, it becomes evident that these
writers represent artistic qualities with which Kennelly is prepared
to ally himself. What they share is an ambitious attempt fully to
understand what it means to be a human being, and to offer a clear
artistic expression of their understanding. 'The question "How to
live?"', Kennelly argues in his 'W.B. Yeats: An Experiment in Living',
especially written for this volume, 'becomes increasingly inseparable
from the problem "How to write?"' (244). 'The act of re-writing
words on a page', he continues, 'is inseparable from the conscious,

disciplined re-moulding of the self, that interesting mess which is always capable of being shaped and re-shaped by a vigilant and vigorous imagination' (238). In other words, life shapes writing, writing shapes life. To write becomes a way in which to make sense of life; to live becomes a way in which to write.

This existential approach to literature does not mean that Kennelly constantly points to the innumerable details from a writer's life, although he believes that the person and the life behind the work *are* important. What it does mean, and as the reader will notice, is that he sees literature through life and the often harsh experiences which produced the work. Therefore, life, in all its splendour and in all its ugliness, is frequently referred to in the essays, for instance in 'Seán O'Casey's Journey into Joy':

> To read through his plays – or better still to see them – is to become increasingly aware of O'Casey's reverence for life, his respect and affection for those who add to it, usually by their gaiety, and his savage scorn for those who diminish it, usually by their callous application of the heartless standards of mechanical moralities. (211)

If life and writing are closely connected in a 'consciously experimental' (217) and exploratory outlook on existence, it follows that writing is a celebration of all aspects of life lived and experienced. 'By paying attention', Kennelly philosophises, 'constant attention, poetry discriminates, defines, and celebrates what it discovers' (31). Genuine creative writing, therefore, stems from being emotionally honest when facing the world's horrors and their consequences. 'Irish history is so riddled with violence', Kennelly forcefully argues in 'Poetry and Violence', 'so packed with horrors and persecutions of various kinds, that any significant body of poetry *out* of Ireland *must* take account of both that violence and its consequences' (33). Or, as he writes on Beckett in 'A View of Irish Drama', 'it is never enough for a writer simply to be aware of horror and distress; he must create and communicate his vision of it' (96).

Kennelly's fascination with 'violence and its consequences' reflects one concern to which he returns with increasing intensity, namely the suffering and distress inflicted by forces which are prepared to prevent all aspects of life from being explored. This kind of oppression stifles the search for identity, and could be of a physical nature, like poverty, hunger, bad apartments and bad landlords, or psychological, such as lack of emotional space preventing growth and fulfilment, and pressures from religious institutions, like the spoken and unspoken codes set up and enforced by the Roman Catholic Church. It is that hostile climate, those 'heartless standards of mechanical moralities' (211), Kennelly suggests, which must be challenged and opposed. The writer becomes the one who can and must criticise and offer alternative moralities, individual and collective. In his criticism, Kennelly is sympathetic to writing which attempts to expose pettiness and injustice of all kinds. In 'Patrick Kavanagh's Comic Vision', for example, he compares Kavanagh with Blake, who, Kennelly argues, 'had a disturbing habit of slamming whatever he believed to be hypocritical, phoney, and mediocre. Kavanagh had this quality in terrifying abundance' (111). Kennelly goes on to point to Kavanagh's satires in which the targets are 'Dublin's pretentious poetasters, its bumptious "intellectuals", its complacent middle-class, its vicious sentimentality...' (118). And in the essay 'Satire in Flann O'Brien's *The Poor Mouth*', Kennelly focuses on the effects of extreme poverty and places O'Brien's short novel on the same level as Kavanagh's long poem *The Great Hunger*, and pronounces O'Brien's 'satirical genius [as] equal to that of Swift' (182). More importantly, however, he argues that, similar to Kavanagh, O'Brien's target is 'the pretentious and the ridiculous' and his aim 'the eradication of the pompous and the hypocritical' (186). Yet again, in 'Louis MacNeice: An Irish Outsider', MacNeice's qualities as a social critic in his poetry are pointed out, as he 'has a profound respect for the integrity of the individual and a vehement hatred for the forces which violate that respect' (142). George Moore and Liam O'Flaherty, to mention but two, are other writers articulating the intense protest and confrontation which Kennelly finds necessary and which he is prepared to praise. Much of Moore's writing, Kennelly holds, attacks 'the stultifying influence of the Roman Catholic Church in Ireland' which has developed 'from an inspired love of creation to a resolute distrust of life' (152). Similarly, some of O'Flaherty's short stories are passionate responses to what Kennelly refers to as 'the enemies of Irish freedom' (206), chief among whom are the clergy and and the politicians.

Thus, it is evident that external oppression and rigid, stultifying moral systems, which prevent the individual from growing as a human being, must be challenged and exposed. However, the writer cannot and must not escape exploring his/her own inner feelings and all the hidden selves, all the hidden voices waiting to be heard, nor escape looking 'into the abyss of [one]self ' (233),[5] 'Because poetry is, among other things, an interrogatory art, an art of relentless questioning' (36). One of its principal functions, Kennelly suggests, is to 'disturb, challenge, even threaten' (44) what he describes as 'conventional morality' (42).

This kind of exploration must include the uncomfortable confrontation with the violence in the self. Writers have for long realised the creative potential opened up by channelling their inherent violence into art. So, too, Kennelly, whose poetry frequently depicts violence, for example, killing for survival, cruelties in war, oppression, but also the more subtle forms of violence done to oneself by betraying one's own convictions, and to others, by betraying their trust. Kennelly insists that violence is a strong force behind creativity, and it is worth pointing out that this is the main reason why he has frequently led creative writing work-shops in prisons, since he believes that criminality is misdirected creativity.

Consequently, Kennelly's is an approach to literature which puts emotions in the foreground, rather than intellectuality. 'Poetry', he programmatically states, revealing that he subscribes to Romantic aesthetics, 'pays attention to feelings; and it finds its life in these feelings' (31). Fully supporting and encouraging a literature of feelings, Kennelly seems to admire O'Casey's achievements:

> Any poem or play that ignores or lessens the importance of feeling is to O'Casey an act of artistic perversion, a heartless attempt to turn the theatre into a morgue...It follows from this that O'Casey will try to create a drama in which there is as much "life" and "feeling" as possible. It follows too that he must be fascinated by whatever force or forces cripple or kill this feeling and life. (87-88)

This artistic position does not take kindly to false emotions such as sentimentality; instead, what is sought is a literature which is honest to the writer's emotions and therefore to the reader.

It is striking that a relatively large number of the essays in this collection deal with loneliness, explicitly or implicitly. In Kennelly's own creative writing, this is arguably one of his deepest concerns; his earlier as well as later production represents figures who for various reasons are shut out from society, such as the old, the mad, the handicapped, tinkers, all in one way or another victims of prejudice. In his later production, the best examples are the long poems *Islandman* (1977; 1992) [6] – which is one of the most moving poems by Kennelly so far – and *A Small Light* (1979; 1992).[7] Even in *Cromwell* (1983; 1987) [8] and *The Book of Judas* (1991) [9] loneliness is one of the strongest forces: in *Cromwell*, the whole poem takes place in Buffún's psyche. Buffún's harsh and hellish mental landscape is of Dantesque proportions, but whereas Dante had a friendly guide in his hell, Buffún is alone with his demons. Similarly, *The Book of Judas* is permeated with a sense of isolation and fragmentation, Judas himself being the most emblematic outcast in the Christian tradition.

It would seem inevitable that Kennelly's sensitivity to loneliness is reflected in his criticism. Thus, for instance, he writes warmly about George Moore's explorations of loneliness, arguing that 'An important aspect of Moore's genius is that he continually sees loneliness as an integral part of ordinary life' (147). He even goes further in his praise of Moore, claiming that 'It is not unfair to say that George Moore gave Irish short story writers that theme of human loneliness which has so fascinated their imagination' (145).

By focussing so much on loneliness and detachment and their consequences, Kennelly highlights what is a prominent feature in Irish and Anglo-Irish literature: the inability of relating to and connecting with other people. The Irish *are* great talkers, Kennelly jokes – 'talk (always talk)' (30) – but he also suggests that they do not really communicate, that is, they do not manage to get through to each other. In many of the works discussed in the essays we can find, for example, that it is easier for people to relate to the dead than to the living; we find that lives are lived in the head rather than in a daily interaction with others; we find disruptions and betrayals of relationships; we find utter isolation and a sense that communication with other people is completely impossible; we find a strong feeling of imprisonment, both in the self and more physically in crippled bodies, in the prison of marriage without divorce, and occasionally in actual prisons. This kind of isolation is a tragic state, bordering on madness, especially if the individual is conscious of his/her situation. Kennelly almost seems to suggest that the Irish and Irish society are mad, or at least not very far from it. 'In both Moore and Joyce', he argues in 'George Moore's Lonely Voices', 'one of the chief effects of a fully realised loneliness is the brutal moment of self-knowledge that is merciless and complete' (146). The writings of Synge, O'Casey, Joyce, Kavanagh, Beckett and Behan, again to mention but a few, all deal with human isolation, where people suffer and endure in an anonymous existence and where they are forced to live with lost illusions and unfulfilled dreams and ambitions and a strong tragic sense of 'what-might-have-been'.

Furthermore, in 'Louis MacNeice: An Irish Outsider', he comments that 'To some extent, every poet is an outsider, almost by definition' (137). As with his emphasis on a literature of feelings, this view of the writer's position in society has Romantic overtones, and it is not unusual that it is the tension between being an outsider not participating in everyday human activities and the strong wish to break down that sense of isolation which produces literary works. Kavanagh, Joyce, Yeats and Mahon offer keys to an understanding

of what kind of outsidership Kennelly has in mind. Kavanagh's
artistic aim was to be 'utterly himself' (112), which in turn, Kennelly
suggests, originated in his distancing himself from the world; in
that act of detachment, Kennelly proposes, Kavanagh found 'sanity,
and therefore...the rare ability to see things as they are' (124). Joyce's
uncompromising self-exploration and total refusal to accept established norms, moral and otherwise, made him seek what Kennelly
calls an 'unsupported spiritual life, the unscaffolded spiritual life'
(221), interpreted by many of his contemporaries as 'non-belief'
(221). However, in seeking 'the loneliness and mystery and rich
potential of language itself' (221), Joyce instead showed his 'urgent
commitment' (218) to his art and to finding an '*unsupported* perspective on the casual loneliness of men and women' (221). Yeats
represents to Kennelly a similar artistic stance, as Yeats, too, in
his 'experiment in living'[10] sought an absolute integrity, a 'pursuit
of isolationism, [a] conscious removal of himself and his art from
"ordinary" people' (232).

It is an attitude to life and art which has its roots in a firm unwillingness to trust established moral, political, cultural or any
other authorities which, if allowed, would frustrate all attempts to
explore life and the self, 'to make oneself human'. Central to this
stance, therefore, is scepticism, and in 'Derek Mahon's Humane
Perspective', Kennelly points to both MacNeice's and Mahon's
insistence on seeing alternatives; the older poet, he argues, '*is a source
of alternatives*, another way of seeing, another way of experiencing.
MacNeice perceives, tolerates, cherishes and celebrates *difference*'
(128; emphasis BK). In Mahon's poetry, scepticism manifests itself
in 'words at war within themselves, or at least in argument with
each other' (129), but also in 'peripheral appreciation': 'There is',
Kennelly suggests, 'something in his art which is peripheral, watchful, measured, spectatorial, ardently uninvolved, articulately sidelined...It gives it, in fact, the authority of a certain kind of distance,
a certain intellectual chastity...' (131).

3

Emotional honesty is the true sign of a good writer, Kennelly
insists. If 'mechanical moralities' are to be resisted and replaced
by alternative moralities, 'conscience, scrupulously examined' (132)
becomes the serious writer's principal concern. Writing produced
by that kind of minute examination, also referred to in 'James Joyce's
Humanism' as an 'articulate contact with self' (220), will almost
inevitably, Kennelly believes, be candid. Reflecting on the idea that

clarity is essential in the act of meaningful communication, Kennelly
relies on Ibsen's dictum that 'Poetry is a court of judgement on
the soul' [11] and articulates his own credo:

> I believe he was talking about the merciless retribution exacted by lan-
> guage on moments of sloppiness, lazy imprecision, emotional evasiveness,
> bombast and rhetorical pomposity. Such moments are in all of us but
> the writing of poetry tends to emphasise the need to be precise…Are
> there not moments when the mind betrays the heart, the heart the mind,
> in such a way that we may increasingly try to convince ourselves that
> a manageable emotional fog, a viable confusion, is the least disturbing
> way to live? The unsettling clarities of poetry are a constant challenge
> to that way of thinking… (244)

Commenting on Flann O'Brien's achievement in *The Poor Mouth*,
Kennelly claims that O'Brien's 'love of verbal precision is the expression of an essentially moral imagination' and continues: 'Cliché
is not only the truth worn dull by repetition; it can also be a form of
immoral evasion, a refusal to exercise the mind at a moment when
it should be exercised, even to one's own discomfort or distress' (184).

There is no doubt that Kennelly supports a literature of lucidity
and simplicity, in language and style as well as in vision and ideas;
'obscurity', he polemically argues in 'Patrick Kavanagh's Comic
Vision', 'is simply a failure of the poet's imagination, a sanctuary of
the inadequate' (112). Not surprisingly, Kavanagh, Joyce and Yeats
once again represent the writer's search for candour. In Kavanagh's
case, it is a search for 'simplicity' (112). It is a simplicity, Kennelly
further proposes, 'that stems from a totally coherent and lucid
vision…only the man who sees completely can be completely simple'
(112). Joyce's ruthless insistence on self-exploration and on a 'denial
of support' (229) results in similar creative heights. Echoing his statements on O'Brien, Kennelly reaffirms the idea that morality and
candour are strongly connected, as Joyce's 'morality is a morality
of candour. The candid heart speaks for itself' (224); his 'white,
glistening style', furthermore, 'reflects the soul's wish to be candid'
(224). Another example of praiseworthy clarity is Yeats, whose works
reflect an 'urgent need for emotional precision', a 'constant attempt
to be accurate about what he feels and thinks [which] has to do with
the knowledge that any kind of dishonesty in poetry is ruthlessly
avenged by language itself' (244)

However, it would be too simplistic to argue that self-scrutiny
is automatically followed by clarity. For example, a writer much
admired by Kennelly for his courage to face inner conflicts is Joseph
Plunkett, whom he describes as 'probably the least known of the
Rising poets' (103). Kennelly defends Plunkett's poetic achievements

and to a certain extent moves away from the established notion that he is 'a poet of promise [rather] than of achievement' (103). 'Plunkett', Kennelly argues, 'is at his best when he is making a decisive statement, arrived at through a deliberate choice made as a result of inner conflict...[which] sweeps vagueness and imprecision aside...' (105). Kennelly admits, however, that Plunkett's inner struggle does not always lead to clarity, but very often to the opposite, and claims that he is 'frequently confused and obscure...often guilty of vagueness, ragged diction, feeble poeticisms, strained imagery, ineffectual use of symbols, cumbersome inversions' (104). These aspects, Kennelly suggests, are due both to the sense that 'his mystical experiences overwhelm his power of articulation' and to the fact that 'his technical ability is simply incapable of communicating what is genuinely felt' (104). Nevertheless, despite Plunkett's weaknesses, Kennelly defends the poet's attempts, and, because they aim at honesty, prefers them to what he labels 'superficial clarities' (104).

4

Brendan Kennelly's essays reveal two dominant aspects of Irish and Anglo-Irish literature: firstly, an obsession with isolation and detachment, and secondly, a search for clarity. But there emerges a third important aspect which has to do with the function of literature, namely its insistence on hope and joy. In 'Seán O'Casey's Journey into Joy', Kennelly argues that 'There is an intriguing tendency common to some of the most interesting Irish writers... we might describe this tendency as a journey into joy'. It is a journey which involves the 'transfiguration of experience, through language, into works of art, which, because their livingness derives from their attempt to understand and express the nature of suffering, become, in themselves, images of joy' (209). Thus, someone who is close to suffering is potentially also close to gaiety and laughter, and paradoxically it is sometimes the very suffering which makes writers and others more strongly aware of beauty and which makes them celebrate the small, everyday wonders. Kennelly perceives this tendency in writers who are intensely aware of the hardships of the human condition and points to the group of Yeats, Joyce, O'Casey and Kavanagh, but also to Moore and O'Brien, and, in 'Irish Poetry Since Yeats', to Austin Clarke and Paul Durcan. What they all share, in Kennelly's opinion, is a comic outlook on life, a kind of 'comic vision' (109), as in the case of Kavanagh. O'Casey, for example, has, Kennelly suggests, 'an awareness that even in moments of the most savage cynicism, compassion should be allowed its life; an adamant, agile refusal to dwell too long in sorrow' (213). This philosophy celebrates the small wonders of the ordinary, everyday world, and it includes giving an identity to the underdog. By creating a space for 'ordinary' people and activities, love for a forgotten and neglected creation is shown; the writer laughs with the world as well as at it, and it is the laughter of someone who has come to terms with existence, at least temporarily.

There is no denying that part of the process of moving from sorrow to joy is therapeutic: honestly confronting the nature of suffering could mean that the writer will come out at the other end of the darkness, liberated from it. Because it is therapeutic it is a journey into self-discovery, and because it is a journey into self-discovery it is also a journey into clarity of vision and joy. The reader is invited on this journey, and because the writer is honestly representing the complexities of life, as in, for example, O'Casey's plays, the experience for the reader is cathartic. Interestingly, Kennelly openly distances himself from modern critical theory, provocatively expressing his dismay over 'boring, arid theories about poetry, theories often expressed in language that is pedantic and leaden' (238). Nevertheless, articulating his belief in poetry as experience, he states that

> one of the most valuable abilities of poetry [is that] it extends the reader, sometimes against his or her will. This extension of tolerant awareness can be inspired by poetry that is insulting, outrageous, boorish, deliberately provocative; or by poetry that is serene, reflective, peaceful. What matters is the change, however temporary, in the reader. (233)

By taking that position, Kennelly comes close to some theories in relatively recent reader-response criticism, theories which, Jane P. Tompkins points out, are 'therapeutic' and which aim at 'leading to fuller knowledge of the self and even to self-creation'. Their 'practical goal', Tompkins continues, is 'to achieve knowledge of the self, of its relation to other selves, to the world, and to human knowledge in general'. Consequently, the literary work is not viewed as an object but as an experience.[12] Thus, by accepting the invitation to join in, the reader is taken to a new perspective, via ugliness, violence and loneliness. But for him/her, too, self-discovery, clarity of vision and joy are at the end of the process. Commenting on Kavanagh's insistence on transforming suffering into 'gaiety', Kennelly programmatically states: 'That, I believe, is what genuine art is all about. Millstones becoming stars' (209).

5

Written over a period of almost thirty years, Brendan Kennelly's essays in this volume deal with twentieth century Irish writers (except in the first part of the essay 'A View of Irish Poetry') and focus on these writers' attempts to come to terms with violence, suffering, loneliness, history, myth, the tragic, the comic, the function of literature.

The broad scope shows not only Kennelly's sensitivity to complex and multi-layered problems of Irish life, which most works treated in the essays deal with; it also shows his deep insight into how some of the greatest creative minds in Ireland have worked, what their obsessions have been and what they have aimed for in their art. The writers focused on are, admittedly, exclusively from the male Irish canon, although Kennelly is eager to open up the canon to include the radical voices of women writers. In 'Irish Poetry Since Yeats', and indeed elsewhere,[13] he does not hide the significant role played by women, 'whose work', he believes, 'has brought a new wave of excitement into Irish writing' (58). He particularly points to the achievement of Eavan Boland, but also to that of Medbh McGuckian, Nuala Ní Dhomhnaill and Paula Meehan, to name but a few. What they have in common, Kennelly argues, is 'a defiant, dignified sense of creating their own forms of independence' (65), and he predicts that 'Poetry by Irish women will...elicit...strong responses in the future' (65).

For obvious reasons, the largest number of the essays deal with poetry, although Kennelly is increasingly interested in the stage as an expression of conflicts and the complexities of existence (and it must be remembered that much of his creative writing has strong dramatic elements in it). It should be pointed out that some material was left out of this volume, material which would have shown Kennelly's explorations of other literatures and literary periods, such as a vast body of shorter essays, newspaper articles and reviews, many of which are interesting in their own right but more journalistic in style. Furthermore, there are the many lectures on, for example, modern world drama he has given, and gives, as part of Trinity College courses. These longer and shorter pieces will hopefully see publication in a second volume in a not too distant future.

The majority of the essays included here are out of print, a couple of them were only published abroad, and others in journals with a very limited availability. Two essays, 'Irish Poetry Since Yeats' and 'W.B. Yeats: An Experiment in Living', were especially written for this volume. Kennelly writes about poetry: 'If the poem isn't

shared it's not alive'.[14] In the present work he shares his broad reading experiences and thoughts in searching, undogmatic and warm
analyses which do not go beyond 'the ordinary reader', yet challenge
and provoke long after being read. In short, they are unmistakeably
and uniquely Kennellian.

ÅKE PERSSON

Poetry and Violence

I would like to begin this essay with a poem – a translation into English of a poem originally written in Irish. It is called 'Caoineadh Airt Uí Laoghaire – A Cry for Art O'Leary.' The poem was written by a woman, Eileen O'Connell. It is a cry of grief, of revenge, of love, of hatred, and of a deep, frustrated passion for justice. Art O'Leary was Eileen O'Connell's husband. He was shot by a man named Morris because he refused to sell his horse to Morris for five pounds. According to the 18th century penal law in Ireland, a Catholic had to sell his horse to a protestant, if the protestant asked him, for five pounds or under. O'Leary refused to sell his horse. Morris shot him. Eileen O'Connell composed her *Caoineadh* – her *cry* for her man. I chose this poem because it is a poem about various forms of violence – sexual, religious, political, forms of violence that occur again and again throughout Irish writing. But it is far more than that: here, the woman's passion is fiercely real; this fierce, passionate, violent reality creates the poem's momentum, its primal, driving, driven rhythms. It is, above all, a *cry* – a violent cry, *beyond* words, put *into* words. It intrigues me most of all for the way the woman's violent feelings are somehow changed even as they are expressed in this unrelenting rhythmical momentum.

Remember that the poem is a *cry* – the heart's pure violence, dragged down into language, elevated *by* it, and transfigured *in* it.

A Cry for Art O'Leary
(*from* The Irish of Eibhlin Dubh Ní Chonaill)

My love
The first time I saw you
From the top of the market
My eyes covered you
My heart went out to you
I left my friends for you
Threw away my home for you

What else could I do?

You got the best rooms for me
All in order for me
Ovens burning for me
Fresh trout caught for me
Choice meat for me

In the best of beds I stretched
Till milling-time hummed for me

You made the whole world
Pleasing to me

White rider of love!

I love your silver-hilted sword
How your beaver hat became you
With its band of gold
Your friendly homespun suit
Revealed your body
Your pin of glinting silver
Glittered in your shirt

On your horse in style
You were sensitive pale-faced
Having journeyed overseas
The English respected you
Bowing to the ground
Not because they loved you
But true to their hearts' hate

They're the ones who killed you
Darling of my heart

My lover
My love's creature
Pride of Immokelly
To me you were not dead
Till your great mare came to me
Her bridle dragging ground
Her head with your startling blood
Your blood upon the saddle
You rode in your prime

I didn't wait to clean it
I leaped across my bed
I leaped then to the gate
I leaped upon your mare
I clapped my hands in frenzy
I followed every sign
With all the skill I knew
Until I found you lying
Dead near a furze bush
Without pope or bishop
Or cleric or priest
To say a prayer for you

Only a crooked wasted hag
Throwing her cloak across you

I could do nothing then
In the sight of God
But go on my knees

And kiss your face
And drink your free blood

My man!
Going out the gate
You turned back again
Kissed the two children
Threw a kiss at me
Saying 'Eileen, woman, try
To get this house in order,
Do your best for us
I must be going now
I'll not be home again.'
I thought that you were joking
You my laughing man

My man!
My Art O'Leary
Up on your horse now
Ride out to Macroom
And then to Inchigeela
Take a bottle of wine
Like your people before you
Rise up
My Art O'Leary
Of the sword of love

Put on your clothes
Your black beaver
Your black gloves
Take down your whip
Your mare is waiting
Go east by the thin road
Every bush will salute you
Every stream will speak to you
Men and women acknowledge you

They know a great man
When they set eyes on him

God's curse on you, Morris
God's curse on your treachery
You swept my man from me
The man of my children
Two children play in the house
A third lives in me

He won't come alive from me

My heart's wound
Why was I not with you
When you were shot

That I might take the bullet
In my own body?
Then you'd have gone free
Rider of the grey eye
And followed them
Who'd murdered me

My man!
I look at you now
All I know of a hero
True man with true heart
Stuck in a coffin
You fished the clean streams
Drank nightlong in halls
Among frank-breasted women

I miss you

My man!
I am crying for you
In far Derrynane

In yellow-appled Carren
Where many a horseman
And vigilant woman
Would be quick to join
In crying for you
Art O'Leary
My laughing man

O crying women
Long live your crying
Till Art O'Leary
Goes back to school
On a fateful day
Not for books and music

But for stones and clay

My man!
The corn is stacked
The cows are milking
My heart is a lump of grief
I will never be healed
Till Art O'Leary
Comes back to me

I am a locked trunk
The key is lost
I must wait till rust
Devours the screw

O my best friend
Art O'Leary
Son of Conor
Son of Cadach
Son of Lewis
East from wooded glens
West from girlish hills
Yellow nuts budge from branches
Apples laugh like small suns
As once they laughed
Throughout my girlhood
It is no cause for wonder
If bonfires lit O'Leary country
Close to Ballingeary
Or holy Gougane Barra
After the clean-gripping rider

The robust hunter
Panting towards the kill

Your own hounds lagged behind you
O horseman of the summoning eyes
What happened you last night?
My only whole belief
Was that you could not die
For I was your protection

My heart! My grief!

My man! My darling!

In Cork
I had this vision
Lying in my bed:
A glen of withered trees
A home heart-broken
Strangled hunting-hounds
Choked birds
And you
Dying on a hillside
Art O'Leary
My one man
Your blood running crazily
Over earth and stone

Jesus Christ knows well
I'll wear no cap
No mourning dress
No solemn shoes
No bridle on my horse
No grief-signs in my house
But test instead
The wisdom of the law

I'll cross the sea
To speak to the King
If he ignores me
I'll come back home
To find the man
Who murdered my man
Morris, because of you
My man is dead
Is there a man in Ireland
To put a bullet through your head?

Women, white women of the mill
I give my love to you
For the poetry you made
For Art O'Leary
Rider of the brown mare
Deep women-rhythms of blood
The fiercest and the sweetest
Since time began
Singing of this cry I woman make
For my man

[*translated by Brendan Kennelly*][1]

When one reads a poem like that, I think one is entitled to ask: what do we *do* with the violence of our emotions? And further – how is it that, so frequently, we, as critics, tend to obscure or hide or minimise the violence that is at the heart of such good poetry? Why do we *kill* poetry with intellectual politeness – with fatuous phrases like 'It seems to me', when we should be saying 'I believe'. But even politeness has an ironic violence. You notice that I wrote (unconsciously) that politeness 'kills'. The poet who, in our times, has the reputation of dealing most frontally with violence is the English poet, Ted Hughes. When asked about violence in his poetry, he has this to say:

> When my Aunt calls my verse 'horrible and violent' I know what she means. Because I know what style of life and outlook she is defending. And I know that she is representative of huge numbers of people in England.
> What she has is an idea of what poetry ought to be...a very vague idea, since it's based on an almost total ignorance of what poetry has been written. She has an instinct for a kind of poetry that will confirm the values of her way of life. She finds it in the milder parts of Words-worth if she needs supporting evidence. In a sense, critics who find my poetry violent are in her world, and they are safeguarding her way of life. So to define their use of the word violence any further, you have to work out just why her way of life should find the behaviour of a hawk 'horrible' or any reference to violent death 'disgusting', just as she finds any reference to extreme vehemence of life 'frightening some-

how'. It's a futile quarrel really. It's the same one that Shakespeare
found the fable for in his *Venus and Adonis*. Shakespeare spent his life
trying to prove that Adonis was right, the rational sceptic, the man of
puritan good order. It put him through the tragedies before he decided
that the quarrel could not be kept up honestly. Since then the difficult
task of any poet in English has been to locate the force which Shakespeare
called Venus in his first poems and Sycorax in his last.

Poetry only records these movements in the general life...it doesn't
instigate them. The presence of the great goddess of the primaeval
world, which Catholic countries have managed to retain in the figure
of Mary, is precisely what England seems to have lacked, since the
Civil War...where negotiations were finally broken off. Is Mary violent?
Yet Venus in Shakespeare's poem if one reads between the lines eventu-
ally murdered Adonis...she murdered him because he rejected her. He
was so desensitised, stupefied and brutalised by his rational scepticism,
he didn't know what to make of her. He thought she was an ethical
peril. He was a sort of modern critic in the larval phase...a modern
English critic. A typical modern Englishman. What he calls violence is
a very particular thing. In ordinary criticism it seems to be confused a
lot with another type of violence which is the ordinary violence of our
psychotic democracy...our materialist, non-organic democracy which is
trying to stand up with a bookish theory instead of a skeleton. Every
society has its dream that has to be dreamed, and if we go by what
appears on TV the perpetual tortures and executions there, and the
spectacle of the whole population, not just a few neurotic intellectuals
but the whole mass of the people, slumped every night in front of
their sets...in attitudes of total disengagement, a sort of anaesthetised
unconcern watching their dream reeled off in front of them, if that's
the dream of our society, then we haven't created a society but a hell.
The stuff of pulp fiction supports the idea. We are dreaming a perpetual
massacre.[2]

In this assiduously-created hell, masquerading as a society, modern
England may well be dreaming 'a perpetual massacre', as it sits
content and stupefied before the TV in a trance of symbiotic terror.
The same is true of a good deal of modern Irish life; Ireland is, in
certain respects, as mummified by television violence and soap-
operas as England or any country. But in Ireland the massacre is
not merely dreamed on television; it is *enacted* in the streets of
Derry and Belfast and other places. The horrors of history are alive
and well; and they have always been investigated, brooded on, and
dramatised by Irish poets. Ireland is a small, relatively poor country
– a small, congested place with a lot of hatred in it. There is a
tourists' Ireland: there is a terrorists' Ireland; there is an Ireland
of sentimentality, nostalgia, four green fields, Cathleen ní Houilhan,
patriotic ballads sung in pubs to the musical accompaniment of
Guinness being gulped; an Ireland of image-making, flawless middle-
class Catholic respectability, flawless Protestant politeness with nice

accents and good taste; an Ireland of endless opinions, comments, judgements, talk (always talk), and letters to *The Irish Times* about the first cuckoo of the year, and the last true Republicans of the century.

And there is an Ireland, increasingly, of money, with all the polished, ruthless violence that money can bring; an Ireland, increasingly, of big business and cut-throat competition; an Ireland that is busy burying peasant superstition and practising a new bourgeois style, with all that *that* means and implies. And meanwhile there are bombs in shops, in streets, outside police barracks; there are assassinations and revenge-killings and corrective kneecappings. And there are always the innocent victims of this savage, tireless historical process, this appetite for death. The kind of violence I'm talking about now, the violence engendered by history, is the violence of hatred. Hatred is a dynamic force, a stimulating, animating power. Hatred hates indifference. Hatred loves its own annihilating expression, wiping out distinction between innocent and guilty, adult and child, man and woman. Hatred tolerates no humane hierarchies of kindness, gentleness, affection, considerateness. Hatred sneers at the futility of intellectual subtlety. And hatred is, above all, a devoted servant to a cause. Hatred revels in devotion, in an act of unswerving service to a cause. In serving that cause, whatever it be, hatred is *exemplary* in its attention to its own unshakeable purpose. Yeats captured the situation when he wrote:

> Out of Ireland have we come.
> Great hatred, little room,
> Maimed us at the start.
> I carry from my mother's womb
> A fanatic heart.
>   ('Remorse for Intemperate Speech')[3]

The beat of that fanatic heart can be heard clearly and frequently in Irish poetry. Here is a typical poem about hatred at work. It is by James Simmons. It is a ballad called 'Claudy'. Terrorists leave a car containing bombs, in a village. They go to a nearby town to telephone a warning. The phone doesn't work. The consequences are horrific. Good poetry captures *consequences*.

Claudy
(for Harry Barton, a song)

> The Sperrins surround it, the Faughan flows by,
> at each end of Main Street the hills and sky,
> the small town of Claudy at ease in the sun
> last July in the morning, a new day begun.

How peaceful and pretty if the moment could stop,
McIlhenny is straightening things in his shop,
and his wife is outside serving petrol, and then
a child takes a cloth to a big window-pane.

And McCloskey is taking the weight off his feet,
and McClelland and Miller are sweeping the street,
and, delivering milk at the Beaufort Hotel,
young Temple's enjoying his first job quite well.

And Mrs McLaughlin is scrubbing her floor,
and Artie Hone's crossing the street to a door,
and Mrs Brown, looking around for her cat,
goes off up an entry – what's strange about that?

Not much – but before she comes back to the road
that strange car parked outside her house will explode,
and all of the people I've mentioned outside,
will be waiting to die or already have died.

An explosion too loud for your eardrums to bear,
and young children squealing like pigs in the square,
and all faces chalk-white and streaked with bright red,
and the glass and the dust and the terrible dead.

For an old lady's legs are ripped off, and the head
of a man's hanging open, and still he's not dead.
He is screaming for mercy, and his son stands and stares
and stares, and then suddenly, quick, disappears.

And Christ! little Katherine Aikin is dead,
and Mrs McLaughlin is pierced through the head.
Meanwhile to Dungiven the killers have gone,
and they're finding it hard to get through on the phone.[4]

Lying under the increasingly bland surfaces of Irish life, are various degrees of pathological hatred.

At this point, I would like to say that I believe that poetry is the language of the heart, shaped, directed, controlled, moulded and ordered by its colleague, the sympathetic, vigilant and discriminating intelligence. Poetry pays attention to feelings; and it finds its life in these feelings. By paying attention, constant attention, poetry discriminates, defines, and celebrates what it discovers. Poetry, like hatred, is therefore a kind of education, demanding dedication. But where poetry is the language of the heart in all its human vacillation and uncertainty, hatred is the language (word language or bomb-language or gun-language) – the language of the heartless in all its stamina and unfeeling devotion. A person in love is potentially happy, or, potentially, a victim; a person in hate is unquestionably beyond such possibility of fulfilment or vulnerability. A person in

hate becomes the instrument of his hatred. His heart is a stone.
And yet it could be argued that political and historical changes
have been brought about by the stony-hearted. So any poem about
this *kind* of violence must confront this problem, this contradiction:
change, the sort of change that brings about new civilizations with,
perhaps, accompanying great works of art, admired by the sensitive,
analysed by structuralists and deconstructionists in a formal, sophisticated idiom – that sort of change is often brought about by men
and women who have precious little time for the sweet fruits of
civilization, the consolations of poetry, the challenges and comforts
of art. At the roots of good taste lies barbarism. In museums reposes
evidence of murder and massacres; enthroned kings and popes rule
and advise, pronounce and pontificate, to a background of blood.
Yeats put it cogently:

> Some violent bitter man, some powerful man
> Called architect and artist in, that they,
> Bitter and violent men, might rear in stone
> The *sweetness* that all longed for night and day,
> The *gentleness* none there had ever known...
>
> ('Meditation in Time of Civil War: I', 225; emphasis BK)

Violence is the begetter of sweetness and gentleness. Murderous
disorder is often the source of that beautiful, unruffled self-possession
and order which are associated with style.

   Men with fanatical political causes embody this contradiction; they,
the agents of change, are driven by a purpose that cannot change.
The most interesting parts of Yeats's poem 'Easter 1916' debate
this problem of change and unchangingness. Yeats cannot solve it.
His moral intelligence as a person is repelled by what his imagination
senses to be brutally true. The law of nature, or the law of God,
is the law of change. In Dublin, Yeats knew men whose lives were
devoted to radical change. He saw these people as 'Hearts with one
purpose alone'. All around them, everything changes in nature,

> Hearts with one purpose alone
> Through summer and winter seem
> Enchanted to a stone
> To trouble the living stream.
> The horse that comes from the road,
> The rider, the birds that range
> From cloud to tumbling cloud,
> Minute by minute they change;
> A shadow of cloud on the stream
> Changes minute by minute;
> A horse-hoof slides on the brim,
> And a horse plashes within it;

> The long-legged moor-hens dive,
> And hens to moor-cocks call;
> Minute by minute they live:
> The stone's in the midst of all... (204)

Creatures that live from 'minute to minute' consciously or unconsciously partake of the universal changes that never cease, either
within or outside them. But if the heart's a stone, what price change?
Yeats says of the revolutionaries that they may have been bewildered
by 'excess of love'. He does not, in this poem, speak of hatred –
and this is, I think, one of the poem's shortcomings. This evasiveness in the poem helps to account for its flag-waving, rhetorical
conclusion. He *does* begin to explore the situation created by the
fact that

> Too long a sacrifice
> Can make a stone of the heart.
> O when may it suffice? (204)

but the poem swerves away from that question and from further
exploration with

> ...enough
> To know they dreamed and are dead... (204)

Well, yes, they dreamed. And they acted too. And they set in motion
these changes that have helped to produce a small, modern country.
But did not that 'excess of love' (if it *was* such, or such *only*) also
lead to, or point the way towards, *both* the new middle-class Irish
society, *and* the 'Northern Troubles', as that warfare is called. The
stony-heartedness that resists change within itself, *because* its sole
purpose is change in society, becomes part of the forces that it helps
to unleash. It has its own messianism. That messianism may, generations later, pick up willing disciples and devotees. In fact, such
discipleship is inevitable, so that the unborn will be burdened, in
their time, with the responsibilities of the 'stony heart'. Irish history
is so riddled with violence, so packed with horrors and persecutions
of various kinds, that any significant body of poetry *out* of Ireland
must take account of both that violence and its consequences.

A contemporary poet, Michael Longley, looks at history, and
sees wounds, the wounds of people, the wounds of history. Longley
is a Northern Unionist; his father fought for the English, with the
Ulster Division, at the Somme. His father survived that war, and
died later when his wounds turned to cancer. Longley links his
father's death and burial with the burial of three young English
soldiers, and the death of a bus-conductor, murdered by a youngster,
a teenager, as the family prepared to watch television, after supper.

I choose this poem, 'Wounds', because it depicts the consequences in a atmosphere of domestic normality. A boy, become the instrument of history's blind hatred, *kills*, because he himself is both victim and instrument. This poem is a striking example of the grotesque normality of that violence which is the consequence of previous violence which is itself the consequence of previous violence – and so on. What is appalling is the reader's realisation of something about the very nature of violence – that is, its fertility, its spawning, helpless fertility, endlessly begetting itself in infinite form, like a demented Proteus.

Wounds

Here are two pictures from my father's head –
I have kept them like secrets until now:
First, the Ulster Division at the Somme
Going over the top with 'Fuck the Pope!'
'No Surrender!': a boy about to die,
Screaming 'Give 'em one for the Shankill!'
'Wilder than Gurkhas' were my father's words
Of admiration and bewilderment.
Next comes the London-Scottish padre
Resettling kilts with his swagger-stick,
With a stylish backhand and a prayer.
Over a landscape of dead buttocks
My father followed him for fifty years.
At last, a belated casualty,
He said – lead traces flaring till they hurt –
'I am dying for King and Country, slowly.'
I touched his hand, his thin head I touched.

Now, with military honours of a kind,
With his badges, his medals like rainbows,
His spinning compass, I bury beside him
Three teenage soldiers, bellies full of
Bullets and Irish beer, their flies undone.
A packet of Woodbines I throw in,
A lucifer, the Sacred Heart of Jesus
Paralysed as heavy guns put out
The night-light in a nursery for ever;
Also a bus-conductor's uniform –
He collapsed beside his carpet-slippers
Without a murmur, shot through the head
By a shivering boy who wandered in
Before they could turn the television down
Or tidy away the supper dishes.
To the children, to a bewildered wife,
I think 'Sorry Missus' was what he said. [5]

What is 'civilised' in us must condemn violence, as leaders of governments do with predictable clichés and platitudes. These do not diminish the sincerity of leaders; but they *do* emphasise the ready-to-hand slogan-like quality of their condemnations, as if leaders sensed something hollow in their own rhetoric of condemnation. If what is 'civilised' in us must condemn, what is exploratory and creative in us must enquire and ponder.

What *is* violence?

As I write this essay the ink from my pen is violating the whiteness of the paper. When I eat, I know (usually) that a creature had to be killed so that my stomach may be satisfied. Beautiful, and unbeautiful, women are often wrapped in the skins of several animals. Men, women and children *walk*, their feet cosily wrapped in death. If, as a teacher, one plants an idea in a student's mind that may be partly responsible for, say, a gesture or act or word from that person which may cause hurt to another, is one violating that person? How much violence is there in education? How many victims of intellectual rape are there in Universities? How much 'happy' home-life depends on silent and silently, mutually agreed on, forms of violence? How violent are so-called passive women? What violence lies in Daddy's concern, his future-moulding concern for his son? How much are children violated by parents, parents by children? What violence begins to be born in us when we are too embarrassed or bland or indifferent to confront the problem of violence in ourselves? And can the 'struggle for control' lead to *other* forms of violence? Above all, perhaps, what violence is there in our *desire* to possess – to possess houses, cars, jobs, each other? One thing is sure - the violence engendered in us as a result of discovery and admission is less damaging than the violence, frequently disguised as morality, engendered in us when we lie to ourselves. That is why the poetry of recognition and admission, no matter how clumsy or awkward, must always be preferable to the poetry of stylish evasion. There are many examples of both *kinds* of poem in the work of the same poet. Yeats, Ireland's greatest poet, is a good example. When Yeats is *talking* about being noble or candid or dignified or distinguished or vaguely aristocratic or honest (God help us!) then I prefer to think that Yeats is – just talking. But, in the next poem or the next breath, Yeats can *admit* the violence in his nature, and, without mentioning a word about candour and honesty, he wins our hearts with his honesty and candour.

> You think it horrible that lust and rage
> Should dance attention upon my old age:

> They were not such a plague when I was young.
> What else have I to spur me into song?
>
> ('The Spur', 359)

There, in a nutshell, is the core of the matter. The imagination of a man or a woman can be *nourished* by the same violent feelings and forces which would most likely repel that same man or woman in his or her attempts to live an ordinary, decent life. The light of poetry often finds its origin in the darkness of our natures. It is no wonder at all that Plato banished poets from his ideal republic. Or so my classical friends tell me.

Because poetry is, among other things, an interrorgatory art, an art of relentless questioning. Ibsen called poetry 'a court of judgment on the soul':[6] when we read poetry, *really* read it, we are putting ourselves on trial. Do some people relegate poetry to the level of mere entertainment, or consolatory escapism, precisely because the close, intense study of it can result in a brutal state of self-revelation? So we condemn what we are prepared to confront.

Because Irish life has so many *kinds* of violence in it, Irish poets have responded in a great variety of ways. So far, I have, for the most part, concentrated on *public* manifestations of violence, and their consequences. Public institutions and the lives of private individuals meet in ways both obvious and subtle. In Ireland, the most powerful single institution is the Roman Catholic Church. Over 95% of the population are Catholic. The Church is omnipresent, omniscient, and, apparently, omnipotent in Ireland. It is a predominantly *male* institution, though there are nuns everywhere. Only recently have Irish women begun to show any defiance against the church; women were content, or *seemed* content, to go along with the fact and the implications of male domination. No divorce! No contraception! Sexual pleasure, outside of marriage, is a sin! Even *within* marriage, the purpose of sex is the begetting of children. And this *must* be the purpose – even if the mother is ill. Serious illness is no excuse. Many Irish women have died because of this kind of tyrannical, male-clerical thinking.

The Irish poet who most confronted and demonstrated this kind of tyranny is Austin Clarke. His autobiography *Twice Round the Black Church* is a stirring account of his own experience in the Catholic Church, and of his life when he left it. In this passage, for example, he describes his first confession at the age of seven. What we witness is a clerical assault on a child's consciousness.

> At seven I made my first confession. I cannot remember how and when I was prepared for the sacrament of penance. No doubt I conned the

penny catechism in class and learned the sixth commandment, which
forbids all looks, words and actions against the virtue of chastity, speech
with bad companions, improper dances, immodest company keeping
and indecent conversation. In eager anticipation I set forth, proud of
having now attained to the theological age of reason and in awe, knowing
that the confessor was the visible representative of Christ. I went up
Mountjoy Street that morning on our side of the street, past the Protestant
orphanage, Wellington Street corner, and glanced up at the big clock
over the public house.

In Berkeley Road chapel, I read the name of Father O'Callaghan
over a confessional and, kneeling down, waited till the last penitents
had left. Then I opened the side door on the left of the confessional
and found myself in the narrow dark recess and, in a minute, the panel
was drawn back. I told my little tale of fibs, disobedience and loss of
temper and then Father O'Callaghan bent towards the grille and asked
me a strange question which puzzled me for I could not understand it.
He repeated the question and as I was still puzzled he proceeded to
explain in detail and I was disturbed by a sense of evil. I denied everything but he did not believe me and, as I glanced up at the grille, his
great hooknose and fierce eyes filled me with fear. Suddenly the panel
closed and I heard Father O'Callaghan coming out of the confession
box. He opened the side door and told me to follow him to the vestry.
I did so, bewildered by what was happening. He sat down, told me to
kneel and once more repeated over and over his strange question, asking me if I had ever made myself weak. The examination seemed to
take hours though it must have been only a few minutes. At last, in
fear and desperation, I admitted to the unknown sin. I left the church,
feeling that I had told a lie in my first confession and returned home
in tears but, with the instinct of childhood, said nothing about it to
my mother.[7]

That little drama begins in a confession-box. One can feel there,
in that poem, the *power* of the priest over the child. And that power
breeds in the child a sense of evil. And so it was, and often still *is*,
not only with priests and children, but with priests and women. I
would like to comment on a poem by Austin Clarke which presents
a woman going to confession, to a Redemptorist priest, a missioner.
She tells him it is ten months since the birth of her last child. The
Redemptorist priest says this is a sin; and he cannot forgive her
until she conceives again. She protests a little, but in vain. She goes
home, her husband makes love to her that Saturday night, she
conceives, she dies giving birth. It is a simple, frightening parable
of the power of priests over women; of the violence done by an
institution against a single, fragile, vulnerable woman. And this
poem is also an excellent illustration of the kind of poem that Austin
Clarke perfected – imagistic, anecdotal, making use of dialogue and
brief, vivid, effective moments of characterisation. The poem is, in
effect, a little drama, a small play in a confession-box as a result

of which the woman dies and the priest goes on his proud, powerful way, self-inflated with rhetoric and images of hell-fire. One gets in this poem a sense of the male conspiracy between priest and husband which has always been strong in Ireland. It is the *woman* who suffers as a result of the violence implicit in the 'morality' of the institution of which she is a member, and in the doctrines of which she, presumably, believes. The violence done to her, her actual death, is brought about by the very fact of her belief. One wonders how many women have died because of their sincerity.

There is a reference in this poem to Adam and Eve's; it is a church in Dublin. The poem is entitled 'The Redemptorist.' It is important to realise that the dialogue takes place in the extremely *quiet* privacy of the confessional.

The Redemptorist

'How many children have you?' asked
The big Redemptorist.
                     'Six, Father.'
                              'The last,
When was it born?'
                             'Ten months ago.'
'I cannot absolve your mortal sin
Until you conceive again. Go home,
Obey your husband.'
                    She whimpered:
                           'But
The doctor warned me...'
                    Shutter became
Her coffin lid. She twisted her thin hands
And left the box.
                The missioner,
Red-bearded saint, had brought hell's flame
To frighten women on retreat:
Sent on his spiritual errand,
It rolled along the village street
Until Rathfarnham was housing smoke
That sooted the Jesuits in their Castle.
'No pregnancy. You'll die the next time,'
The Doctor had said.

                  Her tiredness obeyed
That Saturday night: her husband's weight
Digging her grave. So, in nine months, she
Sank in great agony on a Monday.
Her children wept in the Orphanage,
Huddled together in the annexe,
While, proud of the Black Cross on his badge,

> The Liguorian, at Adam and Eve's,
> Ascended the pulpit, sulphuring his sleeves
> And setting fire to the holy text. [8]

What Austin Clarke gets at, in a ruthless, penetrating way, is the hypocrisy engendered by the violence of the institution of the Church, directed against its members, especially women. Some four thousand Irish girls go to England every year to have abortions there. This suits perfectly. There are, you see, no abortions in Ireland. That means we're pure. But you can have an abortion in England. Aren't the English terrible? As a race, we Irish are so casually hypocritical in such matters that it is almost unbelievable.

And yet, precisely because of this blend of tyranny, hypocrisy and oppression, Irish poets have always celebrated the integrity, energy and heroic common-sense of women. The best of O'Casey's plays are a celebration of women's courage and endurance. Joyce's *Ulysses* finishes with Molly Bloom's torrential affirmation of life. Later novelists such as John McGahern, Brian Moore and Edna O'Brien concentrate much on women's fighting spirit. Beckett's understanding and presentation is profound and comprehensive. And Thomas Murphy's play, *Bailegangaire* (1985) is a wonderfully poetic celebration of the sheer spirit and stamina of women.

Long before any of these writers, however, James Stephens wrote about the way some women fought against the bland tyranny of men (that sort of tyranny, of which even men *themselves* realise they are guilty). I have chosen James Stephens because he is a rather neglected figure. He was a contemporary of Yeats: he was a tiny little man (he has been referred to as a leprechaun); he was an orphan who is said to have been helped, when very young, by various women who took pity on him. In his novels, *The Crock of Gold* (1912), *Deirdre* (1923) and *The Demi-Gods* (1914), in his short stories, especially 'Hunger' (1918, later published in *Etched in Moonlight; Arthur Griffith*, 1922), and in many of his poems, Stephens has his women fight against their oppressive circumstances. Above all, perhaps, he is interested in how certain women fight for their *identity* in a world were so many forces combine to undermine that identity. In exploring woman's identity, Stephens discovers the well-springs of his own compassion as a poet: he finds out the direction of his deepest sympathies. In this poem, 'The Red-Haired Man's Wife,' Stephens reveals the violence inherent in man's sacred structures, such as marriage. These structures are created by man, and sanctioned by man's God. This poem always reminds me of a line from Webster's play, *The Duchess of Malfi*. It is spoken by the Duchess

herself, after she has experienced violence, horror and humiliation.
She says '*I am Duchess of Malfi still*'. Here is Stephens' poem, in
which the woman realises and protests against the bland tyranny
she senses is at the heart of the marriage-union:

The Red-Haired Man's Wife

I have taken that vow!
And you were my friend
But yesterday – Now
All that's at an end;
And you are my husband, and claim me, and
    I must depend!

Yesterday I was free!
Now you, as I stand,
Walk over to me
And take hold of my hand;
You look at my lips! Your eyes are too
    bold, your smile is too bland!

My old name is lost;
My distinction of race!
Now, the line has been crossed,
Must I step to your pace?
Must I walk as you list, and obey, and smile
    up in your face?

All the white and the red
Of my cheeks you have won!
All the hair of my head!
And my feet, tho' they run,
Are yours, and you own me and end me,
    just as I begun!

Must I bow when you speak!
Be silent and hear;
Inclining my cheek
And incredulous ear
To your voice, and command, and behest;
    hold your lightest wish dear!

I am woman! But still
Am alive, and can feel
Every intimate thrill
That is woe or is weal:
I, aloof, and divided, apart, standing far,
    can I kneel?

Oh, if kneeling were right,
I should kneel nor be sad!
And abase in your sight
All the pride that I had!
I should come to you, hold to you, cling to
    you, call to you, glad!

If not, I shall know,
I shall surely find out!
And your world will throw
In disaster and rout!
I am woman, and glory, and beauty; I,
    mystery, terror and doubt!

I am separate still!
I am I and not you!
And my mind and my will
As in secret they grew,
Still are secret; unreached, and untouched,
    and not subject to you. [9]

That, from a woman's viewpoint, is a poem about violence within
a certain kind of marriage. As a rule, Irish poetry (with a few recent
exceptions) has not really begun to explore the actual violence con-
tained in marriage. Almost a hundred years after Ibsen, Irish poets
are still tentative in explorations of 'married' violence. Around
marriage there is an entire mythology of happiness, peace, hygiene,
promise, renewal, generation, valid or legal or legitimate sexuality.
The bride is in white, usually; the man is impeccable. This is the
Big Day, the once-in-a-lifetime event (especially if you happen to be
an Irish Catholic). The implication of the Big Day is that marriage
will lead to various forms of fulfilment. And no doubt it does, in
certain cases. But in many other cases, it leads to other states, other
conditions. It locks two people together in what can be a kind of
violent, exclusive intimacy, a private arena where each can throw
the other to the emotional lions. The *togetherness* of marriage *can*
be based on a recognition of the silent violence of the atmosphere
in which the couple live, discover each other, look at each other,
renew each other. In this respect, violence is a kind of education,
a private enlightenment, a schooling in forms of determination and
continuity. Here is the conclusion of Thomas Kinsella's poem,
'Remembering Old Wars':

Each dawn, like lovers recollecting their purpose,
We would renew each other with a savage smile. [10]

At the back of most of the poems I've discussed is some kind of
response to the violence inherent in sexuality. The Church uses
this violence to keep women down; one man uses it to establish
his own mastery, another to renew both himself and his mate while
his mate does the same. It would appear that poetry tells us that
violence is inevitable and universal, that it has to do with vital and
consequential change, that it appeals to the imagination of a person
even as it threatens or even appalls that same person's daily life. Or
to put it another way: there are certain forces which, simultaneously,
attract the imagination and repel the reason. Yeats's last poem 'Under
Ben Bulben' is a celebration of what violence can lead to.

> You that Mitchel's prayer have heard,
> 'Send war in our time, O Lord!'
> Know that when all words are said
> And a man is fighting mad,
> Something drops from eyes long blind,
> He completes his partial mind,
> For an instant stands at ease,
> Laughs aloud, his heart at peace.
> Even the wisest man grows tense
> With some sort of violence
> Before he can accomplish fate,
> Know his work or choose his mate... (398-99)

The imagination instinctively realises that violence exists everywhere,
and has its own purpose. It goes further: violence is a kind of motive-
power, a sort of emotional fuel, a key to developed action, a source
of creative thinking, a restless, stirring, challenging origin of art
and civilisation.

   Poetry, like the moth to the flame, is drawn towards violence.
But poetry does not perish because of this attraction. In fact, poetry
is animated, vitalised, refreshed by the contact. This is so, I think,
because poetry is neither moral nor immoral. It is amoral, it exists
beyond conventional morality. If poetry merely reflected conventional
morality, it would exist only in Christmas bards and after-dinner
speeches. But poetry creates its own new fierce, vigorous code of
morality. It was Synge who said that 'before verse can be human
again it must learn to be brutal.'[11] This is the real crux. If poetry
is to be real, challenging, primitive and sophisticated at once, then
it must observe and imitate that fundamental principle of life: in a
million different ways, under the guise of politeness, concern, do-
gooding, converting, enlightening, educating, loving – people do
violence to each other. *Not* to perceive and explore this in poetry
is to open the floodgates of sentimentality and sententious moralising.

That is why I personally believe that poetry, far from being consolatory and uplifting like some Victorian pill to send you asleep,
radiant with beautiful thoughts, poetry is dangerous, particularly if
it is constantly and attentively read. Not all of it is like this; but a
surprising amount of it is.

Let us look, for example, at Yeats's 'Leda and the Swan'. It is
a poem about rape. The poem does not condemn rape; neither
does it condone it; it *presents* it. And yet, if the poem could be said
to teeter between condemning and condoning, I think that, after
many readings, it could be argued that phrases such as 'feathered
glory', 'loosening thighs', 'strange heart', 'white rush', and the
sheer power of 'engenders there' – all these veer towards a drama-
tisation of the *energy* of the rapist, and not the plight of the victim.
In the *present* act of violence, the future is born. Violence begets
violence. Agamemnon is dead at the moment of the rape of Leda.
Time and its fierce dramas are concentrated, focussed in that violent sexual act. We are appalled at the barbarism of the truth. The
god, in the shape of a swan, rapes the girl. The poem, beautifully
made, contains this violence within its elegant framework. The
formal elegance makes the violence more savagely real, and forces
the intellect to accommodate, in one mental feat, the co-incidence
of act and consequence. Morality, as we tend to understand it, has
no place here. The present is furiously incensed, that the future
may be unleashed.

> A sudden blow: the great wings beating still
> Above the staggering girl, her thighs caressed
> By the dark webs, her nape caught in his bill,
> He holds her helpless breast upon his breast.
>
> How can those terrified vague fingers push
> The feathered glory from her loosening thighs?
> And how can body, laid in that white rush,
> But feel the strange heart beating where it lies?
>
> A shudder in the loins engenders there
> The broken wall, the burning roof and tower
> And Agamemnon dead.
>   Being so caught up,
> So mastered by the brute blood of the air,
> Did she put on his knowledge with his power
> Before the indifferent beak would let her drop? (241)

Poetry tends to recognise and demonstrate what a conventional
morality will tend to outlaw and condemn. The imagination when
it is probing, serves no system, obeys no law but its own longing

for exciting truth. What we call 'violence' is only a part of that excitement; gentleness, love, pity and mercy also come under its defining and dramatising scrutiny. Many of us tend to be like Ted Hughes's aunt – we tend to find a poetry that *confronts* violence somehow violent in itself, as if a poem were, *totally*, confined to its theme. It is not. A poem is limited only by the extent to which it fails to explore and present, as fully and truthfully as possible, the particular emotional world it has chosen, or been compelled by perhaps very instinctive forces, to explore and present. Ironically, Ted Hughes's aunt may well be a good, albeit reluctant, guide to the value of 'violent' poetry. The more disgusted she is, the better the poem is likely to be. Most of us *do* find violence frightening and disgusting; but this doesn't mean, of course, that a poem successfully presenting that same violence is disgusting and/or frightening. But, long before Victorian times, and certainly *after* Victorian times, there are many people who like to see poetry as 'beautiful', 'consolatory', 'uplifting', 'edifying', 'beneficial to the soul'. It may, indeed, be all these things: but it can also achieve the effect of the *opposite* of all these things; ugly, distressing, dangerous, even degrading, playing havoc with the spirit, if sensitively read. The treatment of violence in Irish poetry tells us that poetry cannot be denied its own full, adventurous, enquiring life. It will not be labelled, safely categorised, put into classified boxes.

Poetry, by definition, is always breaking through boundaries and categories. To try to inhibit or limit that function is to do violence to the very nature of poetry, to make it the sweet, biddable, musical slave of our expectations. The poetry that deals with violence is more concerned with its *own* compulsions than with the expectations of others. It will not flatter or comfort or console; it will disturb, challenge, even threaten. Above all, it threatens our complacency. And, in a world that seems hell-bent on its own destruction, that threat to complacent unawareness is a valuable service. We are brought into closer, more articulate contact with fiercely energetic forces which are at work both within and outside ourselves. The poems I have discussed represent some of these forces; they demand that we look at what we call violence face to face. Reading becomes a kind of encounter with the repulsive, even the unspeakable. Returning from such encounters, we are more aware, more conscious. What we choose to do, or *not* to do, with our state of temporarily extended awareness, is our own affair. 'Violent' poetry, the poetry of uncompromising consciousness, the poetry of hard, raw reality, continues to do its work of dramatic demonstration, of ruthless bringing-to-mind, of accusation and warning. This work, as I hope I have shown, is difficult, discomforting, and increasingly necessary.

A View of Irish Poetry

I. *Irish Poetry to Yeats*

1

In this essay I try to give an idea of the origins and development of the Irish poetic tradition. I want to trace its growth, to show its tough capacity for survival despite long silences and methodical oppression, and to indicate the directions in which I believe it is likely to develop. Some critics may argue that I am in fact talking about two traditions in poetry; the early native Gaelic and the later Anglo-Irish. There is something to be said for this, but I personally believe that both Gaelic and Anglo-Irish combine to create a distinctively Irish tradition.

2

Legends, myths, themes, rhythms and ideas are not like political parties and social groups. They do not thrive on an identity based on a sense of separateness; they fertilise and enrich each other constantly and deliberately in order to create new legends, myths, themes, rhythms and ideas. 'Thus far shalt thou go, and no farther' may be wise words in the mouth of a politician, but in the mouth of a poet they are death. An outstanding example of the fertilising influence of one mode of thought and expression on another is the way in which Yeats took the dust-covered figures of Cuchulain, Conchubar, Maeve and others and proved how totally adequate these products of an ancient mythology were to express the immense complexity of life in the twentieth century. Yeats's achievement alone would justify the fusion of Gaelic and Anglo-Irish into a single, sturdy tradition. It is simply another example of his capacity to discover unity where so many before and after him have perceived and perpetuated discord and division. Today it is clear that although history nearly always sundered Irish from Anglo-Irish, the imagination has nearly always brought them closer together so that now, in retrospect, the cultures they both produced may be seen as a compact imaginative unity.

If I had to generalise about all Irish poetry and say what single quality strikes me most from 'The Deer's Cry' (Eighth Century), attributed to St Patrick, to *The Great Hunger* by Patrick Kavanagh (1942), I would say that a hard, simple, virile, rhetorical clarity is its most memorable characteristic. The Irish mind has never taken kindly to obscurity. It delights in simple, direct, lively expression. Among the virtues of early Irish poetry are accurate observation and precise diction. Those early poets said exactly what they meant, and meant (for the most part) exactly what they said. They never bothered with Celtic Twilight or Pre-Raphaelite ornament. They cut to the bone in a hard, accurate idiom. One of the finest early poems is 'The Old Woman of Beare'. Its difficulty springs not from any inherent obscurity in the verse but from the fact that much of the poetry occurred in prose texts and since this poem has lost its prose framework there are certain references which remain puzzling. In spite of this the poem is an extremely moving lament for lost youth and a haunting outcry against the brutal but inevitable ravages of time:

> The Old Woman of Beare am I
> Who once was beautiful.
> Now all I know is how to die.
> I'll do it well.
>
> Look at my skin
> Stretched tight on the bone.
> Where kings have pressed their lips,
> The pain, the pain.
>
> I don't hate the men
> Who swore the truth was in their lies.
> One thing alone I hate –
> Women's eyes.
>
> The young sun
> Gives its youth to everyone,
> Touching everything with gold.
> In me, the cold...
>
> [*translated by Brendan Kennelly*] [1]

Two other strongly characteristic features of early Irish poetry are its passionate love of nature and its religious intensity. Frequently, these two qualities merge with each other and the result is an exultant spirituality springing from a delight in the natural world:

> I hear the stag's belling
>   Over the valley's steepness;
> No music on earth
>   Can move me like its sweetness.
>
> Christ, Christ hear me!
>   Christ, Christ of Thy meekness!
> Christ, Christ love me!
>   Sever me not from Thy sweetness!
>
>   ('The Sweetness of Nature') [2]

Again, I am struck by the similarity between this early poem and Patrick Kavanagh's *The Great Hunger* where the suspicious peasants, who are usually content to ignore the beauties of the natural world and to treat the supernatural with a blend of scepticism and cunning, occasionally experience a fusion of both, similar to that expressed by the speaker in the early Irish poem. The spanning centuries merely emphasise the similarity:

> Yet sometimes when the sun comes through a gap
> These men know God the Father in a tree:
> The Holy Spirit is the rising sap,
> And Christ will be the green leaves that will come
> At Easter from the sealed and guarded tomb...[3]

In a nation's tradition poets who have never heard of each other are brothers and sisters.

3

History happens in time, and like time, it cures and kills, kills and cures. In any survey of Irish poetry, however brief, history keeps breaking in like the uninvited guest whose rude intrusion is redeemed by his stimulating contribution. English rule in Ireland went a long way towards destroying the Irish language, and, therefore, writing in Irish; but the language never died completely, and in fact is still alive. It is fair to say, however, that the Battle of Kinsale in 1601 brought to an end the glorious native tradition in the literature of Ireland. In the twentieth century there have been many encouraging signs of a renaissance. Today, a new body of impressive literature in Irish is being produced by a number of hard-working poets, novelists and dramatists. History smiles, and tradition revives. It is important also to remember that Ireland was singularly untouched by the Renaissance in Europe; her poets never drank from that particular well of inspiration. If, in this overview, I appear to give relatively short shrift to medieval Irish poetry, it is not because I am unimpressed by its urbane tone, courtly spirit and formal correctness, but because I am eager to talk about the wonderful lament for Art O'Leary by his wife Eileen, and Brian Merriman's *The Midnight Court* (1780-81). Before that, however, mention should be made of the literature of Fionn and the Fianna, an essentially popular literature which is forbiddingly vast in quantity. The best work in it is *Agallamh Na Seanórach*, an epic wrangle between St Patrick and the pagan heroes Oisin and Caoilte.

The English broke the Treaty of Limerick in 1691 and Catholic Ireland became enslaved. The signs and effects of that slavery can be seen in the poetry of Egan O'Rahilly, who saw the new Anglo-

Irish gentry replacing the old Irish aristocracy. Several of his poems
show his agonised sense of the break-up of the native order, and
his profound disgust at the dominance of the 'English upstart'.
O'Rahilly is a great poet, largely because there is pure passion in
his lines which are a heart-broken and heart-breaking outcry against
injustice and disintegration. Almost any one of O'Rahilly's poems
contains this passion. Look, for example, at 'On the Death of William
Gould'. This is not simply a lament for an Irish nobleman; it is
an elegy for Irish generosity:

> All over Ireland – why this chill?
>   Why this foul mist?
> Why the crying birds?
>   Why do the heavens mutter
>   Such wrathful words?
>
> Why this blow to a poet?
>   Why do the Feale and Shannon tremble?
> Why does the wild sky spill
>   Such venomous rain
>   On plain and hill?
>
> What has put song in chains
>   And nobles in bonds?
> Why do God's own bold
>   Servants and prophets
>   Walk shocked and appalled?
>
> The cause of their grief
>   Is that fair William Gould
> Has died in France.
>   Christ! No wonder this pall
>   Darkens the land.
>
> Giver of horses and cloaks,
>   Of silver and gold,
> Silk, wine, meat, bread;
>   This giver, this generous giver
>   Is dead.
>
> [*translated by Brendan Kennelly*][4]

The two great Irish poems of the eighteenth century are, as I
have said, *The Midnight Court* and 'The Lament for Art O'Leary'.
They both spring out of history, but the difference between them
is the difference between the tragic and the comic vision. Both
Merriman and Eileen O'Leary are aware of the frightful legacy of
that history of enslavement. Merriman transforms it into uproarious,
bawdy comedy while Eileen O'Leary's tragic lamentation frequently
reaches a high pitch of visionary intensity. Of the two, I prefer Merri-

man's poem. Like all good comic writing, it is essentially serious. Written in couplets that Pope would have been proud to acknowledge, the poem soars into fantastic laughter at the inhibitions, at once terrible and ludicrous, of Irish puritanism, that dark force which has infuriated so many Irish writers and inspired so much Irish writing. Frank O'Connor's translation of Merriman's poem is, to my mind, the best we have. When it first appeared, it was banned – an ironical proof that early twentieth-century Ireland was as repressive as that eighteenth-century society which produced Merriman's frustrated and furiously articulate women. Its profound insight into human nature in general and Irish character in particular, its compassionate laughter and humanity, its lively dialogue and brilliant technique, make it a monument in Irish poetry. Some critics claim that it is a monument *to* Irish poetry, at once a climax and an epitaph. On the contrary, it points the way into a great deal of modern Irish writing, into the clumsy beginnings of a revival, into its gathering momentum and full flowering. Merriman is not simply a poet to be read again and again. He is a poet to be loved for his comic spirit, his artistic integrity, his gay inspiration.

4

If the eighteenth century was dominated by Merriman, O'Rahilly and Eileen O'Leary, the two leading poets of the nineteenth century are James Clarence Mangan and Sir Samuel Ferguson. Mangan is the better poet – more inspired, more passionate – but the importance of Ferguson's contribution to Irish poetry cannot be overemphasised. It was Ferguson, more than any other single poet, who proved that the old mythology was an almost infinite source of inspiration. In 1834, when Ferguson was twenty-four, nineteen of his translations from the Irish were published in the *Dublin University Magazine*. These translations, mainly love poems, show Ferguson's technical competence and variety, his liking for vigorous rhythms, and his ability to capture the essence of the original. Many years later, Yeats wrote that Ferguson was 'consumed with one absorbing purpose, the purpose to create an Irish school of literature, and overshadowed by one masterful enthusiasm, an enthusiasm for all Gaelic and Irish things'.[5] This passion was the driving-force behind Ferguson's life as a poet and it made him place all his faith in the mythology of his own land. The bulk of his poetry is heroic, though he also produced some fine lyrics. Edward Dowden, the well-known Shakespearean critic, said of him:

> What distinguishes Ferguson as a poet and gives him a place apart is
> that he – and, I think, he alone among Victorian poets – possessed in a
> high degree the genius for epic poetry. He was indeed an epic poet,
> born out of due season.[6]

Ferguson's attempt to write a national epic resulted in the huge
poem, *Congal*, published in 1872, founded on John O'Donovan's
translation of *Cath Muighe Rath* (the Battle of Moyra) which
appeared in 1843. Ferguson spent almost thirty years writing *Congal*
though in the meantime he wrote many other poems of a strongly
heroic character. These poems, entitled *Lays of the Western Gael*,
were published in 1865.

The theme of *Congal* is the conflict between paganism and
Christianity in early Ireland. It is not ultimately a great epic poem.
There are far too many long sections of dull writing, including
tedious digressions, boring speeches and inflated descriptive passages.
Worse again, Ferguson knew in his heart that Christianity had to
win. So it does. Ferguson's heart, however, lies not with the triumphant Christians but with the defeated pagans. The poem suffers from the poet's divided sympathy. Taking these criticisms into
account, *Congal* is still an impressive work; but it proved that
Ireland has no Milton. A better poem is *Conary*, which tells the
story of a king's downfall in taut, precise language. Perhaps the most
remarkable thing in the poem is the restraint with which Ferguson
evokes a terrifying supernatural world, in the frightening light of
which a great man's destiny is spun to its tragic end. It is the work
of a rich, disciplined imagination. I am not able to quote enough
here to do them full justice, but my brief comments on these poems
may help the reader to appreciate better this solid, moving and
enjoyable poet. To the end Ferguson kept his ideals, knowing full
well that his likeliest reward was that, in his own day at least, he
would be largely ignored. He wrote:

> At present, the cultured criticism of the day is averse to the Irish sub-
> ject in any form, and the uncultured will not have it save in that form
> of helotism in which I at least will not present it.[7]

Other poets such as Aubrey de Vere and John Todhunter followed
Ferguson and used Irish mythology to create new poetry. Yeats
openly admitted his admiration for him; and other poets including
James Stephens, George Russell (AE), and the early Austin Clarke
owe something to Ferguson. In *Mesgedra*, one of his longer heroic
poems, Ferguson succinctly stated his aim as a poet:

> the Man aspires
> To link his present with his Country's past,
> And live anew in knowledge of his sires.[8]

In linking Irish poetry with the country's heroic past, Ferguson
showed the way into the future.

   If there is a single quality which characterises Ferguson both as
man and poet, it is his unshakeable solidity. He is at all times firm
and stable. The very opposite is true of James Clarence Mangan,
the most exciting poet in nineteenth century Ireland. Very few poets
have been more chaotic, more consistently lost than this colourful,
eccentric Dubliner who was occasionally driven to madness, frequently
afflicted by illness, and always bedevilled by poverty. Mangan seems
almost a prototype of the *poète maudit*, a lonely figure permanently
dogged by misfortune. The first chapter of his *Autobiography* gives
us a clue to his torment:

> In my boyhood I was haunted by an indescribable feeling of something
> terrible. It was as though I stood in the vicinity of some tremendous
> danger, to which my apprehensions could give neither form nor outline.
> What it was I knew not; but it seemed to include many kinds of pain
> and bitterness – baffled hopes – and memories full of remorse.[9]

This fear entered Mangan's soul and gave him the most astounding
energy. He was a haunted man and he wrote a haunted poetry. Yet
his is not any conventional or predictable kind of Byronic self-
condemnation. It is more a quality of furious self-scrutiny which
brings to mind not a flamboyant figure of late nineteenth-century
romanticism but one like the American poet, Hart Crane, who
burned himself up and finally committed suicide at the age of thirty-
two. Mangan, too, died relatively young, after a lifetime of almost
incessant suffering and deprivation.

   As a writer, Mangan is erratic and impatient. His poetry is extremely uneven in quality, ranging from exquisite lyricism to rhetorical
bombast. He translated from several languages but, of course, in
his own personal, inimitable way. Some translations are beautiful,
some absolutely atrocious. Most important, however, Mangan had
an uncanny knack of self-revelation through translation. Some poets
speak with complete personal directness. Others speak through the
mouths of dramatic personae. Still others choose mythological
characters as their mouthpieces. Mangan spoke through other poets.
This is not to say that he could not be shatteringly direct. He could.
For the most part, though, he poured out the woes of his heart
and soul in poems that came from other languages until they became
unmistakable products of his own tormented sensibility. At his best
Mangan is profoundly moving, even overwhelming. At his worst
he is as bad as any poet can be. But then, that *is* Mangan: a mixture
of inspiration and dullness, ecstasy and eccentricity, marvellous

compassion and embarrassing self-pity. He delights and exasperates, is at once tragic and trivial, profound, silly, infuriating and lovable. He is the greatest Irish poet before Yeats.

The quantity of poetry produced in the nineteenth century is immense; the quality is frequently poor but with always encouraging exceptions. Patriotism and religion inspired a great number of poems, many of which are hysterically nationalistic or gushingly pious. A few are unsentimental and strong. As always, there were the people's poems: ballads that told of love lost and found; death for, in, and out of Ireland; the struggle for the land; the hope of delivery from the oppressor; the vision of a new, exultant Ireland, freed from her chains, rejoicing in the recovery of an ancient, lost identity. They are important not only because they are an accurate guide to the feelings and aspirations of the poeple, or because they turn history into song, but because they also anticipate the ballad rhythms of Yeats, Padraic Colum and F.R. Higgins.

There are always poets who seem to defy any attempt to classify themes and trends. I am thinking of Oscar Wilde and George Darley, two Dubliners whose verse has a vitality which I always find astonishing and admirable. I am particularly fond of Wilde's vigorous 'The Ballad of Reading Gaol' (1898) (rather than any of his short pieces where he tends to simper stylishly like many another *fin-de-siècle* poet) and George Darley's 'Nepenthe', a lyrical outburst of almost epic proportions, a poem that is largely ignored nowadays, though it had a strong influence on the early poetry of Austin Clarke.

It is clear, then, that in nineteenth-century Ireland there was tremendous poetic energy. Yet there was something lacking: a centralising force, a unifying spirit. W.B. Yeats, himself an important part of nineteenth-century poetry, was such a spirit. He had more solid stamina than Ferguson, more fierce intensity than Mangan. He had a vision for Ireland unequalled in her tradition, as well as the intelligence and energy to turn that vision into reality. Carrying his experience of the nineteenth century and its mythology in his heart and head, he stepped into twentieth-century Ireland, a great poet with a great poet's ideals. Never did a country so badly need a poet. Never did a poet work so tirelessly for his country.

5

The Irish literary revival was largely the work of W.B. Yeats. It is not simply that Yeats went from the tinsel brilliance of conventional Pre-Raphaelite verse to a bare, sensual, symbolic poetry; but his development is parallel, almost identical with, his changing views of a changing Ireland. Three poems illustrate this. 'To Ireland in the Coming Times' is youthful and idealistic, and shows the young poet consciously trying to identify himself with the unsung makers of the Irish tradition. 'September 1913' is bitter and disillusioned: Yeats here is middle-aged and openly disgusted by the self-righteous materialism of Irish society. The Easter Rebellion and the Civil War followed; a new Ireland stumbled into existence and Yeats played his part in the uncertain, exciting creation of the young state. In 'The Statues' he applauds the heroism that made this birth possible and asserts Ireland's dignity in the face of the overwhelming 'filthy modern tide'.[10] Yeats is Ireland's greatest poet, not least because he learned to confront the challenging complexities of Irish life. He recognised that Ireland is always capable of treachery and squalor, but he was also aware of its capacity for heroism and nobility. He witnessed and experienced 'the weasel's twist, the weasel's tooth'.[11] Yet he exhorted later generations to be, and to continue to be, the 'indomitable Irishry'.[12]

Around the massive figure of Yeats cluster a number of interesting minor poets: James Stephens, Oliver Gogarty, Padraic Colum, F.R. Higgins, George Russell (AE) and others. They all made vital contributions to the revival.

Though consciously separating himself from Yeats, James Joyce's verse has an unmistakable vitality. Joyce is Ireland's jester, her high-priest of irreverence, her devoted Rabelais. I find Joyce nearer to J.M. Synge than to Yeats both in his art and his life. Just as Synge's drama has drawn attention from his poetry, so Joyce's novels have overshadowed his verse. Though Joyce draws on the city and Synge on the countryside, they are both witty and defiant, tender and vicious.

When Yeats wrote that 'a terrible beauty is born',[13] he had in mind, among others, the poets Patrick Pearse, Joseph Plunkett and Thomas MacDonagh. All three have an intensity lacking in most of the poets who have criticised them adversely.

After Yeats, Irish poets found themselves in a peculiar position. Yeats, it seemed, had exhausted an entire mythology. His heroic-romantic vision overshadowed the visions of all others. He was disturbingly near in time, a colossus breathing down the necks of the younger generation. The problem facing these writers was to revere and understand his achievement and, at the same time, to absorb and transform his influence.

II. *Irish Poetry Since Yeats*

1

Whenever one or two figures seem dominant in a country's poetry, several others are writing in a different but not equally acclaimed or recognised way. When Yeats was at the height of his powers towards the end of his life, an anthology, *Goodbye, Twilight*,[1] was published containing the work of poets who saw themselves as writing a very different kind of poetry from that of Yeats and other distinguished Celtic Twilighters. In 1993, Gabriel Fitzmaurice edited an anthology, *Irish Poetry Now: Other Voices*[2] which, he holds, contains a kind of poetry different from and interesting as the mainstream of contemporary verse in Ireland. Such oppositions, such alternatives, are a healthy sign; they lessen the likelihood that readers may fall into attitudes of lazy categorisation; and they suggest that the scene is more vigorous, varied and complex than we had hitherto realised. Further, they create the possibility that poets in scrupulous opposition to each other may produce better work. There should be fewer cosy coteries, more fierce and intelligent opposition. That's the stuff of which genuine friendship between poets is made.

Yeats's Cuala Press published Patrick Kavanagh's long poem *The Great Hunger* in 1942. Kavanagh went on to denounce Yeats as being 'protected by ritual' in his poem, 'An Insult';[3] he also criticised him severely in several essays. This was Kavanagh's way of distancing himself from Yeats. He went on to explain and express his own vision, a vision which in the end has, ironically, some remarkable similarities to Yeats's. Kavanagh called it 'comedy';[4] Yeats called it 'tragic joy'.[5] Kavanagh's castigating references to Yeats and others helped him to create for himself that space, that freedom from other poets' work (even as they are deeply aware of it) that most poets need. Poets' vicious denunciations of the work of others can be forms of self-liberation.

Creating space is always a problem, particularly, perhaps, in the congested Irish scene. Poets such as Samuel Beckett, Denis Devlin, Brian Coffey and Thomas MacGreevy created this cultural space for themselves in ways which indicate that their poetry is not widely read today. (Why should it be? – some purists will ask.) Much of Beckett's poetry is knotted and ironic; it often transmits the sense of a man muttering to himself in no particular method or order; yet it gives the reader the feeling that he's listening to a private monologue, labyrinthine and tortuous at certain times, at others, comic and self-mocking. It is at once inviting and offputting, like a nutty conversationalist with a kindly countenance. It is particularly striking when read aloud, as indeed all poetry should be, if subtleties of rhythm are to be properly grasped.

Traces of Beckett's oddly fascinating qualities are to be found in the work of contemporary poets such as Tom McIntyre and Hugh Maxton. Paul Durcan's ability to write like a comic Hamlet suggests that he has listened to Beckett at some stage. He has also listened to Kavanagh's call for a comic poetry which, in its spirit of self-criticism allied to criticism of society, brings Swift to mind and reminds poets everywhere that they must avoid becoming pompous or pretentious. Most of the reservations about Yeats's work which I hear expressed here and there throughout Ireland and other places centre on his tendency towards rhetorical pomposity. This tendency may be due to his compulsion to mythologise and dramatise everyone, including himself. His aesthetic compels him to be always at the centre of the poem's action, determined not to fall apart. Beckett and Kavanagh, in their different ways, reject the inflated feelings consequent on dramatic mythologising, Kavanagh especially denouncing Yeats's 'myth of Ireland as a spiritual entity'[6] and proceeding in a defiant and convincing manner to write about the most ordinary situations, events, people: the life of a street, the 'undying difference in the corner of a field',[7] cubicles and wash-basins in a chest hospital, the canal in Dublin, bogs and small 'incurious'[8] hills in Monaghan, pubs, coffee-shops, mundane aspects of life as he saw it about him. All this, however, was coloured by an intense inner life, a religious conviction that 'God is in the bits and pieces of Everyday'.[9] The result is a delightful body of poetry in which the mundane is transfigured by the mystical, and the mystical is earthed in the mundane.

This religious streak in Irish poetry goes back to older poetry in the Irish language and is present, in muted and varied ways, in contemporary poetry. Denis Devlin, deeply influenced by the work of European writers (he translated a considerable amount of French poetry), produced a body of religious verse which grows more fascinating the more one reads it. Compare his poem 'Lough Derg' with poems by Kavanagh and Seamus Heaney on the same topic[10] and it becomes possible to appreciate the varied effects of his deliberate, resonant syntax, his long, evocative lines, his meditative rhythms, his ability to think things through. There is in Devlin a readiness to experiment with language and rhythm that is not very common in Irish poetry which, if I may generalise, tends to be formally conservative and rather cautious in its choices of themes. For such a rebel race, eloquently so, Irish poets can be comically, sadly conservative. Poetry should be adventurous and daring, even offensive at times. It *has* to be, if it is serious in its self-scrutiny and in its response to the abundant casual corruptions and abuses in society, not forgetting the wriggling evils in oneself. The exploration of a deep religious impulse goes hand in hand with the compulsion to satirise its abuses and abusers. This is true of Kavanagh; it is also true of Austin Clarke whose work, helpfully edited by Hugh Maxton in a recent Penguin edition,[11] satirises the hypocrisies and abuses that abound in Irish life even as churches on Sundays bulge with the faithful. Clarke had a lot of courage, and in his satire one can see the outrage suffered by a person who knows what a genuine religious impulse is, and how such an impulse is so often flouted and maimed in a 'religious' society. So Clarke wrote himself into a corner of articulate indignation and rage until, towards the end of his life, he began to write a more 'cheerful' verse. In a note on the Tiresias myth he mentions Tennyson's Victorian respectability and T.S. Eliot's puritan gloom in their treatment of this figure; he then stresses his own 'cheerful' view of the Tiresias drama, and goes on to offer us a sparkling poem.[12] Like Yeats and Kavanagh, like O'Casey in drama, like Joyce in the novel, Clarke's work slowly and tortuously approaches a climax of joy and celebration. I find it honest and convincing because he has brooded on the injustices, abuses, forms of ignorance and prejudice (can they be separated?) inherent in Irish life and yet, in the end, he flies in the face of squalor with poetry that is playful, amusing and sexually exuberant. I find a similiar exuberance in the work of Medbh McGuckian. I'm not saying that she has been directly influenced by Clarke; but influence in poetry is a strangely arbitrary, insidious, floating affair; Clarke helped to create a climate of spontaneity and freedom; poets all through the island have breathed that air. McGuckian is a complex writer, her language has a kind of wild freedom in it that suggests she has coped firmly with conflicts in herself. The writing of poetry is a lifelong bid for freedom from many forces, people, ideas and influences that the poet must be concerned with until, by sheer constant grappling with these forces, people, ideas and influences, he/she liberates himself/herself from their intimidating pressure. Sustained imaginative, sexual sympathy has, in Irish poetry, proved crucial in this liberation. Crazy Jane helps to deliver Yeats. I suspect Molly Bloom did much the same thing for James Joyce. Austin Clarke's lifelong preoccupation with

women in his work helped to create that late, cheerful poetry. In
the imagination, there's a deep connection between feminisation
and freedom. It took Clarke a lifetime to achieve this. Medbh
McGuckian, a young woman, electrifies her poetry with this freedom. So, in a different way, does Nuala Ní Dhomhnaill whose writing has an added comic-mythological dimension which, allied to
her sexual realism, makes her poetry both colourful and penetrating. Some of these young Irish women poets are more relaxed and
free, though no less disciplined in their approach to writing, than
most of their male equivalents manage to be after sixty or seventy
solemn years on this earth that somehow tolerates every conceiv-
able kind of poet and poetry.

Why is poetry so often considered high-falutin by 'ordinary',
intelligent people? I think it has to do, to a considerable extent, with
a certain male pomposity and self-regard which exudes an almost
incredible sense of the incomparable value of the poet himself,
created and sustained by himself, the great untouchable, the victim
who also happens to be an unquestionable master. This attitude of
severed élitism has gone unchallenged for too long. It is the stance
of men who love looking uptight and 'serious', sensitive and man-
ageably oppressed by just about everyone else. That look of special
agony is crucial. It could make the poetry itself more interesting.
On the whole, the women poets of Ireland have little or no time
for this carefully publicised pain. They suffer their confusions alone;
they deliver their clarities to the reading, listening public with style,
frequently with humour. Women poets have done a great deal to
humanise and normalise people's experience of poetry in Ireland:
when Mary O'Donnell's poetry programme on radio is compared
with Austin Clarke's,[13] you know the difference between poetry that
is enjoyed and poetry that is endured. I have genuine admiration
for Clarke's work; it is daring and tenacious; but his presentation
of poetry on radio was pretentious, sloppy and effete. O'Donnell's
is direct, crisp, deeply satisfying.

It is important to say this because poetry, no matter how disturbing, should be enjoyed in its full range without pretence or manipulation on the poet's part.

There are many women poets in Ireland now, in both Irish and
English, whose work has brought a new wave of excitement into
Irish writing. Eavan Boland's work in such books as *The War Horse*,
In Her Own Image, *Night Feed*, *The Journey*, *Outside History* and
In a Time of Violence[14] shows a powerful, questioning intelligence.
Time and again, she places herself not only outside history but

also outside mythology, as created and narrated by men, in an attempt to gain a perspective from which she can witness the places and roles of women in history, myth, in town and country, at home and in public. She is, in fact, making her own myth.

> I am Chardin's woman
>
> edged in reflected light,
> hardened by
> the need to be ordinary.[15]

Like McGuckian and Ní Dhomhnaill, Boland has pondered her situation in depth and at length. She is a superb craftswoman, her poems time and time again exploring complex ideas and situations in lucid, sensuous language. She could be even more hard-hitting; her intellectual stance, her impassioned sense of inquiry and her ability to see different sides of any problem or situation justify the use of more direct mind-blows to Irish society. She is one of the most exciting writers in Ireland today. The rage of time itself is a force in her poetry.

The rage of time. The rage of history. The rage of women. The rage of the oppressed, of the poor against the rich, of the deprived against the privileged, of the uneducated against the educated, of the powerless against the empowered. How much of this rage has been confronted and expressed by Irish poets? Undoubtedly, some of it has. Yeats, Clarke, Kavanagh, MacNeice in 'Autumn Journal', Eavan Boland, Anne Hartigan have expressed rage. Yeats more than any, it must be admitted.

> You think it horrible that lust and rage
> Should dance attention upon my old age...[16]

There is rage in some of Seamus Heaney's work and in a number of Thomas Kinsella's powerfully concentrated poems. James Simmons expresses rage in some of his poems and songs. But where is there a close, passionate statement or evocation of the rage that is making murder a daily event in the North of Ireland? And how close do Irish poets look at *the kinds of responses* from people to these events? How closely *connected* are Irish poets to what is actually going on? How interested are they? Who speaks out? Which poets express the different viewpoints? Is there something offensive to most poets in the notion of taking sides? Patrick Galvin certainly doesn't think so. In a shockingly candid poem entitled 'Letter to a British Soldier on Irish Soil', he concludes:

Go home, Soldier
Before we send you home
Dead.[17]

That's the conclusion to a rather fiercely Nationalist poem. Is there
a similiar Unionist poem? Should there be? Should the war be kept
out of poetry? Out of criticism? Or is poetry expected not to 'take
sides' but to stay on the sidelines, silent, sensitive, agonised, properly inarticulate, as the savage game is played according to its own
murderous rules?

How daring are Irish poets prepared to be? If we live in a murderous society should not our poetry reflect that fact? Does it? Or
do poets create and cherish their own partitions?

It may be, of course, that murder is of limited interest, even when
it is the expression of some ancient, entangled religious hatred or
of a prejudice at once so remote in time and so vile in its current
intensity that any coherent human understanding of it is no longer
possible. Life in Ireland can be like that. Who battered the epileptic
to death and dumped the body in a playground for children to
discover?

2

There are certain words in Ireland that glint, quiver and stick in
people's minds like the thin blades of knives. 'Partition' is one such
word. The political-territorial partition of Ireland intensified further
divisions among Catholics and Protestants, Nationalists and Unionists.
Partition begets partition and endows certain words with a virulent
significance. The word 'North', title of Seamus Heaney's strongest
collection, contains an entire history in itself which, the moment
the book is opened and the poems begin to be read, throws light
and shadows over practically every line. Heaney makes an admirable
effort to be detached from 'the Northern problem', 'the Northern
tragedy', but Heaney's words, attitudes, his tight, slit-eyed rhythms
show him as a Northern Catholic of rural origin with appropriate
political sympathies. And why not?

If partition creates partition, labels create labels: Catholic, Protestant, Unionist, Nationalist, Pan-Nationalist. Can an Irish poet
escape being labelled? One understands why Joyce, wishing to escape
Ireland's labelling congestion, its ruthless 'I know you no matter
what you do or say or write' intimacy, saw himself sitting on a
cloud over the city of Dublin, paring his fingernails in a show of
indifference. But cloud-squatting is not a popular posture among

Irish poets; and the few souls on the island who aspire to the name
of 'critic' are usually loaded with labels when they come to 'evaluate'
a book of poems. Nevertheless, there are a few critics who try to
rise above the label-tyranny.

The Northern poet (I'm starting to use my own little labels now!)
enjoys the advantage of being both Irish and British. This can be ignored or exploited at will. A Catholic Northern poet can be seen as a
victim deserving sympathy everywhere he or she goes; but if he writes
savage poems like Patrick Galvin he won't be much heard of. The
old question recurs: how daring are poets prepared to be? A choice
of theme is a measure of courage. Courage, the no-warning bombing
of one's own cosy limits, is one of the hallmarks of verse alive.

And there is indeed considerable courage in Heaney's poetry, in
the poetry of Derek Mahon, Michael Longley, Seamus Deane,
James Simmons, Medbh McGuckian, Frank Ormsby, Ciaran Carson
and Paul Muldoon. The first thing one must say about these, and
other Northern writers, is that they are darned good poets, some
of whose poems hit you right between the eyes and force you to
think anew about the Northern problem and other matters. And
these forceful poems are not always *directly* about that problem;
yet violence sweeps into Simmons's poems about love and marriage
as well as ballads such as 'Claudy' (which *is* a direct violence-poem);[18]
Longley's versions of the Greek poets as well as poems like 'Wounds'
and 'The Ice-Cream Man';[19] Mahon's bleak, ironic meditations on
loneliness, on being lost; and Muldoon's atrocity-haunted, witty
creations. An older poet like John Montague has a lot to say about
life in Northern Ireland but the fact that he has lived away from it
for so many years, doing his own bit of cloud-squatting here and
there throughout the world, gives his poetry an air of rather sad,
travelled wisdom which makes it calmer, though not less urgent, than
the work of younger poets. This calm, detached note in Montague's
verse, creating space for compassionate meditation on suffering and
emotional entrapment, is deeply attractive. A similar calm concern
marks the work of another Northern poet, Gerald Dawe, whose essays
on contemporary poetry are pithy, incisive and illuminating.[20]

If a sharp-minded anthology were made from the work of these
poets, it would be a forceful, haunting book. A sort of history of
our times and crimes.

Poetry will not solve the Northern problem, but when the terrorists, murderers and assassins decide to call it a day (as they finally
will, when it suits them), poetry will have written its own history
of the horrors. Even the youngsters, the schoolboys and schoolgirls

of Belfast and other places are writing poems in response to the Troubles. A Belfast childhood darkened by terrorism involves us all, even the resolutely complacent middle-classes of the Irish Republic where interest in the North and its distresses could hardly be slighter. Partition is a line dividing suffering from unawareness. And unawareness can be very 'superior'. 'Honestly, darling, have you ever heard of such barbarism?'

And yet the North *must* somehow infiltrate the consciousness of Southern poets (another wee label!). To what degree such infiltration occurs is anybody's guess. There's not much evidence of it in most of the poetry written in the South. Partition is a line beyond which certain imaginations refuse to go.

The critic Edna Longley has tried to cross such lines, such boundaries. There's a visionary quality in some of her criticism which, wittily bitter and insistent, makes many people, including poets, stop and think about the implications of their conscious and unconscious prejudices.

Violence is a form of publicity. The sensationalism that accompanies terrorism may transfer itself to the poetry arising from that violence, giving it a disproportionate prominence, causing the work of quieter poets to be overlooked.

There are three poets of another generation whose work must constantly be brought to mind, particularly in the South: Louis MacNeice, W.R. Rodgers and John Hewitt. The influence of MacNeice, particularly, on poets both North and South, is far-reaching. 'Why do you never sing?' some tone-deaf, ignorant Southern poet said to him once. 'Why do you never think?' replied MacNeice. MacNeice's brief reply constitutes one of the most telling criticisms I know of poetry written in Ireland.

This Southern ignorance takes many forms and is especially strong in Dublin. It springs from what can only be called a deliberately *willed* partition – the line drawn between Dublin and the rest of Ireland. A Southern singer, Donagh MacDonagh, son of the executed 1916 leader, Thomas MacDonagh, a far more gifted poet than his endlessly judgemental son, has a poem called 'Dublin Made Me', a manifesto of that ignorance proclaiming itself as loyalty which is a solid basis for partition. Dublin alone is worthwhile; every other part of Ireland, North, West and South, is dismissed for various 'reasons'. The curious thing about this poem is that it applies not only to poetry, but to many other aspects of culture and living. Dublin *is* a very attractive city; MacDonagh's response to that attractiveness is ignorant and dismissive.

Dublin made me and no little town
With the country closing in on its streets
The cattle walking proudly on its pavements
The jobbers the gombeenmen and the cheats

Devouring the fair-day between them
A public-house to half a hundred men
And the teacher, the solicitor and the bank-clerk
In the hotel bar drinking for ten.

Dublin made me, not the secret poteen still,
The raw and hungry hills of the West
The lean road flung over profitless bog
Where only a snipe could nest,

Where the sea takes its tithe of every boat.
Bawneen and curragh have no allegiance of mine,
Nor the cute self-deceiving talkers of the South
Who look to the East for a sign.

The soft and dreary midlands with their tame canals
Wallow between sea and sea, remote from adventure,
And Northward a far and fortified province
Crouches under the lash of arid censure.

I disclaim all fertile meadows, all tilled land
The evil that grows from it and the good,
But the Dublin of old statutes, this arrogant city,
Stirs proudly and secretly in my blood.[21]

The troglodytic attitudes in that poem still exist but not at all,
I would say, to the same degree. MacDonagh was a prime specimen
of the most close-minded class in Dublin, probably in the Republic,
the Catholic middle class; and many of the best poets in Dublin
today come from a very different Dublin. The Dublin of Paula
Meehan's poetry is startlingly different from that of MacDonagh;
Meehan's is humane, troubled, compassionate, funny, eager to reach
out and touch other aspects of life. A similar openness appears in
the poetry of Dermot Bolger and Michael O'Loughlin. Bolger, a
publisher as well as poet, and an accomplished novelist and dramatist,
brought 'invisible Dublin' into the light, gave a forum to poets
who would almost certainly not otherwise have been heard. Bolger
has always campaigned against partitioning ignorance, one of the
most powerful forces in Irish life, a force that is frequently obvious,
but just as frequently subtle and even stylish in its sinister workings.
It is, for example, quietly rampant in our educational system, especially at University level.

Dublin continues to produce many fine poets. Thomas Kinsella
has written incisively about Dublin, using various parts of the city

as a means of exploring his own dark, complex vision. Gerald Smyth's images of Dublin life are snappy and penetrating as well as reflective. And Michael Hartnett's *Inchicore Haiku*[22] contains unforgettable pictures of Dublin. Some of Paul Durcan's most outrageously vivid poems are set in Dublin; and Macdara Woods charts his Dublin in a spirit of patient affirmation. Woods wrote the introduction to *Collected Poems* of John Jordan,[23] a book containing much wisdom and wit concerning Dublin and its people. In the elegance of its phrasing, in the sharp intelligence of its perceptions, Jordan's work brings to mind the graceful poetry of Val Iremonger. Iremonger's poems about Dublin, particularly those about Sandymount and its people, are full of crisp images that linger in the memory. 'Elizabeth, frigidly stretched, /On a spring day surprised us.'[24] So do Iremonger's poems.

Micheal O'Siadhail's *Hail! Madam Jazz*[25] show a shrewd observer of Dublin life at work in thoughtful, well-made poems. O'Siadhail, like these other younger poets, writes with open heart and sharp intelligence about the uncertainties of living in a capital city that is both ancient and modern.

The poetry emerging from any city is an acute guide to the tolerance of that city's people. By that criterion, Dublin today is a growingly tolerant city. In spite of its increasing crime rate, its many social problems such as poverty, AIDS, drugs, unemployment on an alarming scale, Dublin life is marked, on the whole, by decency, humour and intelligence. The more critical poetry is, the more these qualities tend to emerge. The more savage poetry is, the more humanising its effects. Individual sentimentality is an insult to society, a gross offence to readers. Students in schools and universities should be encouraged to write this kind of cutting, critical poetry so that their vision of their own society may be less clouded, less deceptive. Poets like Meehan and Bolger, Theo Dorgan and Michael Hartnett produce a sharply critical poetry that does much to limit the damaging effects of both the obvious and subtle forms of divisiveness. The poetry that battles against partitionism will open the hearts and minds of people who read it or hear it properly spoken or read at public poetry-readings.

Probably the deepest partition in Irish life is the sexual divide between men and women. The Catholic Church established and exploited this partition for its own ends. Austin Clarke is probably our most combative anti-partitionist in this area; he fought for the dignity of women in his poems. Today, the women poets of Ireland are still fighting that deepest of all partitions. Some fight it with satirical wit, like Rita Ann Higgins, Julie O'Callaghan, and Rose-marie Rowley; others, like Anne Hartigan and Moya Cannon, in steely, defiant poems; others, like Eavan Boland and Eiléan Ní Chuilleanáin, with formidable intelligence; and others still, like Paula Meehan and Katie Donovan, with a spirit at once critical and magnanimous. There are many striking individual differences between these poets but they all have one thing in common: a defiant, dignified sense of creating their own forms of independence. These forms are the forms of their poems. Sinéad O'Connor's full-page poem, 'I am Sinéad O'Connor', in *The Irish Times* in the summer of 1993 [26] was an impassioned statement of that independence and her need for it. The poem drove some people hopping mad; it compelled others to state their admiration in public. Poetry by Irish women will, I believe, elicit such strong responses in the future.

And yet this partition remains widespread and profoundly rooted. Some of its most devoted practitioners don't even know they're promoting and sustaining it. This is the deepest single cultural/emotional/spiritual partition in Ireland. The act of exploring it will produce a more humane poetry from men and women, and ultimately from these young poets in schools, colleges, universities, and from outside these institutions, too. Poetry is the deepest kind of education there is, a conscious, structured, logical, inspiring illumination of the various darknesses in us all. Poetry which is fully alive is always on a threshold, making fresh assaults on ignorance, intolerance and evil so that concepts and practices of tolerance may be endlessly refreshed and re-invigorated, even as intense, rhythmical language is enjoyed and reflected on. This is especially true in Ireland, a society always in danger of succumbing to that paralysis so feared and yet so ruthlessly explored by Joyce; a society, too, permanently menaced by the 'great hatred, little room' [27] noted by Yeats. Paralysis, hatred, poverty, intolerance, cynicism, begrudgery, bored indifference and, most of all, that horrible, effective half-heartedness with its workable lethargy, its viable apathy, its slithery key to 'success' – these should be the targets of poets and poetry. Of poetry, above all. If our society is to be fully alive, self-questioning and realising its potential, poetry must be ruthless and brave. In this small country, where news of terrorism's latest atrocities is served with breakfast, the need for such poetry is deep indeed.

Other forms of partition involve the relative subjugation, or at least quietly pushing into the background, of some genuinely interesting poets. Anthony Cronin is one such. A social critic of remarkable range and depth, a distinguished biographer and literary historian,

an independent-minded critic of literature, he is also a poet whose
work spans several generations of Irish life and writing. Yet his
poems are scarcely available. He is a victim of that aggressive lazy-
mindedness that stems from partition. He is not easily labelled;
therefore, let's not mention him just now. Later, perhaps.

Curious how, in the swirling pool of poetry-politics, some poets
become the victims of critical clichés and labels while others profit
from the same mindless method. And it's curious, too, how Cronin,
a prominent public figure (he was cultural advisor to the former
Taoiseach, C.J. Haughey), seems to be penalised for this. The current
Minister for the Arts, Michael D. Higgins, is a poet of some sub-
stance. It is to be hoped that his public prominence won't diminish
this fact or, more likely, lead to a cartooning of it. Bad criticism is
a form of caricature, a systematic misrepresentation of a poet's real
worth. This malignant approach is rife in Ireland: Brendan Behan
was 'a great bloody character' but he is largely unread. I wonder
how true this is of Flann O'Brien, Patrick Kavanagh and others.
The stage Irishman is not an English but an Irish creation. What
it means is this: 'I want you, the writer, to be colourfully unreal
so that I won't have to listen to what your work has to say. Entertain
me so that I may laugh you out of existence and into absurdity'.

One of the odd consequences of partition is the emphasis it
throws on the figure of the loner in poetry, the man or woman
outside the cliques or mutually back-slapping groups that pop up
here and there in a climate of acclaim for each other. John Ennis
is a good example of the loner. Quiet, undemonstrative, tucked
unobtrusively away 'somewhere in the provinces' (he lives and
works in Waterford) he writes an adventurous poetry with a strong
narrative pulse. Similarly interesting figures are Mary O'Donnell,
Robert Greacen, Fred Johnston, Robert O'Donoghue, Rory Brennan,
Seán Dunne, Gerard Fanning, Ciaran O'Driscoll, John F. Deane,
Francis Harvey, Desmond Egan, Dennis O'Driscoll, Michael Coady,
Peter Sirr, Peter Fallon and the versatile Desmond O'Grady. Over
the years, these poets have worked hard to produce their highly
individual and very readable verse.

Another loner is Padraic Fallon. He was so during his lifetime;
he remains that sort of figure today. Up until recently when a
summer-school began to bring attention to his work at last, Fallon
was a poet you simply had to go in search of. His work is complex,
richly-wrought in a self-conscious way, musical, meditative, absorbing
a lot of influences from the Classical to the Gaelic.

One of the most gifted loner-figures is Richard Murphy. Murphy has never been labelled. What higher praise can an Irish poet be given? In this century, his narrative poems are among the most thrilling of their kind. [28]

But there are other loners. I'm thinking of poets who, instead of becoming embroiled in Ireland's local squabbles, write and work in different parts of the world. Bernard O'Donoghue, Eamon Grennan, Peter McDonald, Greg Delanty, James Liddy, Matthew Sweeney are, literally, outsiders whose work reflects that fact. Ireland is an island washed, in the eyes of many exiles, by nostalgic seas. None of the poets I've mentioned has been a victim of this nostalgia. Each, in his different way, is creating a poetry free of Ireland's turmoil but true to his own experience in the broader world. In that broader world, these poets are relatively free of the partitions that both inhibit and stimulate poets living in Ireland.

3

In the context of what I've tried to present in the second part of this essay, the poetry of personal relationships may tend to be overlooked; but right across the entire spectrum of contemporary Irish poetry, a keen scrutiny of such relationships occurs. Poetry is a solitary art and no amount of engagement with public issues can alter that fact. The number of intense, individual energies in Irish poetry now is impressive, and the style of each of these poets may be savoured for reasons peculiar to each writer. Each poet's moulding of his/her own language is ultimately the most revealing aspect of the work.

A poet's relationship with language is one of the deepest there is. The kind of English spoken and written in Ireland has a twist to it. It can be Janus-faced, crooked, indirect, poisonously comic, inflated, often pretending to a false sophistication, haunted by the Irish language, resenting or cherishing that influence. The English of Dublin is very different from that of Belfast or Cork or Galway. Even within these places there are different Englishes. In poetry, one English is as effective as another, depending on how imaginatively, passionately, skilfully it is used. When these qualities are present it doesn't matter what town, village, city, region or prison a poet is from; the necessary bridge between writer and reader is created. I should point out here, being aware of the approaches of some other poets, that I consider such bridges 'necessary'. An unshared poetry might as well be an unwritten poetry. The silence of the unread poem accuses us all.

Part of the problem of writing an essay entitled 'Irish Poetry Since Yeats' is the fact that each one of an impressive number of poets thinks that he or she is the best Irish poet since Yeats. The rest of the good souls know it. It's an odd business. It's a comical, rubbishy business, full of raised and unraised hackles. I suppose this kind of labelling is inevitable; critics go in for it, too; but if it stimulates somebody to produce better work, well, fair enough! The main problem would appear to be to keep on motoring. Egotism, no matter how deluded, can be the petrol that keeps the poetry-machine ticking over. The *sources* of poetry may be ludicrous, tragic, lonely, self-deceiving, bullying, vile in one way or another; the poetry itself may bring a keen and echoing pleasure.

The important thing for Irish poetry now is to be open to all kinds of influences from cultures all over the world. I know no good study of the effects of insularity on Irish writing, on Irish criticism. Insularity is both a state of severance and a state of self-containment. It can lead to the most inflated view of one's self and the most distorted views of others. Insularity is a shocking revelation of the implications and consequences of the big fish in the small pond situation. It can be a source of the most atrocious smugness and totally believed-in self-delusion. Insularity can be a method of cutting out of one's life the challenging forms of comparison and contrast that help us towards some kind of sane evaluation of who we are, what we are, and what we do. The seas that perpetually wash the shores of Ireland can help to fortify this sad state of affairs. 'Thank God we're surrounded by water' as the song says.

But an intelligent, vigilant, outward-looking insularity, not obsessed with self-protection, open to comparison, learning from contrast, welcoming challenge, developing the sense of proportion, eager to experience *difference* in whatever shape or form, can be a healthy, productive state for a poet. At some fundamental level, there's an ongoing conflict between the cautious, delusive, strong form of insularity, and the open, risk-taking, learning, adventurous kind. I believe this is a challenge that faces many English poets and critics also. It is a complex matter. Closed insularity is often connected with what people take to be love of place, language, rituals, local culture. The open brand challenges this love, its very nature and implications. When love is questioned the battle is bound to be furious.

Part of the problem with Irish poetry is the failure to find a proper balance between these two emotional/cultural/spiritual conditions. This failure to find a balance helps to explain the vicious antagonisms within the Irish poetry scene; the creators of beauty can be a malignant lot, at times. If there is an answer, it must be somewhere in the willingness to open up, to question the function of the seas, to look ever more closely at oneself, the land, its people.

This openness to otherness has implications of a purely thematic and technical kind for poetry. The strangest and most disturbing forms of otherness, often eruptively violent, reside in the self. Equally important is the otherness in thought, feeling, values, beliefs one finds throughout the world. Only in his or her own loneliness can the poet's bridges be created. That bleak need for connection, root of most poetry, is founded in the confrontation of that fact. There are many factors in Irish life working against this confrontation. The significant poets are those who insist on it.

This openness brings in themes that minds largely shaped by closed insularity will find distasteful, ugly, vulgar or simply wrong-headed. I experienced a fair amount of this kind of talk after the publication of *The Book of Judas*.[29] I received letters from friends telling me I was 'a disgrace' and 'a traitor'. I also received letters from strangers saying that the poem had helped them to understand problems in their own lives and in society. I mention this simply to illustrate what happens when poetry ventures into 'forbidden territory' or explores the state of the outcast, the lost, the damned. Irish life shivers and burns with little hells. There are little heavens too. And countless, tacky little purgatories. They should all be explored. Therefore, poetry will be 'offensive' or 'outrageous', as you will, as readers will. Readers read poetry and are in turn read by it. This is one further reason why poetry in Ireland should be more and more open and experimental. It's as if this experimentation at every level is part of a battle against stagnation, half-heartedness, closed insularity, rigid judgementalism, ready prejudice, cosy certainties, unexpressed angers, active hatreds, fear. Fear above all, perhaps. Poetry is a battle against these horrors, even as it is often, surprisingly, rooted in them. This recognition has been made by many poets writing in Ireland today. It helps to account for the vigour and variety of the poetry they produce. It is up to the poets themselves to discover and take measures against the reasons that help to account for its shortcomings. This always involves a necessary return to the hurts and honesty of that solitude where poetry begins and ends and then again, true to its own resilient spirit in a world that usually ignores it and always needs it, begins.

Some Irish poets have been influenced by Yeats but Irish poetry

on the whole has been surprisingly unintimidated by the range
and magnitude of his achievement. This may be because his vision
of Irish society ('Sing the peasantry and then/Hard-riding country
gentlemen')[30] is so silly, so irrelevant to life in contemporary Ireland,
that his verse can be appreciated as something quite apart from
his vision of the country. Besides, the deepest, most far-reaching
aspect of Yeats's achievement must always inspire poets everywhere.
Poetry is hard work. Yeats's real meaning for poets can be put simply:
'Work hard at exploring the abyss of yourself and at clarifying
your discoveries.'

Poetry is trouble. Much of it springs from emotional trouble.
Writing it can be nightmarish though words are fun; dangerous too.
To read poetry properly, in a state of concentrated, fluent attention,
is almost impossible, frequently leaving the reader with a sense of
dissatisfaction, even uncouthness. Reading poetry aloud can be a
painful exercise in personal absurdity. Some souls find it consoling
and enlightening. But trouble is the name of the game. Poets are
addicted to this trouble.

Ireland is a post-colonial island. Trouble. Thousands of years old
and still struggling to be born. I'm a post-colonial scribbler with vast
resources of ignorance, prejudice, misunderstanding and self-deception.
An English poet said to me last year, 'You don't write English,
Brendan, you write an Irish version of my language. I don't know
whether it's rhetorical or real.' I think I know what she meant. On
the other hand, it does no harm to feel homeless in a language, does
it? A language, like any house, can be a source of homely smugness.

The problem is to be at home in the sense of homelessness, to
risk rhetoric, to overcome embarrassment, to forgive oneself for
follies leaping from brain to tongue to pen, to be candid, to try to
achieve a light-filled laughter, to make the trouble lilt and sing
and plant a look of amazement on the face of a youngster who is
convinced that poetry is crap he has to endure for examinations
which he must 'pass' or 'fail', hideous words. Keats and Milton
and Yeats and Eliot make life bloody hard for some people doing
the Leaving Certificate. Poetry is trouble. 'Christ in heaven' a
young man exploded to me some years ago, ' 'Twas a great pity
Keats didn't shoot that fuckin' Nightingale!'

I'd be a fool to try to predict the likely course of Irish poetry. I
hope it develops more of a sense of humour, of comic selfmockery,
thereby admitting its own seriousness and limitations. Our beautiful
world is a horror-pit; how can our poetry not be comic? The kind
of poetry envisaged here would involve a properly savage and sus-

tained act of self-criticism. I hope this poetry reaches out to more and more people without compromising its seriousness or concealing its limitations. I hope it tackles the trouble that walks the streets, teaches in the schools, preaches in the churches, judges in the courts, festers or prospers in prison ('universities of crime' as one prisoner remarked to me), adores the music and songs of U2 and Sinéad O'Connor, speculates on the Stock Exchange, lives with AIDS, is sexually abused, sexually abuses, becomes anorexic, is unemployed, perhaps hopelessly so, condemns or praises the IRA and the UVF, begs in the streets of Dublin and talks to itself endlessly, lips moving with an eloquent, steady desperation that suggests nobody is listening or will ever listen.

I hope the troublesome art and craft turn all this trouble into a thoughtful word-music that will, even for a brief while, make sense to whoever reads or listens. I hope it will give some people the courage to sit alone and listen to their own neglected voices. I hope it will make them remember and prepare. But most of all I hope it will bring them joy, sharp and deep, the kind of joy that often co-exists with deepened feelings of sadness or pain. More than anything else, poetry is a celebration of certain hard-won clarities arising from trouble and confusion. In today's world, these clarities can be won only by a poetry that is open, experimental and so serious it doesn't give a hoot about anything except what it dreams it believes it is struggling to suggest or say.

A View of Irish Drama

Introduction

There are many reasons for the distinctive character of Irish drama. The first is obvious: Ireland is a small, poorish island in the Atlantic, close to Britain, with which country it has had a long and troubled relationship (is that the proper word?) for almost a thousand years. One would hardly think that a rather impoverished insularity would help to breed a world-renowned drama, but it has, because drama thrives on that trouble and conflict which are as much a tragic part of Irish life today as they have ever been. During the past twenty years, several fine plays have been written about the 'Northern troubles'. Irish drama presents a continuous re-creation of Irish history.

This insularity breeds a particular kind of intensity in talk, humour and human relationships. It nourishes gossip rather than thought, encourages anecdotes rather than philosophy. It creates an atmosphere of congestion that is frequently bitter and, more often than not, bitterly articulate. It helps to spawn what is known in Ireland as 'begrudgery', that is the state of envying other people whatever progress they may make in their lives, particularly in Ireland. One may be forgiven for improving one's lot abroad, but not at home. An oppressed people for centuries, we Irish frequently give evidence of that vicious slave-mentality noted, in different but definite ways, by all the dramatists in this anthology. Much of this begrudgery is accompanied by humour that is often savage and derisive or even downright destructive. Anything for a laugh, as the man said. This is also noted by the seven dramatists whose work I will discuss. The quality and consequences of the laughter in most Irish plays should be closely looked at.

It may be an aspect of this insularity that there is a sense in which these plays seem at times to be the work of inevitable outsiders. Reality is often viewed and explored from an odd perspective, an arrestingly different angle. Not being of the 'chief' or 'pure' tradition in English drama, these plays will strike readers for the freshness of their perspectives, the athletic freedom of their language, the articulate oddness of many of the human relationships they depict.

There is a considerable amount of drama in Irish life itself. The impulse to dramatise experience is especially noticeable in the *talk* of people on our damp island. Whoever said that Ireland is an open-air debating society wasn't far off the mark. This sense of a furiously talkative people is especially strong in the plays of Shaw, Synge, O'Casey, Johnston and Behan. Much of the talk is concerned with complaint, scandal, abuse, judgements of spontaneous and varying severity. Much of it is remarkable for its spirit of banter, for its word-play, for its light, rippling mockery. Some of it is a striking mixture of cleverness and bitterness, as if one's waking hours were at best an opportunity to hone one's satirical intelligence. And much of it is incisively, memorably funny, packed with merry poisons and smiling jibes.

These talkative people are too busy talking, it seems, to prevent the pollution of their landscape just now. It is one of the most beaut-iful landscapes in the world and its presence is real and pervasive in most of the plays. In Synge's drama, for example, the landscape seems as much a character as any of the people on stage. Language and landscape reflect each other.

Ireland's economic poverty has had, and continues to have, a deep influence on its dramatists. Writers like Congreve, Wilde, Shaw, O'Casey and Beckett left Ireland for several reasons; and it's a safe bet that the casual, insidious degradations of poverty were one strong reason for their deliberate exile. Poverty too plays an important part in nearly all plays I will discuss.

But the most important influence on Irish drama is the way the Irish people live their lives, or are seen to live their lives, by individual playwrights. When Synge said that art is a collaboration I believe he meant, among other things, that the writer is the people's truest voice, and probably never more so than when his art offends his people. All the writers in this anthology draw inspiration from the lives of the people among whom they themselves lived and grew and changed. 'A people alone,' Yeats said, 'are a great river'.[1] There is a deep sense in which Irish life, or more particularly Irish lives, flow through these plays.

The pressures of history and mythology are further factors to be taken into account when one is trying to describe or define the special character of these works. Political and religious realities are present everywhere and at nearly all times. The 'relationship' with Britain, or more particularly with England, is vital and is perhaps most obvious in the work of Shaw, Synge, O'Casey and Behan.

Even these few reasons will help us to appreciate both the back-ground and the content of these seven plays. If, taken together, they suggest a collectively distinctive character, it is hardly surprising to find that each writer has his own individual voice and vision, ensuring that each play is a compelling imaginative creation.

John Bull's Other Island by **Bernard Shaw** (1904)

John Bull's Other Island is about Ireland or, more precisely, about
Irelands – the different Irelands in the minds of the various characters.
For Broadbent, the Englishman whose 'first duty is his duty to
Ireland',[2] that country is the stage on which he can witness charm
and wit, comedy and fecklessness, humour, captivating feminine
innocence and lyrical natural beauty in an unpolluted landscape. It
is also the place where he can grab a seat in Parliament and plan
to turn that same lyrical landscape into a lively tourist area in which
even the most interesting and complex figure in the play, Peter
Keegan, will become a tourist attraction. For Broadbent, Ireland is
a stage. His English naïveté, his 'eupeptic jollity', breezily automatic
sense of superiority and invincible sentimentality, are equalled only
by his shrewd business instinct for turning not merely wild beauty
into exploitable territory but for presenting a visionary human
being as a colourful local eccentric. The entrepreneur in Broadbent
is powered by the sentimentalist. Most forms of sentimentality are
repugnant because the sentimentalist is not only committed to the
cheapest form of self-deception (it literally costs him nothing) but
also because sentimentality is usually a mask for cruelty, callousness
and instinctive exploitation. Broadbent proposing to Nora Riley is
a slobbering lump of sentimentality; Broadbent using Nora's attractiveness as a way of getting votes is a cold-blooded politician who is,
one feels certain, on the threshold of developing a passion for kissing
babies in public. Broadbent is aptly named by Shaw; he is certainly
broad in the scope of his ambition, and undeniably if acceptably
bent in his manner of achieving it. 'What I really dread,' he says,
'is misunderstanding.' His capacity for sentimental misunderstanding
is, however, the real source of his strength because it prepares the
way for his ruthless vision of power in the magnificent final scene
with Larry Doyle and Peter Keegan.

For Larry Doyle, Ireland is a more complex matter. Broadbent's
power derives from his ignorance of Ireland; Doyle's strength comes
from his knowledge of it. He has genuine insight into certain crippling
aspects of Irish life. Such insight must result from self-knowledge;
hence the savage, self-loathing violence of Doyle's expression when
he lashes out to Broadbent about Irish dreaming. This is the dreaming that Doyle escaped from as a youngster; yet there is an element
of fascination running through his fierce denunciation:

> Oh, the dreaming! the dreaming! the torturing, heart-scalding, never
> satisfying dreaming, dreaming, dreaming, dreaming! No debauchery
> that ever coarsened and brutalised an Englishman can take the worth

and usefulness out of him like that dreaming. An Irishman's imagination
never lets him alone, never convinces him, never satisfies him; but it
makes him that he can't face reality nor deal with it nor handle it nor
conquer it: he can only sneer at them that do, and be 'agreeable to
strangers', like a good-for-nothing woman on the streets. It's all dreaming,
all imagination. He can't be religious. The inspired Churchman that
teaches him the sanctity of life and the importance of conduct is sent
away empty; while the poor village priest that gives him a miracle or a
sentimental story of a saint, has cathedrals built for him out of the
pennies of the poor. He can't be intelligently political: he dreams of
what the Shan Van Vocht said in ninety-eight. If you want to interest
him in Ireland you've got to call the unfortunate island Kathleen ni
Hoolihan and pretend she's a little old woman. It saves thinking. It saves
working. It saves everything except imaginaion, imagination, imagination;
and imagination's such a torture that you can't bear it without whisky...
(Act I; 84-85)

Even more perceptive on Doyle's part is his statement about the
nature of some Irish laughter. This same mocking, derisive laughter
was noted by Joyce in *Dubliners* and *Ulysses*, by Yeats in poetry
('Come let us mock at the good'),[3] by O'Casey in his plays and autobiography, as well as by Flann O'Brien, Patrick Kavanagh and
others including Synge, Denis Johnston and Brendan Behan. Shaw
must have had some bitter personal experience of this laughing
derision when he lived in Ireland because Doyle's words are haunted,
authentic and unmistakably personal:

And all the while there goes on a horrible, senseless, mischievous laughter.
When you're young, you exchange drinks with other young men; and
you exchange vile stories with them; and as you're too futile to be able
to help or cheer them, you chaff and sneer and taunt them for not doing
the things you daren't do yourself. And all the time you laugh! laugh!
laugh! eternal derision, eternal envy, eternal folly, eternal fouling and
staining and degrading, until, when you come at last to a country where
men take a question seriously and give a serious answer to it, you deride
them for having no sense of humor, and plume yourself on your own
worthlessness as if it made you better than them. (Act I; 85)

Though Doyle has left Ireland, Ireland has not left Doyle; and
when he returns with Broadbent to effect a commercial conquest as
well as to see Nora Riley, his relationship with country and woman
defines him as an intelligent, eloquent, perceptive man who can best
cope with Ireland by rather crudely cutting Nora out of his life and
by endorsing and sharing Broadbent's vision of a tourist emerald isle.
Shaw never quite presents Doyle as being scared of sexual contact;
and yet it is impossible not to see in Doyle the kind of Irish flight
from sexuality that actually gives a certain acid to his eloquence, a
bitchy venom to his invective.

Both Broadbent and Doyle are, in their different ways, essentially cold fish impassioned by ambition. Peter Keegan is a passionate man made thoughtfully detached by his experience. Keegan is a visionary, perhaps a saintly one; he is tolerant, loving, critical, jocular in his special way: 'My way of joking is to tell the truth. It's the funniest joke in the world' (Act II: 1; 101). Keegan is, above all, sane in that his insistence on detecting and practising what seem to him to be the most worthwhile human values leads to his being an outsider, a defrocked priest in a society that pays lip-service to these values but often treats them with that derisive laughter so well described by Larry Doyle. In such a society, Keegan's sanity is what makes him a 'madman'; and his final confrontation with Doyle and Broadbent, in which he expresses his vision of heaven, a vision connected with his conviction that 'this world is hell', is in his own words 'the dream of a madman'. On the contrary, it is the dream of a deeply humane person with a vision of unity necessarily 'mad' to those whose lives are deliberately and savagely fragmented in the pursuit of self-interest. And yet, Keegan's dream is impossible; but is Shaw not implying that a passionate dream sharpens the sense of reality, broadens and invigorates the mind's horizons, and vitalises rather than deadens the potential of the individual? The dream, in this sense, pushes a person's capacity for self-knowledge towards its limits. Keegan's Ireland may well be hell, but it is also the raw material of his dream of heaven. As well as that, his final words reveal the dramatic power of Shaw's innate capacity for paradox. The Irish 'hell of littleness and monotony' begets the heaven-dream of magnanimity and justice. Heaven and hell, and the Ireland that symbolises both, dwell in Peter Keegan's heart and mind:

> In my dreams it is a country where the State is the Church and the Church the people: three in one and one in three. It is a commonwealth in which work is play and play is life: three in one and one in three. It is a temple in which the priest is the worshipper and the worshipper the worshipped: three in one and one in three. It is a godhead in which all life is human and all humanity divine: three in one and one in three. It is, in short, the dream of a madman. (Act IV: 2; 177)

As the curtain falls on Broadbent's 'I feel sincerely obliged to Keegan: he has made me feel a better man: distinctly better. I feel now as I never did before that I am right in devoting my life to the cause of Ireland' (Act IV: 2; 177), we feel that Keegan's dream must yield before the combined energies of Broadbent and Doyle; and yet it lingers vividly in the memory.

The other characters, too, are pre-occupied in their varying minor yet important ways with Ireland. For some, Ireland echoes with

the wrongs and sufferings of history, the evils of absentee landlordism.
For others, it is a small stage where life is a struggle and the struggle
gives value to life. For others, Ireland is land, land to be fought
for, to be owned and worked; and as the land is worked, it clarifies
the workers' capacity for industry and greed, for enlightened co-
operation and rapacious individualism. For all, Ireland is an image
that absorbs their days, moulds their dreams and defines their notions
of, and capaciy for, success and failure. Silent Ireland defines its
speaking people. Like Godot in Beckett's play, like the wild duck
in Ibsen's, and like the quare fellow himself of Behan, Ireland never
speaks in *John Bull's Other Island*; and yet its silence measures and
judges the value and consequence of the words of all those whose
lives are entangled with the rich, mysterious life of that 'other island'
which fascinated Shaw throughout his entire life. Written out of
the deepest recesses of his nature, this is one of Shaw's finest plays.
It is beautifully structured, the large cast of characters is effectively
orchestrated, the Irish-English problem of the tragedies and comedies
of mutual misunderstanding is deftly and penetratingly handled,
political issues are seen as part of the characters' everyday lives not
as remote parliamentary abstractions, and the language, always lucid
and pertinent, does justice to Shaw's complex relationship with the
land of his birth and, to a lesser extent, with the land that enabled
him to explore and develop his cheeky, compassionate genius. An
essential element of that genius is Shaw's need to explain himself,
his world, himself in relation to his world, his ideas, beliefs, dis-
beliefs, attitudes, opinions, prejudices, judgements and hopes. Hence
his prefaces, that vast bulk of explanatory literature which is an
eloquent indication of Shaw's terror of being misunderstood, and
also, perhaps, of misunderstanding himself, his work and the meaning
of his work for other people. He wrote four prefaces to *John Bull's
Other Island*. Readers of these and other prefaces can hardly be
blamed for thinking that in Shaw the passion to explain might well
have stifled the impulse to dramatise. It has not. Shaw's energy of
mind, body and imagination is such that one can only marvel at
the fact that far from stifling his dramatic impulse, his tireless
preface-writing deepened and enriched it. *John Bull's Other Island*
is a fully realised dramatic achievement; and the preface to it is a
model of lucid, urgent prose.

The Playboy of the Western World by J.M. Synge (1907)

J.M. Synge is one of the most poetic dramatists of this century;
he creates complex imaginative worlds which are genuinely rich

and strange. The word 'rich' is, in fact, one of Synge's favourite words whenever he seeks to describe his view of drama (the italics are mine). In the 'Preface' to *The Playboy of the Western World* he writes:

> ...there is little doubt that in the happy ages of literature, striking and beautiful phrases were as ready to the story-teller's or the playwright's hand, as the *rich* cloaks and dresses of his time.[4]

or again:

> ...where the imagination of the people, and the language they use, is *rich* and living, it is possible for a writer to be *rich* and copious in his words, and at the same time to give the reality, which is the root, of all poetry, in a comprehensive and natural form. (vi)

Synge's determination to embody reality in a richly copious language led to his desire to create plays marked by the kind of '*rich* joy' which is found 'only in what is superb and wild in reality' (vi).

This 'richness' has several fascinating ingredients. Two of its most essential elements are its musicality and its health. The musicality of Synge's language is inseparable from his view of art as 'collaboration'; he literally draws his inspiration from the people he meets and observes. Synge, like Pinter, has a tape-recorder in his brain; and he is quick to acknowledge the help which he, as a patient, vigilant, listening outsider, gets from the community in which he moves. He constantly acknowledges this in his prose works, *The Aran Islands* (1906) and *In Wicklow, West Kerry and Connemara* (1911). And he states it bluntly in the opening sentence of the 'Preface' to *The Playboy of the Western World*:

> In writing *The Playboy of the Western World* as in my other plays, I have used one or two words only that I have not heard among the country people of Ireland, or spoken in my own nursery before I could read the newspapers. (v)

It is not sufficient, at the same time, to present Synge's drama merely as a kind of distilled collaborative music. This musicality has deeper sources in Synge; it is profoundly personal; it is inseparable from his view of life itself. His brief *Autobiography* begins:

> Every life is a symphony, and the translation of this life into music, and from music back to literature or sculpture or painting is the real effort of the artist. The emotions which pass through us have neither end nor beginning – are a part of the sequence of existence – and as the laws of the world are in harmony it is this almost cosmic element in the person which gives great art, as that of Michelangelo or Beethoven, the dignity of nature.[5]

This is very different from Pater's neat dictum that 'All art constantly aspires towards the condition of music'.[6] Synge's conviction *is* that each human life is music. The dramatist who would present that human life must, therefore, discover and perfect an appropriate music. An examination of the various drafts of Synge's plays reveals precisely this: the scrupulous struggle of a writer to discover and reveal the minutely appropriately heart-music, mind-music and soul-music of *each* of his characters. In this struggle, Synge is nearly always successful; his output of plays is small but his work is as close to perfection as that of the greatest modern dramatists.

The second element of Synge's 'richness' is his sense of the drama as being a source of imaginative and spiritual health, of giving us a certain 'nourishment' which, he says, is 'not very easy to define'; but it is precisely this 'nourishment' that helps our imaginations to 'live'. It is significant that Synge himself was in poor health for many years; and there is what amounts to an obsession with sickness and death in his plays. But there is also a passionate concern with the opposite; with robust health, vigorous well-being, and a kind of emotional exuberance which, when expressed in Synge's soaring but always appropriate language, is nothing short of electrifying.

'We should not' writes Synge in his 'Preface' to *The Tinker's Wedding*, 'go to the theatre as we go to a chemist's or a dram-shop, but as we go to a dinner where the food we need is taken with pleasure and excitement'.[7]

It is hardly surprising that in these uniquely musical plays of which *The Playboy* is the most consistently sublime, Synge sees humour as a necessary ingredient in that 'nourishment' which he considered vital for the healthy life of the imagination. Synge's belief in the power of humour is more relevant in our polluted, nuclear-bomb-threatened world than it has ever been. Across the years, his words ring with sanity and a kind of singing common sense:

> Of the things which nourish the imagination humour is one of the most needful, and it is dangerous to limit or destroy it. Baudelaire calls laughter the greatest sign of the Satanic element in man; and where a country loses its humour, as some towns in Ireland are doing, there will be morbidity of mind, as Baudelaire's mind was morbid.[8]

Morbid images abound in *The Playboy of the Western World*, yet the overall effect is of a marvellously comic play. Jimmy Farrell may talk of 'the skulls they have in the city of Dublin, ranged out like blue jugs in a cabin of Connaught', and Philly O'Cullen may speak of the 'remnants of a man' whose 'shiny bones' he puts together for fun on 'many a fine Sunday' (Act III; 57), but the imagery

of skulls and bones is more a vivid part of the story being told than
it is evidence of a morbid preoccupation with death and its work.

One feels, on reflection, that *The Playboy* should, in fact, be
morbid. It is set in a poor, remote, severed if self-contained community; and it concerns the fate of a tired, frightened, dirty little
man who tells how he killed his father with the blow of a loy. Far
from being morbid, however, this is an exhilarating play, a genuinely
complex comedy. When it was first produced it led to riots in the
Abbey Theatre, proof that it cut to the bone with Irish audiences.
After the riots an interview appeared in which Synge was represented
as saying that the play was merely an 'extravaganza' and that he
'did not care a rap' for the public's reaction. In a letter to *The Irish
Times* in January 1907, Synge said of that interview:

> ...The interview took place in conditions that made it nearly impossible
> for me – in spite of the patience and courtesy of the interviewer – to
> give a clear account of my views about the play, and the lines I followed
> in writing it. *The Playboy of the Western World* is not a play with 'a
> purpose' in the modern sense of the word, but although parts of it are,
> or are meant to be, extravagant comedy, still a great deal more that is
> behind it is perfectly serious when looked at in a certain light. That is
> often the case, I think, with comedy, and no one is quite sure today
> whether 'Shylock' and 'Alceste' should be played seriously or not. There
> are, it may be hinted, several sides to 'The Playboy'.

The more one reads and sees this play, the more one realises
the truth of Synge's statement that 'there are several sides to "The
Playboy"'. It can be seen in different ways. One may say, for example,
that it is a play about an outsider (a recurring figure in Synge's
plays) whose presence in a small, tightly-knit society has, because
of the story he tells and the way he tells it, profound and far-reaching
consequences. To this extent, it is a play about the transfiguring
power of the imagination itself, the ways in which the story creates
the man with a power as wonderful and effective as that of the man
creating the story; the fact that the story is one of patricide merely
adds to our sense of Synge's ability to involve his audience in the
fabulous skill and wonder of the story itself; morality is burned up
in Christy's fiery poetry; the audience, as well as the other characters
in the play, are lifted beyond the accepted fact of murder into the
marvel of a tale captivatingly told by Christy Mahon who changes
from being a dirty, frightened weakling into a towering champion
capable of shaping his own destiny. We are witnessing the growth
of a poet's imagination; and we delight in that rare, inspiring spectacle.

We may also say that the play is a lyrical and moving love-story
with a sad, almost tragic ending, certainly an ending marked by a

deeply cutting and consciously felt sense of loss. Or it may be
asserted that *The Playboy* vividly demonstrates that the world evoked
by the poetic imagination is both fabulous and fragile; fabulous,
because it has an enchanting, liberating effect on all who permit it
to touch their hearts; fragile, because the magical world evoked by
the story is diminished, even destroyed by an action which fulfils
in dreary fact what had been mesmerically narrated in fiction. When
Christy finally kills his father (only he doesn't), he turns to Pegeen,
his love and his inspiration, and he asks:

> And what is it you'll say to me, and I after doing it this time in the
> face of all? (Act III; 81-82)

Pegeen's reply is not only a dismissal of a man capable of murderous action, 'a dirty deed'; it is also a defence of the poetry which
had won her heart.

> I'll say, a strange man is a marvel, with his mighty talk; but what's a
> squabble in your back yard, and the blow of a loy, have taught me that
> there's a great gap between a gallous story and a dirty deed.
> (Act III; 82)

There is a genuine feeling of let-down, of sadness, disappointment
and loss, at the end of *The Playboy*. In his 'Preface' to the play,
Synge wrote: 'On the stage, one must have reality and one must
have joy' (vi). Much of *The Playboy* is deeply thrilling because of
the joyful reality of its poetry and the exuberant reality of its comedy;
but the reality of its final lines from Pegeen is stinging and sad;
and that final sadness, pithy and undeniable, seems, as we contemplate
this play of 'many sides', to enrich and deepen its many moments
of comic vigour and lyrical beauty.

> PEGEEN. Oh, my grief, I've lost him surely. I've lost the only Playboy
> of the Western World. (Act III; 86)

That word 'only' may be the key to the nature and extent of
Pegeen's loss. She has indeed lost somebody unique, somebody she
will never replace. Her consciousness of the loss of a unique human
being, her 'only playboy', adds to the 'richness' of Synge's comedy,
throwing back on the preceding action a dark shadow that stresses
the wild laughter, the abandoned but accurate language of so many
memorable scenes. Ultimately, *The Playboy of the Western World*
defies strict categorisation; but its swirling energies of imagination
and language make it an increasingly fascinating play. Like a great
poem, it turns the reader's sense of familiarity into a deepening
sense of freshness and wonder.

On Baile's Strand by **W.B. Yeats** (1904)

When in January, 1907, rioting crowds disrupted the first production
of Synge's play at the Abbey Theatre, W.B. Yeats came quickly to
the dramatist's defence. Yeats, a passionate lover of freedom and a
ruthless champion of what he believed to be artistic excellence,
showed heroic grit in defending Synge's work against some of the
most repressive forces in Irish society. That word 'heroic' can never
be far from the lips of any critic trying to assess Yeats's achievement
in poetry and drama. In fact, right from the start of his career, Yeats
was concerned, even obsessed, with the idea and image of the hero,
the man who leads a brief, passionate, egotistical, free, adventurous
life, scorning a long lifetime of secure mediocrity and pensionable
caution. In art, Synge was one of Yeats's heroes, living and writing
with the fiery simplicity and integrity that Yeats admired.

In his quest for the heroic, a quest that implied a scorn for
realistic art, Yeats turned to Irish mythology where, thanks to the
translations by scholars such as Standish O'Grady and by other writers
like Lady Gregory, he discovered the heroic figure of Cuchulain,
the Achilles of Ireland, the focal character of the old Irish epic,
Táin Bó Cuailgne. Yeats determined to create a number of plays
based on incidents in Cuchulain's life. Writing about his play *On
Baile's Strand*, he says in his 'Preface' to *Plays in Prose and Verse*:
'It makes one of a series of plays upon events in the life of Cuchulain,
and if placed in the order of these events the plays would run: 1.
'The Hawk's Well' (*Four Plays for Dancers*); 2. 'The Green Helmet';
3. 'On Baile's Strand'; 4. 'The Only Jealousy of Emer' (*Four Plays
for Dancers*): but they were so little planned for performance upon
one evening that they should be at their best on three different
kinds of stage.'[9] There is a fifth play, *The Death of Cuchulain* (1939),
which Yeats finished near the end of his life.

These Cuchulain plays may, as Yeats says, be performed separately,
but they are also an intriguing dramatic unity which Yeats may not
have consciously intended. In the late 1950s, I saw a production of
the five plays in the course of a delightfully lengthy evening in the
Players' Theatre, Trinity College, Dublin. It was an unforgettable
theatrical experience. The five plays fused into a single, multi-
faceted, heroic-dramatic image. At the centre of that image stood
the proud, passionate and ultimately tragic figure of Cuchulain.

My concern here is with *On Baile's Strand* in which the High
King Conchubar, desiring to harness Cuchulain's individual bravery
and strength in the interest of firm government, persuades Cuchulain

to swear an oath of obedience to him as a result of which the hero
is forced to fight and kill his own son although, at the moment of
combat, Cuchulain does not know his son's identity. This son is
the child of Aoife, a warrior-woman of Scotland, whom Cuchulain
had overcome in battle and then loved. When he *does* discover his
son's identity, Cuchulain goes mad and fights the waves of the sea,
believing in his madness that the foamy crown of every wave is
the crown on King Conchubar's crafty head.

   On Baile's Strand is a tragic drama. Yeats saw tragedy as 'a
moment of intense life';[10] he held that 'passion and not thought makes
tragedy',[11] and that tragedy, in fact, 'is passion alone'.[12] Indeed, for
Yeats, 'the subject of all art is passion, and a passion can only be
contemplated when separated by itself, purified of all but itself,
and aroused into a perfect intensity by opposition with some other
passion.'[13] In *On Baile's Strand*, Cuchulain's passion for self-assertion
is brought into conflict with Conchubar's passion for strong government, for the need to establish and maintain a reliable defence of
his country, and above all, perhaps, for the desire, at once civilised
and primitive, to pass on to his children a stable and well-ordered
society. Yeats saw this kind of passionate conflict as being essential
to tragedy which 'must always be a drowning and breaking of the
dykes that separate man from man'.[14] The tragic experience carries
one 'beyond time and persons to where passion, living through its
thousand purgatorial years, as in the wink of an eye becomes wisdom;
…as though we too have touched and felt and seen a disembodied
thing.'[15]

   On Baile's Strand is indeed a play of extraordinary passion. This
passionate effect is achieved through a deliberate, coherent structure.
Although the play is a continuous rhythmical entity, undivided into
scenes, I suggest that a helpful way to see how Yeats achieves his
passionate effect is to strip the play into the different sections or
scenes that constitute its peculiar rhythm.

   1. A Fool and a Blind Man open the play. (They will end it
also.) From the beginning, we realise that the Blind Man, clever
and resourceful, harnesses and directs the Fool's energy so that he,
the Blind Man, will not be short of food. The Fool's energy is
necessary for the Blind Man's survival just as Cuchulain's heroic
drive is essential to Conchubar's vision of strong government. Not
a word is wasted in this play: each word works for the next, each
scene echoes and deepens preceding and following scenes.

   In this opening section we learn that the Blind Man knows the
identity of the Young Man who is challenging Conchubar's warriors.

Indeed, the Blind Man knows who the Young Man's father is:

> BLIND MAN. Listen. I know who the young man's father is, but I won't
> say. I would be afraid to say. Ah, Fool, you would forget everything
> if you could know who the young man's father is.[16]

Much of the impact of this opening section is due to the Fool's
soaring fantasies. Yeats, indeed, dedicated the play to the actor
William Fay 'because of the beautiful fantasy of his playing in the
character of the Fool' (246).

2. This second section, tense with the sense of the High King's
determination to make the hero swear an oath of obedience to him,
is a kind of passionate debate between Conchubar and Cuchulain.
As the debate proceeds we become aware of the conflict between
the man who believes in government, succession and heredity and
the man who lives gloriously and unapologetically for himself, out
of a real passion for the thrills of open, adventurous living. The
High King's aim is clear:

> CONCHUBAR.   I would leave
>   a strong and settled country to my children. (255)

Cuchulain refuses to be bound. He will dance or hunt, or quarrel
or make love, wherever and whenever he has a mind to. He says
he has no need of children; he is even glad he has none:

> CUCHULAIN: I think myself most lucky that I leave
>   No pallid ghost or mockery of a man
>   To drift and mutter in the corridors
>   Where I have laughed and sung. (256)

This is the proud boast of Cuchulain the son-killer. When his son
does turn up, Cuchulain is immediately attracted to him. But that
is not yet.

3. All the Kings gather to try to persuade Cuchulain to take the
oath of obedience to Conchubar. Three women attend who will sing
their strange prayer-song when the hero finally agrees to take the
oath.

4. Cuchulain has scarcely taken the oath when the Young Man
turns up and challenges the hero. Cuchulain immediately feels
affection for the Young Man and plans to make him his friend.
Conchubar will not permit this friendship; Cuchulain, angry, lays
hands on the High King. The other Kings say this violence done
to the High King's person is a result of witchcraft. Cuchulain accepts
this and, throwing aside his instant, instinctive affection for the
Young Man, insists on fighting him. He kills him.

5. The women predict Cuchulain's death. This brief scene sends the most gripping reverberations backwards and forwards through the play. When, for example, the First Woman says,

> Life drifts between a fool and a blind man
> To the end, and nobody can know his end. (271)

we realise the same could be said of the play itself.

6. Cuchulain learns from the Fool's prattle that he has killed his own son. He goes mad with grief for his deed and with rage against the High King, and he goes to fight the sea. The Fool describes to the Blind Man how the hero cuts the head off each wave. The use of repetition in this final scene is hypnotically effective, clarifying the ironic fact that the hero's death prepares the way for thieving opportunism:

> FOOL: There, he is down! He is up again. He is going out in the deep water. There is a big wave. It has gone over him. I cannot see him now. He has killed kings and giants, but the waves have mastered him!
> BLIND MAN: Come here, Fool!
> FOOL: The waves have mastered him.
> BLIND MAN: Come here.
> FOOL: The waves have mastered him.
> BLIND MAN: Come here, I say.
> FOOL: (*coming towards him, but looking backwards towards the door*). What is it?
> BLIND MAN: There will be nobody in the houses. Come this way; come quickly! The ovens will be full. We will put our hands into the ovens. (*They go out.*) (278)

Each of these six scenes or sections plays its part in creating that passionate rhythm, initiated and completed by the hunger and rapacity of the Fool and the Blind Man, which makes *On Baile's Strand* such a compelling play. Yeats's preoccupation with re-writing his poems and plays is almost legendary among scholars and critics; but the real point of all his re-writing is to establish an inner resonance in his work which adds greatly to its appeal. This becomes clearer each time one reads or sees *On Baile's Strand*. Also, far from being an obscure writer, Yeats is forever struggling to make difficult yet lucid connections between different parts of his poems and plays. If, for example, we read *On Baile's Strand* and then read his poem 'The Circus Animals' Desertion', we can think about not only the deep themes of this play itself, or its relationship with certain other of Yeats's plays, but also its place in Yeats's entire work. So we can appreciate both its special significance for Yeats and its status as a poetic play about heroism in an age when poetry is at a low ebb in the theatre:

> And when the Fool and Blind Man stole the bread
> Cuchulain fought the ungovernable sea;
> Heart-mysteries there, and yet when all is said
> It was the dream itself enchanted me...[17]

Well, 'when all is said', what matters most about *On Baile's Strand* is that it is a many-layered, well-structured play by a great dramatic poet. For its language alone, *On Baile's Strand* is worth reading and re-reading. Here, for example, is Cuchulain's description of Aoife, mother of the son he kills. Aoife is both the source of his love and of his madness:

> CUCHULAIN. Ah! Conchubar, had you seen her
> With that high, laughing, turbulent head of hers
> Thrown backward, and the bowstring at her ear,
> Or sitting at the fire with those grave eyes
> Full of good counsel as it were with wine,
> Or when love ran through all the lineaments
> Of her wild body – although she had no child,
> None other had all beauty, queen or lover,
> Or was so fitted to give birth to kings. (258-59)

Yeats is not just a distinguished poet who wrote plays with the intention of adding dramatic fire and fibre to his lyric verse. He is an important dramatist who spent much of his life trying to bring poetry back into the theatre. I believe that Yeats's plays, with their profound insights, tight structures and distinctive language will become more and more significant with time.

The Silver Tassie by Seán O'Casey (1929)

Fighting and war play an important part in Yeats's plays about Cuchulain. Seán O'Casey's drama *The Silver Tassie* is also about war. Yeats's rejection of that play for the Abbey Theatre is now part of theatrical history. O'Casey had given three excellent, popular plays to the Abbey – *The Shadow of a Gunman, Juno and the Paycock* and *The Plough and the Stars*. These plays had dealt with war, drunkenness, ignorance and poverty in the Dublin slums. They were boisterous, tender, comic, tragic and extremely powerful. The Dublin crowds rioted against *The Plough and the Stars* as they had against *The Playboy of the Western World*. And, just as he had defended Synge, Yeats now defended O'Casey. When, however, O'Casey submitted his anti-war play, *The Silver Tassie*, to the Abbey, Yeats rejected it. O'Casey, living in England at this stage, did not write for the Abbey again, although he produced many more plays.

What sort of dramatist is this Seán O'Casey, child of the Dublin slums, self-educated socialist, actor, docker, stone-breaker, builders' labourer, opinionated hater of injustice and cant? I would say that first and foremost he is a writer who believes in the dignity and courage of ordinary men and women even as he witnesses apparently endless human suffering and pain. In an essay called 'Immanuel', O'Casey writes:

> Man's real fight has always been against sorrow of every kind, a fight to banish it out of sight, out of feeling, out of the earth altogether: to abolish the weariness of hard work, the sorrows of insufficient food, the misery of cold clothing, of misery-making homes, of the pains of illnesses, and, when possible, the unhappiness of death to life before life is ripe enough to discard the care of going.[18]

We are immediately into what is central to O'Casey's dramatic vision: a spirit of fighting gaiety, a profound awareness of human misery and sorrow equalled only by a fierce determination to make laughter triumph over trouble and despair. It is difficult to avoid calling O'Casey an emotional idealist; that in fact is what he is. This man who had seen human misery somewhere near its worst in the slums of Dublin had an unshakeable faith in the power of gaiety and laughter to help people survive all kinds of misfortune. O'Casey's genius lies in his ability to make his audience accept and admire those powerful surges of feeling that show people waging an incessant war 'against sorrow of every kind'. O'Casey consciously and aggressively gives us a passionate, personal Theatre of Feeling. He responds strongly to what he considers over-intellectualised writing and eloquently re-states his view of the primacy of feeling in life:

> Feeling, rather than thought or detachment, seems to dominate the world of life. It was not thought but feeling that led the way to human development, for the meaning of the word is based on the word 'to grope', and life, in its first stage of withdrawal from the world's waters, must have felt, groped its way in to the land. When hands grew handier, we groped our way forward more accurately, and, even today, with all our knowledge and our dependence on mind, the fingers retain an amazingly delicate sense of touch. We usually trust our feelings. How does one feel towards this or that? How often the question is asked! 'I felt sympathy towards him or her: I felt obliged to do that or this; I felt it was time to go; I feel something is bound to happen': the examples of the use of feeling are a multitude, and there is no escape from them, even in a snarl of a poem or snarl of a play, for cynicism itself is prompted by the feeling that there is little or no hope in humanity.[19]

Any poem or play that ignores or lessens the importance of feeling is to O'Casey an act of artistic perversion, a heartless attempt to turn the theatre into a morgue:

> Feeling is a faculty common to all living things…So since we can't take
> this feeling away, this emotion that is common to all things – even to
> those who taboo them – to banish it from poem or play is to banish it,
> not from life, but to banish life from the poem and the play.[20]

It follows from this that O'Casey will try to create a drama in which
there is as much 'life' and 'feeling' as possible. It follows too that
he must be fascinated by whatever force or forces cripple or kill
this feeling and life. War is such a force, 'the one great calamity,'
according to O'Casey, 'fashioned by the stupid mind and fumbling
hand of Man.' O'Casey rails against war:

> Life becomes a tale of an idiot when nation is set against nation, and
> war flames in our face to a clamor of sound and fury, signifying nothing;
> and life becomes an idiot's babble when we watch the few having so
> much, while many have so little.[21]

In his three early Abbey Theatre plays, O'Casey had demonstrated
the tragic futility and waste of war as he had witnessed it in Ireland
during the 1916 Uprising, the War of Independence and the Civil
War. But now, O'Casey wanted to show the horror, carnage and
consequences of the First World War. In his *Autobiographies*, he
tells how he first heard the song, 'The Silver Tassie', and how that
song became the title of his new anti-war play:

> The Silver Tassie
> Gae fetch to me a pint o' wine,
> An' full it in a sulver tossie;
> That I may drink before I gae
> A service tae my bonnie lossie…
>
> But it's no' the roar of sea or shore
> Wad mak' me langer wish tae tarry;
> Nor shout o' war that's heard afar
> It's leavin' thee, my bonnie lossie.
>
> Seán was startled. Aaron's rod had budded. A riotous and romantic song
> had drifted up…He hummed it in his tiny flat in South Kensington;
> he hummed it in the dead of night, strolling down the Cromwell Road.
> He would give the title of the song to his next play. He would set down
> without malice or portly platitude the shattered enterprise of life to be
> endured by many of those who, not understanding the bloodied melody
> of war, went forth to fight, to die, or to return again with tarnished
> bodies and complaining minds. He would show a wide expanse of war
> in the midst of timorous hope and overweening fear; amidst a galaxy of
> guns; silently show the garlanded horror of war. However bright and
> haughty be the burning of a town; however majestic be the snapping
> thunder of the cannon-fire, the consummation is the ruin of an ordered,
> sheltering city, with the odious figure of war astride the tumbled build-
> ings, sniffing up the evil smell of the burning ashes. The ruin, the squeal

of the mangled, the softening moan of the badly rended are horrible,
be the battle just or unjust; be the fighters striving for the good or
manifesting faith in evil.
    And he would do it in a new way.[22]

Doing it 'in a new way' meant that O'Casey no longer gave
audiences the kind of play that had packed the Abbey Theatre when
The Shadow of a Gunman, Juno and the Paycock and *The Plough
and the Stars* had appeared there. This departure from his early
style was a conscious decision on O'Casey's part:

> There was no importance in trying to do the same thing again, letting
> the second play imitate the first, and the third the second. He wanted
> a change from what the Irish critics had called burlesque, photographic
> realism, or slices of life, though the manner and method of two of the
> plays were as realistic as the scents stealing from a gaudy bunch of
> blossoms.[23]

The conscious throwing-aside of 'photographic realism' allows
O'Casey a whole range of exciting new possibilities in *The Silver
Tassie*. Most significant of the new developments is the use of a
dramatic chant in the play, especially in the powerful second Act,
set in the war zone, in the 'jagged and lacerated ruin of what was
once a monastery'.[24] This is where we hear 'the bloodied melody
of war' and witness 'the garlanded horror of war'.
    What an apt phrase is 'the bloodied melody of war' to describe,
for example, the strong misery-chant of the wounded soldiers in
Act Two. This full, musical expression of misery would be unthink-
able in a realistic play. O'Casey's 'bloodied melody' is a sensuous,
disciplined chant that reveals horror in a ritualised word-music.
The chant gives an ironic religious dimension to the horror, as if
the soldiers were maimed but articulate celebrants at some High Mass
of destruction and death in this old ruined monastery, this broken
relic of Christianity. The Wounded on the Stretchers chanting:

> Carry on, carry on to the place of pain,
> Where the surgeon spreads his aid, aid, aid.
> And we show man's wonderful work, well done,
> To the image God hath made, made, made,
> And we show man's wonderful work well done
> To the image God hath made!
>
> When the future hours have all been spent,
> And the hand of death is near, near, near,
> Then a few, few moments and we shall find
> There'll be nothing left to fear, fear, fear,
> Then a few, few moments and we shall find
> There'll be nothing left to fear.

The power, the joy, the pull of life,
The laugh, the blow, and the dear kiss,
The pride and hope, the gain and loss,
Have been tempered down to this, this, this.
The pride and hope, the gain and loss,
Have been tempered down to this. (48)

The Silver Tassie, in four Acts, has an effective structural rhythm. Act One is vibrant with the boisterous enjoyment of a victorious football team of which the hero is Harry Heegan. Here is what O'Casey calls 'the sweet and innocent insanity of a fine achievement' (25); but all this celebration, this drinking from the Silver Tassie, takes place on the threshold of hell, the edge of war. Act Two plunges us into that hell; we go swiftly from the spectacle of joyous victory to a weirdly effective music of war's obscenity and abomination. If there is music in hell, this is it.

In Act Three, set in hospital, we meet some of the men who have returned from war 'with tarnished bodies and complaining minds'. The football-hero, Harry Heegan, is a bitter cripple in a wheelchair, sexually frustrated, jealous and hopeless. His friend Teddy Foran, the frightening bully of Act One, is a blind shadow of himself. Sylvester Heegan and Simon Norton who have not been to war provide the kind of mild comedy that underlines the bitterness of the war-victims. Harry's bitterness has a black, lyrical intensity.

> HARRY (*with intense bitterness*). I'll say to the pine, 'Give me the grace and beauty of the beech'; I'll say to the beech, 'Give me the strength and stature of the pine.' In a net I'll catch butterflies in bunches; twist and mangle them between my fingers and fix them wriggling on to mercy's banner. I'll make my chair a Juggernaut, and wheel it over the neck and spine of every daffodil that looks at me, and strew them dead to manifest the mercy of God and the justice of man! (77)

In the final Act, set in a room of the dance hall of the Avondale Football Club, that crippled bitterness is contrasted mercilessly with the health and gaiety of the dancers. Although at the end both Harry Heegan and Teddy Foran resolve to 'face like men' (102) whatever lies before them, it is Susie who, changing throughout the play from self-righteous hot-gospeller to self-consciously sensuous beauty, is given the hard, necessary words of truth by O'Casey. The bloodied melody of war must always be replaced by the sweet music of continuing life:

> SUSIE (*to Jessie*) ...Teddy Foran and Harry Heegan have gone to live their own way in another world. Neither I nor you can lift them out of it. No longer can they do the things we do. We can't give sight to the blind or make the lame walk. We would if we could. It is the

misfortune of war. As long as wars are waged, we shall be vexed by woe; strong legs shall be made useless and bright eyes made dark. But we, who have come through the fire unharmed, must go on living. (103)

Most important of all, however, is the fierce, surging, musical power with which O'Casey's hatred of war and his love of humanity come through. The deepest war in this play is between the forces of destruction and the forces of creativity. O'Casey presents both, but there is no doubt as to which side he is on. The mature dramatist who had as a boy witnessed in the Dublin slums various kinds of human misery extracted from that youthful hardship an unshakeable appreciation of human grit and gaiety, and a kind of fierce good-will towards all creative power.

O'Casey is not a subtle thinker; his use of language often proves this; he cannot handle an argument like Shaw or achieve the pure lyricism of Synge; but he has the whole-hearted faith and the warm affections of an instinctive celebrant of life's irrepressible beauty and strength. He is a flawed, lovable writer whose heartening wish for humanity's welfare and happiness is more needed and pertinent today than it has ever been.

The Old Lady Says 'No!' by Denis Johnston (1929)

When Denis Johnston submitted his play, Shadowdance, to the Abbey Theatre, it was returned to the playwright with the words 'The Old Lady Says No' scribbled across the manuscript's front page. The 'old lady' in question was Lady Gregory; and her rejection provided Johnston with a new, and more striking, title for his play.

Johnston's readiness to change the scrawled rejection into the play's title gives us a good idea as to the actual nature of the play itself. One thing that the four plays we have already looked at have in common is that they each have a plot, a definite narrative line which leads with firm dramatic logic to a conclusion. In his delightful play, Denis Johnston seems more to anticipate Samuel Beckett than to echo Shaw, Synge, Yeats and O'Casey, although in fact The Old Lady Says 'No!' owes a lot to these writers in the sense that their achievements, readily acknowledged and applauded by Johnston, are also the objects of his considerable genius for parody and satire. A tradition begins to be mature when its masterpieces are mocked with sharp perception and critical affection; and while The Old Lady Says 'No!' is a distinguished addition to the Irish dramatic tradition it is also a tribute to the achievements of most of the writers it satirises. This play is written out of that restless and fertile frame of mind which rebels against what it most admires. It is a rebel's play – vivacious, experimental, satirical, mocking, consciously having a go at the sacred cows and the enthroned gods not only of the theatre but also of society and its institutions. It is one of those rare plays in which the spirit of fun and mischief is quite inseparable from the more serious satirical purposes and methods of the drama. *The Old Lady Says 'No!'* is quite zany at times, full of moments of inspired nonsense and uproarious confusion; anything can happen and there are moments when anything does; but all this is not to obscure or deny the deep-lying seriousness of the play. I say this despite Johnston's stated reservations concerning plays which are 'About' something:

> In English-speaking countries...the tradition of Pinero, Barker and Shaw, culminating in the 'Problem Play', is still well entrenched in the path of any further development of the theatre. We have the Play that leaves you with a Thought. What would I do if I met an Escaped Convict? How would I like it if Father married a Prostitute? Is War Right? I need hardly say that as a natural consequence nobody can go to an ostensibly serious play without feeling that he must concentrate upon what it is all About.
>
> But surely this is all wrong, just as it would be in the case of music! All that is needed to enjoy and appreciate a work, such as e.e. cummings' *Him*, is a simple faith, a little human experience, and a receptive state of mind attained by a process the reverse of concentration. This being the normal condition of my own mind I need hardly say that I find little difficulty in preferring Strindberg's *Dream Play*, to *Emperor and Galilean*.[25]

For Johnston, it is only a short step from this to say that 'the real play must be regarded as what goes on in the mind of the audience. What, therefore, a play is about depends entirely on who is listening to it.'[26]

The audience is a vital aspect of the play itself, playing its part in that atmosphere of animated experiment, ultimately controlled, which enables weird and wonderful things, as well as cynical and sinister things, to happen. Johnston has always stressed the importance of the role played by the director in the play's success:

> It is, of course, a director's play written very much in the spirit of 'Let's see what would happen' if we did this or that. We were tired of the conventional three-act shape, of conversational dialogue, and of listening to the tendentious social sentiments of the stage of the twenties, and we wanted to know whether the emotional appeal of music could be made use of in terms of theatrical prose, and an opera constructed that did not have to be sung. Could dialogue be used in lieu of some for the

scenery, or as a shorthand form of character-delineation? Could the
associations and thought-patterns already connected with the songs and
slogans of our city be used deliberately to evoke a planned reaction from
a known audience? [27]

The 'city' referred to is, of course, Dublin. Johnston says 'This play,
if plays must be about something, is about what Dublin has made
a good many of us feel.' [28]

In *The Old Lady Says 'No!'* the actor playing the part of Robert
Emmet, the famous, romantic young patriot executed for his part in
the rebellion in 1803 gets a blow on the head which leaves him
concussed. This concussed actor/patriot, known as the Speaker,
slipping from one identity to another with stunned and stunning
unpredictability, fumbles and orates his way through the play, finding himself in all sorts of situations, quoting from poems and speeches.
The Speaker is at once dazed and articulate, but always a determined,
somewhat ludicrous Romantic seeking the love of his heart, one
Sarah Curran of The Priory, Rathfarnham, a village outside Dublin.

Both Irish life and literature are myth-haunted. Shaw, Synge,
Yeats and O'Casey acknowledge this fact, in different ways, in their
plays. None of these writers, however, has the mischievous attitude
to myth that Denis Johnston has. Johnston has a deeply ironic
intelligence; and he is profoundly aware of the Irish tendency to
mythologise the past, to glamorise its famous figures, to put patriots
on pedestals. This is, of course, a human tendency and is not confined to Ireland. But Johnston believes that this tendency has a
special power and prominence in Ireland; and he questions the effects
and consequences of that tendency. His comments on one of Ireland's
most Romantic patriots are ironic and, one feels, true:

> So we all love Robert Emmet. Yeats and De Valera loved him, each in his
> own fashion. I do too; and so did Sarah Curran...We all agree that it was
> a pity that some of his supporters had to murder one of the most liberal
> judges on the bench, Lord Kilwarden, and that the only practical outcome
> of his affray was to confirm the Union with England for about a hun-
> dred and twenty years. Our affection is not affected by these details.[29]

Johnston writes of his myth-riddled, myth-haunted city of Dublin
with an irony at once blistering and affectionate. In doing so, he
shows a deep, intimate knowledge of Ireland's literature, and he
makes effective dramatic use of that knowledge. He writes:

> The play with which the first part opens, and which crops up again at
> intervals, is almost entirely composed of well-known lines from Mangan,
> Moore, Callanan, Blacker, Griffin, Ferguson, Kickham, Todhunter and
> a dozen more. The voices of the Shadows are the easily recognisable

words of some of Dublin's greatest contributors to the World's knowledge of itself. The long speech with which the play concludes contains
suggestions from Emmet's speech from the dock, the resurrection thesis
of the Litany, and the magnificent though sadly neglected Commination
Service of the Anglican Church.[30]

By what is literally a stroke of genius, Johnston treats his con-
tributing audience to a most revealing view of Irish life, history
and mythology as experienced and expressed by a concussed actor.
So the play is not only a hilarious send-up of everything and everybody it encounters, it is also a satirical swipe at the theatre itself,
at the very notion of theatrical illusion, the willing suspension of
disbelief for which we pay our hard-earned cash to look at people
pretending to be other people while we pretend to believe the entire
illusory exercise. By setting aside 'the long predominance of narrative drama', by allowing the receptive audience to be active partici-
pants, by simultaneously undercutting and extending the peculiar
nature of the theatrical illusion, Johnston enjoys all the advantages
of an irreverent approach to drama. Does he also, one wonders,
suffer from its disadvantages?

Is *The Old Lady Says 'No!'* an inbred play, demanding a prior
knowledge of Irish life, literature, mythology and history? Is it provincial in its assumptions? Is it too 'literary'? Is it indulgently pedantic?

I cannot pretend to answer for others but while I would say that
the knowledge mentioned above would be an asset to anybody view-
ing the play for the first time, I would add that the deeper life of
the play lies in the marvellously daft ways in which the concussed
speaker, dazed and drunk as history itself is when you try to grasp
it in its bewildering complexity, meets and tries to cope with people
and situations. This is the only comedy I know where the 'hero' is
both semi-stunned and expressive. Whether he is talking with the
Statue of Grattan or the old Flower Woman or conversing with Joe
whom he has shot or making a singular mess of an encounter with
two girls or simply trying to catch the bus to Rathfarnham, we find
ourselves delighted by this dazed, glamorous, romantic figure.
Concussed patriots are excellent company.

Satirical though much of the play is, it has a very touching,
lyrical ending, a love-poem to the ciy of Dublin, city of Joyce, Shaw,
Synge, Yeats, O'Casey and Behan. And, of course, of the bold
Robert Emmet, the dazed darling of Erin!

SPEAKER.
 Strumpet city in the sunset.
 Suckling the bastard brats of Scots,
   of Englishry, of Huguenot.

> Brave sons breaking from the womb, wild
>   sons fleeing from their Mother.
> Wilful city of savage dreamers,
> So old, so sick with memories!
> Old Mother
> Some they say are damned,
> But you, I know, will walk the streets of Paradise
> Head high, and unashamed.[31]

The Old Lady Says 'No!' is a proud, ironic, loving hymn to a city and its people; a rebellious, irreverent appraisal of the culture of that city and that people; a satirical stab at 'narrative' drama. But, it is also, in its own right, a most enjoyable, youthful play, packed with critical laughter and thoughtful comedy.

All That Fall by Samuel Beckett (1957)

Among the reasons why Samuel Beckett is widely considered one of the most important writers of the twentieth century is the fact that his works give evidence of unusual courage and unusual comedy. Harold Pinter has noted Beckett's courage:

> The farther he goes the more good it does me. I don't want philosophies, tracts, dogmas, creeds, way outs, truths, answers, *nothing from the bargain basement.* He is the most courageous, remorseless writer going and the more he grinds my nose in the shit the more I am grateful to him.[32]

Beckett is sometimes referred to as a gloomy, even a despairing writer. He is not. He writes of gloom and despair but not in a despairing, gloomy way. He writes of pain, distress, suffering, hardship, various forms of affliction; and yet a sensitive person will come away with a profound sense of the value of human grit and endurance. Beckett was once asked by an American critic, Tom Driver, if his plays were concerned with those aspects of human experience with which religion is also involved. Beckett's reply was:

> Yes, for they deal with distress. Some people object to this in my writing. At a party an English intellectual – so-called – asked me why I write always about distress. As if it were perverse to do so! He wanted to know if my father had beaten me or my mother had run away from home to give me an unhappy childhood. I told him no, that I had had a very happy childhood. Then he thought me more perverse than ever. I left the party as soon as possible and got into a taxi. On the glass partition between me and the driver were three signs: one asked for help for the blind, another help for orphans, and the third for relief for the war refugees. One does not have to look for distress. It is screaming at you even in the taxis of London.[33]

This is one of the most important things to grasp about Beckett. His entire being is saturated in a consciousness of human distress. *Waiting For Godot* is the creation of a writer whose awareness of that distress in so many painful and bewildering ways is close to being Christ-like. A friend of mine who recently spent some time with Beckett said to me, 'The man is a saint'. I never met Beckett but I know from his writing that he, of all the modern writers I know, allowed into his being a truly shattering awareness of the agonies, disasters, tragedies and humiliations of the twentieth century. I would say to anybody approaching Beckett that he or she should sit in a darkened room, alone, for a considerable while and think about the many appalling horrors of our 'civilisation'. Then that person should ask himself or herself, 'which writer most truthfully reflects the reality of the world we and our ancestors have created?' Many people would, I believe, come up with the name of Samuel Beckett.

But it is never enough for a writer simply to be aware of horror and distress; he must create and communicate his vision of it. And he must do that in the way most appropriate to his genius. Beckett's way is comedy – but a very special kind of comedy, and *All That Fall* is a good example of Beckett's comedy of distress.

All That Fall was first written for radio, commissioned by the BBC and first broadcast in the Third Programme on 13 January 1957. The play is made of sounds, silences, words, pauses. Beckett is as much a poet of silence as he is of sound. Very few dramatists equal him in his cunning and effective uses of silence. Such uses of silence give an added intensity to the sounds of *All That Fall*. Primary among these sounds is that of shuffling human feet, shuffling onward, ever onward through wind and rain and all weathers. It is the sound of human pain and human endurance. But there are many other sounds; the sound of sheep, bird, cock, cow, music, cartwheels, trains, a man welting a horse, bicycle-bell, squeal of brakes, thunderous rattles of a motor-van, cooing of ringdoves, woman sobbing, bumping bicycle, wild laughter, panting, violent slapping, hard breathing, slamming doors, violent unintelligible muttering, motor starter, roaring engine, grinding gears, feet quick-ening receding ceasing, handkerchief loudly applied, hymn-humming, nose-blowing, guffaws stifled and unleashed, bells, whistles, hissing of steam and clashing of couplings, blind man's stick thumping ground, ejaculations, curses, braying of donkey, children's cries, and always the dragging steps of the blind couple, Mr and Mrs Rooney trudging home from the station where Mrs Rooney has gone to meet her husband off the train.

The other major sound in this play is the sound of words, the sound of language. Mrs Rooney is dissatisfied with her language. She says to Christy the dung-carter:

> Do you find anything...bizarre about my way of speaking? (*Pause.*) I do not mean the voice. (*Pause.*) No, I mean the words. (*Pause. More to herself.*) I use none but the simplest words, I hope, and yet I sometimes find my way of speaking very...bizarre.[34]

Shortly afterwards, Mrs Rooney says 'I am not half alive nor anything approaching it' (11).

Mrs Rooney's consciousness of her half-livingness extends to her uses of language. As so often in Beckett, *All That Fall* is riddled with the sense of deadness of language in people's mouths. It is as if Beckett were saying that a person is language; therefore, if a person suffers pain and depression, his language must suffer depression and pain also. This sense of language being afflicted, even crippled at times, is one of Beckett's chief obsessions.

The vitality of Beckett's language springs from his awareness of the ways in which language is brutalised, fatigued, corrupted and endlessly abused by most of us today. It is as though he were so aware of the appallingly normal *deadness* of language in our society that his imagination, in recording and exploring that deadness, discovered a paradoxical freshness, even beauty, in the battered carcase of language. Lilies sprout from the guts of corpses.

Sounds of affliction fill *All That Fall*; yet it is essentially a comic play. If people and language are afflicted or crippled, language and people are made to speak of that fact in a specially eloquent way. It is a stilted, arch eloquence, even ludicrously pedantic at times, rooted in desperation, unleashing a deep sense of frustration with a dogged, ironic fluency, refusing to give in to the sense of being battered, refusing to shrivel up and expire in the face of incessant insult and injury, refusing to die, refusing to live, just going on and on with an obstinacy laced with despair, with a persistence mingled with futility:

> MRS ROONEY. I feel very cold and faint. The wind – (*whistling wind*) – is whistling through my summer frock as if I had nothing on over my bloomers. I have had no solid food since my elevenses.
>
> MR ROONEY. You have ceased to care. I speak – and you listen to the wind.
>
> MRS ROONEY. No no, I am agog, tell me all, then we shall press on and never pause, never pause, till we come home to haven.
>
> *Pause.*
>
> MR ROONEY. Never pause...safe to haven...Do you, know, Maddy,

> sometimes one would think you were struggling with a dead language.
>
> MRS ROONEY. Yes indeed, Dan, I know full well what you mean, I often
>   have that feeling, it is unspeakably excruciating.
>
> MR ROONEY. I confess I have it sometimes myself, when I happen to
>   overhear what I am saying.
>
> MRS ROONEY. Well, you know, it will be dead in time, just like our own
>   poor dear Gaelic, there is that to be said. (*Urgent baa.*)
>
> MR ROONEY (*startled*). Good God!
>
> MRS ROONEY. Oh the pretty little woolly lamb, crying to suck its mother!
>   Theirs has not changed, since Arcady. (31-32)

That is not, given Mr and Mrs Rooncy's situation, realistic language; nor was it meant to be. Beckett's comedy far outstrips the
aggressive grime and abundant blood of realism, and yet he makes
hilarious and effective use of slapstick and music-hall antics. The
feat of getting Mrs Rooney into the car, and then getting her out
again, is a nice example of Beckett's love of rumpus.

The dark comic intricacies of *All That Fall* form the core of
the drama. There is something sinister in it all, expecially towards
the end. Mrs Rooney speaks of attending a lecture 'by one of these
new mind doctors', hoping 'he might shed a little light on my lifelong preoccupation with horses' buttocks'. She speaks of 'the troubled
mind' and 'mental distress' (33). The tone is bitingly light. Mr
Rooney, a little earlier, had asked her:

> Did you ever wish to kill a child?
> (*Pause.*) Nip some young doom in the bud. (28)

At the end of the play we learn that Mr Rooney's train was late
because, as young Jerry tells Mrs Rooney, 'It was a little child fell
out of the carriage, Ma'am. (*Pause.*) On to the line, Ma'am. (*Pause.*)
Under the wheels, Ma'am' (37).

And that is it. No more words. No more explanation. Nothing
but the *sound* of dragging steps as Mr and Mrs Rooney trudge
homewards through a 'tempest of wind and rain' (37). Horrors of
all kinds come and go but the old blind couple must try to drag
on home together. We get a tempestuous elemental conclusion to
a drama so deeply human it brings home to all of us a painful sense
of the reality of our situations. *All That Fall* is a blistering revelation
of human inadequacy in many forms; it also contains some dark
suggestions about the nature of evil; but it is above all a comic
hymn to human endurance in a savage, crass, battering world.

The Quare Fellow by Brendan Behan (1954)

It would be hard to imagine a more striking contrast than that
between the austere, remote Samuel Beckett and the boisterous
figure of Brendan Behan, poet, drinker, talker, hell-raiser and gifted
if ultimately undisciplined playwright. Much of Behan's early life
was spent in English and Irish jails. An active member of the IRA
at one stage of his brief and turbulent life, he frequently fell foul
of the law and because of his outrageous behaviour and quick wit
appeared regularly in newspapers and on television. Born in 1923,
he died forty-one years later in Dublin, a broken man, a total legend,
a writer whose work is marked by honesty, humour, intelligence
and compassion. *The Quare Fellow* is his best play.

When it was first produced in London in 1956 Kenneth Tynan
wrote in the *Observer:*

> The English hoard words like misers, the Irish spend them like sailors
> and in Brendan Behan's tremendous new play language is out on a spree,
> ribald, dauntless and spoiling for a fight. In a sense of course this is
> scarcely amazing. It is Ireland's sacred duty to send over every few
> years a playwright who will save the English theatre from inarticulate
> dumbness. And Irish dialogue almost invariably sparkles.[35]

Tynan puts his finger on one of the most vital aspects of Behan's
genius – his ability to write sparkling dialogue. And this sparkle is
deeply comic, for the most part. As in Beckett, it is the nature of
the comedy which, on reflection, strikes us as being appallingly,
heartbreakingly funny.

A man is about to be hanged in a Dublin prison. Some other
prisoners and a number of warders talk about that fact, among
various other matters. There are tensions among both the prisoners
and the warders. There is a visit from an official of the Department
of Justice, named Holy Healey. The Chief Warder and Governor
of the prison appear and contribute to the atmosphere. So do the
hangman, slightly drunk, and his assistant, remarkably sober. The
quare fellow is hanged amid a ferocious, howling hullaballoo.

The theme is grim. The treatment of the theme is, for the most
part, humorous and humane. When Kenneth Tynan wrote that
Behan could 'move wild laughter in the throat of death' he was
pinpointing Behan's ability to extract the most energetic comedy
from characters literally on the edge of the grave. During the entire
second Act, prisoners hop in and out of the grave being dug for
the quare fellow. The situation is bizarre; but the secret of Behan's
comic genius is that all his characters behave with complete 'normality', doing on the edge of the grave, or even *in* it, what they

would do in a pub if they were free in the city. They bet, boast, taunt, banter, smoke, are kind, cruel, lying, truthful. It is this air of unquestioned normality in a bizarre situation that seduces the audience to laugh at what, in their own concept of 'normal' circumstances, would horrify them. An important part of Behan's genius is his ability to turn the appalling into the hilarious without letting his audience forget how appalling the situation really is. However, with Behan, the more horrifying the situation the more comic the language. Far from creating confusion, this unlikely mixture drives home to the audience the horrors of hanging; and yet there's not a moment of obvious or aggressive propaganda in the play. Behan works through implication, suggestion, conversation and laughter. But there is no doubting the humanity of his message. Hanging the quare fellow is merely murdering the murderer. And we, laughing our heads off, are all involved. Our sense of responsibility sharpens as our laughter deepens.

This play has a deep and abiding effect on readers and audiences. The dialogue and peculiar comic tone of the work are two important reasons. So is the characterisation. Each of the prisoners, though simply named A, B, C etc, comes vividly alive, particularly the pair known as Neighbour and Dunlavin. So do the warders, especially Regan who performs his duties scrupulously but whose mind and heart are steeped in that understanding and compassion which form one of the most attractive aspects of Behan's writing. Warder Regan has seen many hangings. He will be present too, along with a new young warder, Crimmin, at the hanging of the quare fellow. Many people, from the Chief to the most seasoned old prisoners, have a strange reliance on Warder Regan.

> CHIEF. I don't know what we'd do without you, Regan, on these jobs. Is there anything the Governor or I could do to make things easier?
> WARDER REGAN. You could say a decade of the rosary.
> CHIEF. I could hardly ask the Governor to do that.
> WARDER REGAN. His prayers would be as good as anyone else's.
> CHIEF. Is there anything on the practical side we could send down?
> WARDER REGAN. A bottle of malt.
> CHIEF. Do you think he'd drink it?
> WARDER REGAN. No, but I would.
> CHIEF. Regan, I'm surprised at you.
> WARDER REGAN. I was reared among people that drank at a death or prayed. Some did both. You think the law makes this man's death someway different, not like anyone else's. Your own, for instance.
> CHIEF. I wasn't found guilty of murder.
> WARDER REGAN. No, nor no one is going to jump on you in the morning and throttle the life out of you, but it's not him I'm thinking of. It's myself. And you're not going to give me that stuff about just

shoving over the lever and bob's your uncle. You forget the times
the fellow gets caught and has to be kicked off the edge of the trap
hole. You never heard of the warders below swinging on his legs
the better to break his neck, or jumping on his back when the drop
was too short.

CHIEF. Mr Regan, I'm surprised at you.

WARDER REGAN. That's the second time tonight.

Tapping. Enter Crimmin.

CRIMMIN. All correct, sir.

CHIEF. Regan, I hope you'll forget these things you mentioned just now.
If talk the like of that got outside the prison...

WARDER REGAN (*almost shouts*). I think the whole show should be put
on in Croke Park; after all, it's at the public expense and they let it
go on. They should have something more for their money than a bit
of paper stuck up on the gate.

CHIEF. Good night, Regan. If I didn't know you, I'd report what you
said to the Governor.

WARDER REGAN. You will anyway.

CHIEF. Good night, Regan.[36]

As well as the dialogue, comic tone and characterisation, there
is another factor which plays an important part in creating the
astonishing effect of this play. The character at the centre of all
the talk and all the action, the quare fellow himself, never actually
appears on stage. And yet his presence dominates this play just as
comprehensively as Godot, who never makes an appearance in
Beckett's drama, dominates the atmosphere of *Waiting for Godot*.
Both these characters figure in the titles of these two plays; and
though they are physically absent throughout, they are the most
crucial figures in both works. Their very invisibility is the deepest
source of their fascination for audiences. The quare fellow has
committed a terrible crime; and the law is about to kill him in the
name of the people. But he is nowhere to be seen, his voice cannot
be heard. Who will speak for the quare fellow? Will anyone plead
for the helpless, condemned man? Such are the thoughts born in
the minds of the audience as they realise they will not see the man
about to be hanged; they will only hear the other characters, un-
forgettably visible and audible, speak of the invisible victim.

This invisibility gives almost unbearable dramatic tension to
the play. Details sustain this tension – details like the digging of
the grave, the hangman's calculations about the height of the drop,
the likely strength and thickness of the quare fellow's neck, his
weight, 'twelve stone, fine pair of shoulders on him' (65), the stratagems necessary to avoid telling him the time, the slitting of the
hood, the holy oils used for anointing a Catholic, the procession

to the place of execution, the Gaelic song the quare fellow asked for. All these details associated with the hanging of the invisible man are searingly present and memorable. They haunt the audience with a peculiar intensity, as does the entire play itself, as boisterous as it is compassionate.

This essay begins and ends with plays by two remarkable humanists – Shaw and Behan. Ireland was and is a poorish country in economic terms, but it has produced writers who have made rich contributions to literature in the English language. Brendan Behan, like Seán O'Casey, knew all about poverty. Lacking O'Casey's discipline and self-restraint, Behan embraced life with ultimately self-destructive passion and gusto. Imprisoned for many years, he knew and cherished the value of every living moment. That sense of value throbs through every word of *The Quare Fellow*, one of the most moving of all Irish plays and a searching contribution to world drama.

The Poetry of Joseph Plunkett

Joseph Plunkett is probably the least known of the Rising poets. Comparatively little has been written about his work, and his few critics have tended to treat him more as a poet in the making than as a finished artist. This is fair enough, but in thinking of Plunkett more as a poet of promise than of achievement, we should remember that he had a unique visionary intensity; that some of his best poetry is born out of deep inner conflict; that he was concerned with the problems of good and evil in a way that Pearse and MacDonagh were not; and that occasionally, despite all his uncertainties, he speaks with a mystic's certainty, insight and authority.

Plunkett is first and foremost a mystical poet. Plotinus said that the mystical state involves 'the flight of the alone to the Alone'; it involves also a knowledge of the real and an aspiration to the ideal; it is distinguished not by its vague visions but by its precise if astonishing insights. The true mystic suffers no delusions; he has a profound realisation of the complexity of his own nature, and of the relationship of that nature to the nature of God and man. He is especially conscious of the gulf between human capacity and human aspiration. He is not deterred or discouraged by this; on the contrary, this consciousness is part of his fortitude. And so Plunkett, realising his own limitations, writes in 'Daybreak':

> But I beneath the planetary choir
> Still as a stone lie dumbly, till the dark
> Lifts its broad wings...[1]

In the very next poem, however, 'The Splendour of God', that same pathetic manhood is seen to possess a divine stature:

> Immovable things start suddenly flying by,
> The City shakes and quavers, a city of mud
> And ooze – a brawling cataract is my blood
> Of molten metal and fire – like God am I... (164)

This tension between the sense of his own greatness and the sense of his own littleness runs through 'Occulta', the first section of Plunkett's *Collected Poems*.[2] 'Initiation' concerns pathetic human limitation and unshakeable human resolution:

> Our lips can only stammer, yet we chant
> High things of God. We do not hope to praise
> The splendour and the glory of his ways,
> Nor light up Heaven with our low descant:
> But we will follow thee... (166)

The same tension is conversely stated in 'Aaron':

> I am the Poet, but I cannot sing
> Of your dear worth, mortal or divine... (167)

Because the mystical poet explores profound problems and relationships, he is more liable to be confused and obscure than a poet who is content with superficial clarities. The worst of Blake is better than the best of Namby-Pamby Philips[3] because Blake's confusion is more indicative of a complex poetic sensibility than Philips' contemptible lucidity. Joseph Plunkett is frequently confused and obscure, but one feels that this is so because his mystical experiences overwhelm his power of articulation, or that his technical ability is simply incapable of communicating what is genuinely felt. Plunkett is often guilty of vagueness, ragged diction, feeble poeticisms, stained imagery, ineffectual use of symbols, cumbersome inversions. Occasionally, also, he is guilty of an even worse fault. He takes what is essentially a meagre idea and inflates it to fill the sonnet form, like so much air swelling a balloon. Poems such as 'The Little Black Rose Shall be Red at Last', 'Your Songs', 'The Vigil of Love' and 'Die Taube' are painful examples of this. Sometimes, too, the exigencies of metre and rhyme distort what he has to say and reduce his poem to a syntactical embarrassment. For example, his technical immaturity is agonisingly obvious in 'Your Fear', where the difficulty and delicacy of internal rhyme simply defeat him:

> I try to blame
> When from your eyes the battle-flame
> Leaps: when cleaves my speech the spear
> For fear lest I should speak your name:
>
> Your name that's known
> But to your heart, your fear has flown
> To mine: you've heard not any bird,
> No wings have stirred save yours alone... (180)

It is difficult to prise a meaning from such confusion; the order, or rather, the disorder of the words that constitute the phrase 'when cleaves my speech the spear' is a grim necessity for the internal rhyme with 'fear' in the next line. This is poetry suffering its growing pains, not the full expression of a mature artist.

His long poem 'Heaven in Hell' is riddled with faults; it has practically all the defects mentioned above. Yet – and this is Plunkett's peculiar strength – when it describes moments of conflict, it has the precision of the true mystic:

> In the dark innocence of night
> I fought unknown inhuman foes
> And left them in their battle-throes,
> Hacked a way through them and advanced,
> To where the stars of morning danced
>
> In your high honour... (173)

His own dream-battle, which was to become a grim reality, is symbolic of the struggle between good and evil in the heart of man. Conquering in his dream, he resolves to continue his personal struggle while recognising that in the conflict between good and evil, the real problem is to see, sanely and precisely, what exactly is evil and what is good; to know also that opposites such as these are marked not so much by their difference but by their disturbing intimacy:

> Still must I fight, but now a gleam
> Of hope comes to me like a dream...
> And I have learned in deepest Hell
> Of Heavenly mysteries to tell...
> I alone of the souls I know
> In Hell and Heaven am high and low,
> High in Heaven and low in Hell:
> From pit and peak inaccessible
> To all but Satan and seraphim,
> My song gains power and grows more grim... (174)

Plunkett is at his best when he is making a decisive statement, arrived at through a deliberate choice made as a result of inner conflict. That Plunkett, like Pearse, was driven by a kind of messianic compulsion is beyond doubt; the poetry that springs from such compulsion sweeps vagueness and imprecision aside, and we are confronted with the authoritative statement of a man who knows exactly where he is going. The certainty of 'The Dark Way' is the certainty of one who has something important to do and who intends to do it at any cost:

> Rougher than Death the road I choose
> Yet shall my feet not walk astray,
> Though dark, my way I shall not lose
> For this way is the darkest way...
>
> Now I have chosen in the dark
> The desolate way to walk alone
> Yet strive to keep alive one spark
> Of your known grace and grace unknown.
>
> And when I leave you lest my love
> Should seal your spirit's ark with clay,
> Spread your bright wings, O shining dove –
> But my way is the darkest way. (184-85)

The certainty achieved through inner struggle is unshakable in
its strength and simplicity. One of Plunkett's best poems, 'The Spark',
begins in doubt and ends in conviction. It moves with growing
resolution until Plunkett treats death with a kind of laughing fervour,
seeing it as a gay ally, vital to his mission:

> Because I know the spark
> Of God has no eclipse,
> Now Death and I embark
> And sail into the dark
> With laughter on our lips. (188)

Practically every poet, particularly in the early stages, is influenced
by the work of other writers. Plunkett is no exception. Tauler,
Keats, Francis Thompson and St John of the Cross helped to form
his thought and style. Dante also influenced him. Plunkett's 'Nomina
Sunt Consequentia Rerum' is translated from the *Vita Nuova*; it
is a competent translation, marred by a couple of clumsy phrases
– 'think all honour me to show' and 'even as retelleth memory'.
But probably the deepest single influence on Plunkett is Blake, one
of the most exciting of all poets. Blake's dictum 'Without contraries
is no progression'[4] is at the very core of Plunkett's thought; it is
what sustains one of his longest poems, 'Heaven in Hell', in the
last couplet of which Plunkett sees:

> A gleam and gloom of Heaven, in Hell
> A high continuous miracle. (175)

Blake is the deepest influence on Plunkett not simply because
he helps to mould his thoughts and technique, but because Plunkett's
profoundly mystical sensibility discovered a startling kinship in
Blake's massive spirituality. They are of the same spiritual fibre
and though Blake is an immeasurably greater poet, Plunkett sometimes approaches the English mystic's passionate simplicity and
penetration. Again, as with many young poets, there are identifiable
echoes in Plunkett's verse – echoes, for the most part, of those
writers already mentioned. But all these influences are completely
justified when we discover a poem which strikes us as being essentially
and unmistakably Plunkett's own, a poem, that is, which is the
expression of a sensibility formed by many influences that have
been fastidiously absorbed and appropriately transformed until they
are an organic part of the writer's own sensibility and vision of
existence. Such a work is 'I See His Blood Upon the Rose', a poem
which has survived both the Irish secondary school system and
the brutalising familiarity of many anthologies:

I see his blood upon the rose
And in the stars the glory of his eyes,
His body gleams amid eternal snows,
His tears fall from the skies.

I see his face in every flower;
The thunder and the singing of the birds
Are but his voice – and carven by his power
Rocks are his written words.

All pathways by his feet are worn,
His strong heart stirs the ever-beating sea,
His crown of thorns is twined with every thorn,
His cross is every tree. (192)

The mystic's loves are manifold and interwoven love of God, love of man, love of country, love of nature, love of woman. All these loves are deeply explored and subtly fused in Plunkett's poetry. His love of country is not passionately overt and aggressive as in Pearse; it mingles with his other loves. Although he dedicated one book of poems to Caitlín Ní Uallachain, the poems in that book are not forcefully patriotic but are rather subdued in their devotion. Many of them, in fact, are love-poems to Grace Gifford[5] and, though passionate, are characteristically quiet. Though he refers to himself as 'that mad heart' and 'this madman', the ultimate impression of these poems he wrote to the woman he married in the condemned cell is of a reverent reticence, a delicately hushed ardour:

Silence is the only song
That can speak such mysteries
As to earth and heaven belong
When one flesh has compassed these.
                        ('Prothalamion', 215)

Of the three well-known Rising poets, Plunkett is easily the most confused. I have tried to show that such confusion resulted not from a lack of talent or vision but from a rich questing poetic sensibility which, because it was not fully formed, was never wholly articulate. It is impossible to say and vain to speculate about what Plunkett might have achieved, had he lived. He himself had no doubt about his powers:

My songs shall see the ruin of the hills,
My songs shall sing the dirges of the stars.
                  ('When All the Stars Become a Memory', 207)

The truth is that Plunkett was just beginning to learn to speak with his own voice when he was executed; he was just entering that stage in his poetic development when he was beginning to have a detached, full view of his own powers and limitations, that point of calm confidence which is the threshold of achievement. The necessary uncertainties, the flounderings, the impassioned half-utterances were beginning to yield to skill, depth of insight and mature authority. But time, tuberculosis, and his own political convictions were against his development. One of his last poems begins with the line, 'There is no deed I would not dare' (212). Plunkett proved this at Easter 1916. But every situation has its irony, and the birth of the martyr meant the death of the poet. A thought that Plunkett – and Blake – would have appreciated.

Patrick Kavanagh's Comic Vision

1

There are certain poets of whom it can be said that they have a unique personal vision – Blake and Yeats for example – and one knows immediately what is meant. They have a new, inimitable, disturbing way of looking at life and, at their best, they communicate this vision successfully. In twentieth century Ireland, one poet (apart from Yeats) possesses such a vision – Patrick Kavanagh – who, for some unaccountable reason, is one of the most misunderstood and undervalued poets of our time. It is with Blake and Yeats that Kavanagh must be compared, for he is a visionary poet and towards the end of his life he claimed that he had achieved a truly comic vision:

> There is only one muse, the Comic Muse. In Tragedy there is always something of a lie. Great poetry is always comic in the profound sense. Comedy is abundance of life. All true poets are gay, fantastically humorous.[1]

Comedy then, meant for Kavanagh something very definite and profound, but sometimes what is perfectly clear to a poet is confused to a critic because the poet lives poetry and his discoveries are inevitable and organic. They are one with the beat of his blood. It is the purpose of this essay to clarify what Kavanagh meant by the comic vision; to show how comedy appears in his poetry; and in so doing to trace his development.

Fewer modern poets have undergone such a deep, dynamic development as Kavanagh. The trouble with Thomas Hardy, for example, is that his poetry, at the deepest level, the level of visionary intensity, does not develop. What we get from him is a series of sincere repetitions of a few basic perceptions. At the end of Hardy's career, he is saying, in more or less the same way, exactly what he was saying at the beginning and his greatness is that he manages to move us by his repetition. It is his sincerity which prevents his repetition from becoming platitude; but as we witness Hardy's integrity, we also see his shortcomings, chief of which is that his vision does not undergo any vital development or change. So there is little or no growth in his poetry. There is instead a kind of intrepid stasis that commands attention. R.S. Thomas, the Welsh poet, is another who is stuck in this peculiar rut of static honesty. He seems to be writing the same poem always. After reading his poems, I feel as if I had listened to somebody with whom a perception has become an obsession and who is so convinced of its importance he has to repeat it *ad infinitum*. A poet's perception has a quality of brutal stamina that will not permit him to remain at rest with one statement. He must tell it to all the world all the time. However, with Hardy and Thomas, what is told doesn't change very much. In the case of Kavanagh, it changes a great deal. His was one of the most moving, coherent, and profound visions in modern poetry.

2

With a great number of poets who undergo this change the beginning is naïve, the conclusion wise.

The poems in Kavanagh's early work, *Ploughman and Other Poems*, are beautifully simple. Yet they contain certain elements which endure into his later work, though in a transfigured way. In the note to his *Collected Poems*, Kavanagh tells us that, for him, poetry is 'a mystical thing, and a dangerous thing'.[2] It is mystical because it is concerned with man's dialogue with God, the foundation-stone of all Kavanagh's work, the source of his humour and sanity:

> If I happened to meet a poet – and I have met poets – I would expect him to reveal his powers of insight and imagination even if he talked of poultry farming, ground rents or any other commonplace subject. Above all, I would expect to be excited and have my horizons of faith and hope widened by his ideas on the only subject that is of any real importance – Man-in-this-world-and-why.
> He would reveal to me the gay, imaginative God who made the grass and the trees and the flowers, a God not terribly to be feared. (*CPr*, 233)

Belief in that gay, imaginative, unfeared, creative God vitalises Kavanagh's early work. It is this spirit of positive belief that makes such simple lyrics as 'To A Blackbird' so authentic and buoyant:

> O pagan poet you
> And I are one
> In this – we lose our God
> At set of sun.
>
> And we are kindred when
> The hill wind shakes
> Sweet song like blossoms on
> The calm green lakes.
>
> We dream while Earth's sad children
> Go slowly by
> Pleading for our conversion
> With the Most High. (3)

In that poem is, in genetic form, another vital aspect of the comic vision achieved by Kavanagh towards the end of his life: his separateness, his detachment, the sense that he can participate but never belong. Kavanagh was to speak many years later of the poet's 'kink of rectitude' (CPr, 230), that blessing and burden of integrity that makes a lot of people hate the poet. Blake had this 'kink of rectitude'. He had a disturbing habit of slamming whatever he believed to be hypocritical, phoney, and mediocre. Kavanagh had this quality in terrifying abundance and his newspaper, Kavanagh's Weekly, which was totally honest and therefore short-lived, is immortal for its moral probity, humour, and outspokenness. These qualities spring from his detachment which in turn originates in his belief in a gay, imaginative God, which is also the source of his later philosophy of 'not caring' (CPr, 20). Kavanagh quite rightly saw that the sense of importance a number of people suffer from is a form of insanity – they invest the trivial things to which they are committed with what is in fact a ludicrous sense that it all matters a great deal. Co-existing with the sense of man's insignificance, however, is the sense of his grandeur – something that Kavanagh never lost though 'malignant Dublin' (CPr, 14) disillusioned him considerably, at least for a time:

> There is nothing as dead and damned as an important thing. The things that really matter are casual, insignificant little things, things you would be ashamed to talk of publicly. You are ashamed and then after years someone blabs and you find that you are in the secret majority. Such is fame. (CPr, 19)

This is another aspect of his vision which needs to be stressed: the significance of the casual and the apparently insignificant. In this attitude is the refusal to be deceived by anything, the determination to accept himself, and by so doing, to forget himself:

> The poet's secret, which is not a secret but a form of high courage, is that he, in a strange way, doesn't care. The poet is not concerned with the effect he is making; he forgets himself. (CPr, 28)

In the best of his early poems Kavanagh looks into himself, desiring this detachment, the key to not-caring about the 'important'. He is trying, in the poetic sense, to keep his soul pure. He looks out from himself at the natural beauty of Monaghan and sees the black hills that do not care, that are 'incurious'. A certain kind of curiosity not only killed the cat and turned Lot's wife into salt – it could also mar the detachment of the poet, and meddle with the happiness that comes from observation and expression.

> My black hills have never seen the sun rising,
> Eternally they look north towards Armagh
> Lot's wife would not be salt if she had been
> Incurious as my black hills that are happy
> When dawn whitens Glassdrummond chapel.
>
> ('Shancoduff', 30)

Kavanagh said once that a poet's journey is the way 'from simplicity back to simplicity' (CPr, 278). The simplicity of Kavanagh's
'Shancoduff' is the simplicity of Blake's 'London', the simplicity
that stems from a totally coherent and lucid vision. In an essay
called 'Pietism and Poetry', Kavanagh says that 'The odd thing
about the best modern poets is their utter simplicity' (CPr, 244). I
would further add that only the man who sees completely can be
completely simple. Kavanagh knew this in his heart, and it can be
said of him that he is the only great modern poet who never wrote
an obscure poem. He recognised that, in most cases, obscurity is
simply a failure of the poet's imagination, the sanctuary of the inadequate. (In a couple of cases, such as Wallace Stevens and some
of Yeats, it is a measure of the depth of their enquiry.)

This simplicity, present from the beginning in Kavanagh's work,
is characteristic of his achieved comic vision. He saw that his simplicity was a gift from the gay, imaginative God; that it was the
most difficult thing in the world to achieve; and that if sophistication
has any meaning at all (and no word in the English language is
more abused or misunderstood) it means that the poet has the courage
to be utterly himself, his *best* self, and that nothing else will do.
In 'Shancoduff', Kavanagh is simple in this sense. He obviously
thought a great deal about the nature of simplicity and came up
with a few sentences that should be stamped on the brow of every
modern poet and critic:

> There are two kinds of simplicity, the simplicity of going away and the
> simplicity of return. The last is the ultimate in sophistication. In the
> final simplicity we don't care whether we appear foolish or not. We
> talk of things that earlier would embarrass. We are satisfied with being
> ourselves, however small. (CPr, 20-21)

Because Kavanagh passionately believed in his own conception
of simplicity, he was impatient, both in his own work and in the
work of others, with whatever violated that conception. A poet's
critical judgements are always, at bottom, necessary justifications
of his own most dearly held aesthetic. Yeats's dismissal of Wilfred
Owen is a daft assessment of Owen but an acute justification of
Yeats. Blake's contempt for verse with a single meaning is essentially

an assertion of the symbolic and therefore an attack on the literal. And this is fair: a poet can't be expected to advocate principles and ideas which he doesn't intend to follow. At the same time, in the interests of objective fair play, poetry should frequently be saved from the judgements of the poet who created it. Passionate belief is certainly the source of whatever achievement lies in the future; it is also the reason why poets are sometimes compelled to distort their accomplishments in the past. Because of his beliefs, Kavanagh was guilty of this distortion in his evaluation of *The Great Hunger*. He somehow failed to see that this splendid though rather uneven work was a vital stage in his journey toward the comic vision. Kavanagh had to write *The Great Hunger*, and, in his own time, he had to dismiss it. At this point, we may say that what is confused to the poet is clear to the critic, and from an objective standpoint, this is right. *The Great Hunger* is a necessary realistic outburst from an essentially transcendental imagination; it is a furious episode in a story that is fundamentally passive, reposed and serene; it is an angry protest from one who really believes in calm statement; it is a fierce hysterical digression in the journey from simplicity to simplicity. Kavanagh dismissed it and from his own viewpoint he was right to do so. But he was also wrong. *The Great Hunger* has a proud place in the larger story. Since it is the purpose of this essay to show the unity of Kavanagh's vision, *The Great Hunger* must be treated as a necessary part of that unity.

3

Patrick Kavanagh knew the meaning of poverty, and so he never tried to sentimentalise it. Seán O'Casey was another man who knew what poverty was, and his picture of it in his three great realistic early plays gets the bare, brutal treatment which the man who knows that world of viciousness, deprivation, and squalor at first-hand can give with complete authority. O'Casey rejected that world and created a different drama. It was as though he had purged himself of a consuming intimacy with a deprived world, and then proceeded to create another world distinguished for its fulfilment, vitality and joy. In *The Great Hunger* Patrick Kavanagh writes out of this sense of consuming intimacy with that crude barbaric world in which:

> Clay is the word and clay is the flesh
> Where the potato-gatherers like mechanised scarecrows move
> Along the side-fall of the hill – Maguire and his men.
> If we watch them an hour is there anything we can prove

> Of life as it is broken-backed over the Book
> Of Death? Here crows gabble over worms and frogs
> And the gulls like old newspapers are blown clear of the hedges, luckily.
> Is there some light of imagination in these wet clods?
> Or why do we stand here shivering? (34)

The Great Hunger is about a man who can trust nothing: not the gay imaginative God, nor life itself, not men, nor women, nor his own heart and soul. Patrick Maguire is married to his fields and animals instead of to a woman. Dominated by his mother, servile to his Church, committed to his meadows, his life is a sad farce of slavish work, furtive masturbation, crude pretence, increasing mindlessness, decreasing manhood and the drab inevitable advance towards old age. The bitter irony of his existence is that he is devoted to a shocking self-deception that began in boyhood and can end only with his death.

In portraying the appalling life of this central, solitary figure, Kavanagh presents the two major tensions of the poem. There is first, the tension between Christianity and a fertile, pagan or completely natural world.

> The pull is on the traces, it is March
> And a cold black wind is blowing from Dundalk.
> The twisting sod rolls over on her back
> The virgin screams before the irresistible sock.
> No worry on Maguire's mind this day
> Except that he forgot to bring his matches.
> 'Hop back there Polly, hoy back, woa, wae,'
> From every second hill a neighbour watches
> With all the sharpened interest of rivalry.
> Yet sometimes when the sun comes through a gap
> These men know God the Father in a tree:
> The Holy Spirit is the rising sap,
> And Christ will be the green leaves that will come
> At Easter from the sealed and guarded tomb. (38)

The second tension re-enforces the first. It is between the increasing impotence of Maguire's physical and spiritual being, and the irrepressible rebel bloom of the fields and meadows. The inanimate world is sure of an annual re-birth; spring's promise is eternal. Nothing but winter faces Maguire:

> Another field whitened in the April air
> And the harrows rattled over the seed.
> He gathered the loose stones off the ridges carefully
> And grumbled to his men to hurry.
> He looked like a man who could give advice
> To foolish young fellows. He was forty-seven,

And there was depth in his jaw and his voice was the voice of a great
    cattle-dealer,
A man with whom the fair-green gods break even.
'I think I ploughed that lea the proper depth,
She ought to give a crop if any land gives...
Drive slower with the foal-mare, Joe.'
Joe, a young man of imagined wives,
Smiles to himself and answered like a slave:
'You needn't fear or fret.
I'm taking her as easy, as easy as...
Easy there Fanny, easy, pet.'

They loaded the day-scoured implements on the cart
As the shadows of poplars crookened the furrows.
It was the evening, evening. Patrick was forgetting to be lonely
As he used to be in Aprils long ago.
It was menopause, the misery-pause. (47)

What Kavanagh insists on most of all in this poem is the appalling
normality of Maguire's fate. Underlying the two tensions mentioned
is the theme to which Kavanagh returns again and again, both by
direct statement and by implication. This is Maguire's devouring
sexual frustration, the agony he suffers from the 'impotent worm
on his thigh' (37). Maguire is a tragic figure. He is a man who,
sentenced to a horribly lingering death, is compelled to watch the
natural world reproduce itself with spendthrift fertility while he
shrivels into barren anonymity:

The cows and the horses breed,
And the potato-seed
Gives a bud and a root and rots
In the good mother's way with her sons;
The fledged bird is thrown
From the nest – on its own.
But the peasant in his little acres is tied
To a mother's womb by the wind-toughened navel-cord
Like a goat tethered to the stump of a tree –
He circles around and around wondering why it should be.
No crash,
No drama.
That was how his life happened.
No mad hooves galloping in the sky,
But the weak, washy way of true tragedy –
A sick horse nosing around the meadow for a clean place to die. (53)

The final picture of Maguire emphasises his sheer emptiness. It
is a frightening portrait of a man and his world utterly devoid of
hope; and Kavanagh explicitly states that this is not simply a personal tragedy. The darkness and guilt touch everybody on the land:

He stands in the doorway of his house
A ragged sculpture of the wind,
October creaks the rotted mattress,
The bedposts fall. No hope. No lust.
The hungry fiend
Screams the apocalypse of clay
In every corner of this land. (55)

The Great Hunger is one of the most striking and memorable long poems of this century, and yet its creator totally rejected it on at least two separate occasions. In his *Self-Portrait*, Kavanagh said that 'There are some queer and terrible things in *The Great Hunger*, but it lacks the nobility and repose of poetry' (*CPr*, 21). And in the note to his *Collected Poems*, he is even more emphatic in his rejection of the poem:

> *The Great Hunger* is concerned with the woes of the poor. A poet merely states the position and does not care whether his words change anything or not. *The Great Hunger* is tragedy and tragedy is underdeveloped comedy, not fully born. Had I stuck to the tragic thing in *The Great Hunger*, I would have found many powerful friends. (xiv)

The most important point here, and one extremely relevant to my argument is that 'Tragedy is underdeveloped Comedy'. If this is not a totally unique way of seeing tragedy, it is certainly a unique way of putting it. But we must remember that Kavanagh wrote the note to his poems in 1964 and that *The Great Hunger* was written in 1942. In the twenty-two years that intervened, Kavanagh's comic vision developed to its full maturity. Personal suffering and physical illness played a vital part in that development. He was now living in Dublin where he had to endure 'the daily spite of [that] unmannerly town',[3] and, of course, give his share in return. This Kavanagh could do extremely well. The next stage in his development shows him exploring the two strains that arise inevitably out of the early poems and *The Great Hunger* – the satirical and mystical strains that form the essence of *A Soul For Sale*. It is quite natural that the poet who wrote *The Great Hunger* should become a satirist; and the mystical strain in Kavanagh is present from beginning to end.

4

One of the most attractive things about Kavanagh's comic vision is his sense of the vulgarity of analysis. He disliked the assumption behind the work of many analysts, especially literary analysts, that whatever is analysed can be totally known. Like Yeats, Kavanagh knew that nothing can be fully known, and the man who assumes it can is committing a crime against wonder, violating that sacred sense of mystery that is at the source of all poetry. We revert to his fundamental belief in a gay, imaginative God and understand why, in 'Pegasus' when he has offered his soul for sale to the Church, the State, the 'crooked shopkeepers' (59) and the rowdy, bargaining tinkers, and nobody will have him, he realises that nothing matters but his own freedom and the integrity of his imagination:

> ...'Soul,' I prayed,
> 'I have hawked you through the world
> Of church and State and meanest trade.
> But this evening, halter off,
> Never again will it go on.
> On the south side of ditches
> There is grazing of the sun.
> No more haggling with the world...'
>
> As I said these words he grew
> Wings upon his back. Now I may ride him
> Every land my imagination knew. (60)

For Kavanagh, at this stage, the rewards of this liberty are twofold. First of all, his sense of wonder deepens, and his expression of it – in 'Advent' – becomes more assured:

> We have tested and tasted too much, lover –
> Through a chink too wide there comes in no wonder...
> Won't we be rich, my love and I, and please
> God we shall not ask for reason's payment,
> The why of heart-breaking strangeness in dreeping hedges.
> Nor analyse God's breath in common statement.
> We have thrown into the dust-bin the clay-minted wages
> Of pleasure, knowledge and the conscious hour –
> And Christ comes with a January flower. (70)

The second reward for the liberated, independent imagination is a kind of savagery which is inextricably involved with the deepened sense of wonder. Both elements are present to some extent in the well-known lyric of accusation, 'Stony Grey Soil' (82-83), but they appear in a far more vital way in that very powerful poem, 'A Wreath for Tom Moore's Statue'. Moore is Ireland's so-called National Poet, but in comparison with Kavanagh, he is a poor popsinger, a facile gaudy entertainer. In one savage line, Kavanagh endows Moore with an immortality of shame: 'The cowardice of Ireland is in his statue...' (85). But, towards the end of the poem, there is a note of hope. Salvation lies in expressed wonder:

> But hope! the poet comes again to build
> A new city high above lust and logic,
> The trucks of language overflow and magic
> At every turn of the living road is spilled... (86)

At the end of *A Soul for Sale* Kavanagh is faced with a choice: satire or celebration? Living in an essentially unsympathetic society, he is understandably attracted towards satire. His natural inclinations as a poet, however, draw him towards celebration. It is not an easy choice, but ultimately a choice will have to be made. Although his evolving comic vision tells him that satire is not enough, before he can consciously formulate its inadequacy, he must exhaust its potential. As a satirist, Kavanagh came to the conclusion that satire was simply 'unfruitful prayer' ('Prelude', 132) to the gay, imaginative god of comedy.

5

Kavanagh satirises those events, people and ideas we would expect him to satirise: Dublin's pretentious poetasters, its bumptious 'intellectuals', its complacent middle class, its vicious sentimentality, and its 'insincere good-nature' ('Tale of Two Cities', 115). Dublin is the largest village in Europe, a gossipy hive where the bees of slander buzz about busily day and night. Literary quarrels and tensions assume a quite disproportionate magnitude in the minds of people involved, and as Kavanagh said the standing army of poets is never less than ten thousand. The pubs are bursting at the seams with unwritten masterpieces, though the amount of writing actually produced is surprisingly little. (The disparity between declared drunken intention and finished sober achievement *is* usually enormous.) In 'The Paddiad or The Devil as a Patron of Irish Letters' Kavanagh lashes out:

> In the corner of a Dublin pub
> This party opens-blub-a-blub
> Paddy Whiskey, Rum and Gin,
> Paddy three sheets in the wind;
> Paddy of the Celtic Mist,
> Paddy Connemara West,
> Chestertonian Paddy Frog
> Croaking nightly in the bog.
> All the Paddies having fun
> Since Yeats handed in his gun.
> Every man completely blind
> To the truth about his mind... (90)

Kavanagh hits at the sentimental self-congratulation typical of the provincial Dublin mentality that James Joyce had parodied with such wicked accuracy. Kavanagh is no less savage in 'The Defeated':

> Drink up, drink up, the troughs in Paris and
> London are no better than your own,
> Joyce learned that bitterly in a foreign land.
> Don't laugh, there is no answer to that one!
> Outside this pig-sty life deteriorates,
> Civilisation dwindles. We are the last preserve
> Of Eden in a world of savage states... (97)

Kavanagh satirises sentimentality not only because it is a fear of real feeling, but also because it would divert the poet from his true responsibility:

> The poet's task is not to solve the riddle
> Of Man and God but buckleap on a door
> And grab his screeching female by her middle
> To the music of a melodeon (preferably), roar
> Against the Western waves of Connemara
> Up lads and thrash the beetles... (98)

The same dishonesty and unreality come under fire in the 'Adventures in the Bohemian Jungle', in which the Countryman, Kavanagh's moral voice, gradually comes to recognise the rottenness and sheer deadness of the world in which he finds himself. In the end, he sounds like a rural Faustus brought face-to-face with the hell of hypocritical mediocrity:

> ...here in this nondescript land
> Everything is secondhand
> Nothing ardently growing,
> Nothing coming, nothing going,
> Tepid fevers, nothing hot,
> Nothing alive enough to rot;
> Nothing clearly defined...
> Every head is challenged. Friend,
> This is hell you've brought me to.
> Where's the gate that we came through?... (108)

Other strong satires are 'Irish Stew' (109-10), 'The Christmas Mummers' (111-14) and 'Tale of Two Cities' (115). In 'Who Killed James Joyce' he satirises the magnates of the Joyce industry. This parody of 'Who Killed Cock Robin?', with its giddy little metre, is a successful demolition of all those pompous, solemn academics whose idea of happiness is the discovery of some trivial allusion in *Ulysses* or *Finnegans Wake*:

> Who killed James Joyce?
> I, said the commentator,
> I killed James Joyce
> For my graduation.
>
> What weapon was used
> To slay mighty Ulysses?
> The Weapon that was used
> Was a Harvard thesis... (117)

It becomes increasingly clear that Kavanagh is not really at home in satire. In the magnificent poem 'Prelude' he shows his competence as a satirist and then proceeds to declare his sense of its inadequacy:

> ...satire is unfruitful prayer,
> Only wild shoots of pity there,
> And you must go inland and be
> Lost in compassion's ecstasy
> Where suffering soars in summer air -
> The millstone has become a star (132)

Ultimately, satire is for Kavanagh 'a desert that yields no' ('Living in the Country: II', 170). In an earlier poem, 'Living in the Country: I' he also states his rejection of satire and informs us of his deeper intention:

> ...I protest here and now and forever
> On behalf of all my people who believe in Verse
> That my intention is not satire but humaneness,
> An eagerness to understand more about sad man,
> Frightened man, the workers of the world
> Without being savaged in the process.
> Broadness is my aim, a broad road where the many
> Can see life easier – generally... (167)

The choice is finally made. Satire falls away because it is not an enduring part of the comic vision. It is at best a necessary digression. I return to the note to the *Collected Poems*.

> I have a belief in poetry as a mystical thing, and a dangerous thing... Tragedy is under-developed Comedy, not fully born. Had I stuck to the tragic thing in *The Great Hunger*, I would have found many powerful friends...
>
> But I lost my messianic compulsion. I sat on the bank of the Great Canal in the summer of 1955 and let the waters lap idly on the shores of my mind. My purpose in life was to have no purpose. (xiii-xiv)

Kavanagh has almost completed the journey from simplicity to simplicity. The angry protest of *The Great Hunger* is over; the sword of satire is blunted in his hand. He has achieved an ideal of vigilant passivity, a belief in poetry as a mystical dangerous thing, a resolution to be at once humorous and humane. He sees the privileges and responsibilities of observation, has a profound understanding of the nature of love, and recognises one of the most fascinating and complex subjects for poetry and the poet. Out of his life, his digressions, failures, sufferings, disappointments and triumphs, he has hammered a superbly lucid and rarefied poetry that is the pure product of the comic vision. I shall now examine these poems.

6

Speaking of the poet in 'From Monaghan to the Grand Canal', Kavanagh says that 'All his life's activities are towards the final fusion of all crudeness into a pure flame' (*CPr*, 225). There is indeed 'a pure flame' of inspiration in a number of Kavanagh's later poems. There is also a certain amount of trivial verse which on first reading, would appear not to have been written by the same man. Yet if we re-read bad poems such as 'A Summer Morning Walk' and 'Sensational Disclosures – Kavanagh Tells All' (188-90) (where he tells singularly little, apart from the fact that he knows the names of a few poets and publishers) we shall see that they have a certain lightness of touch and tone, but are completely devoid of any visionary impact. Speaking about an early poem of his which begins

> Child do not go
> Into the dark place of soul
> For there the grey wolves whine,
> The lean grey wolves...
>   ('To a Child', 9)

Kavanagh said: 'In that little thing I had become airborne and more; I had achieved weightlessness...poetry has to do with the reality of the spirit, of faith and hope and sometimes even charity. It is a point of view...A poet is an original who inspires millions of copies' (*CPr*, 22). There are times when Kavanagh writes as if he were somebody else imitating Kavanagh's originality, as though he were indulging in a frivolous parody of his own vision. So when we read lines like

> Out of weakness more than muscle
> Relentlessly men continue to tussle
> With the human-eternal puzzle
>
> There were gulls on the road in St Stephen's Park
> And many things worth a remark
> I sat on a deck-chair and started to work
>
> On a morning's walk not quite effectual
> A little too unselectual
> But what does it count in the great perpetual?
>   ('A Summer Morning Walk', 182)

we seem to be listening to a bad imitation of some of Kavanagh's
favourite themes: the 'human-eternal puzzle'; the startling significance
and beauty inherent in casual things; the sense of his own dignity
and littleness in the face of 'the great perpetual'. But the rhymes
are forced, the metre giddy, the diction sloppy, the rhythm ragged.
In his attempt to become 'airborne' and to achieve 'weightlessness'
he has managed at best a rather frivolous lightness before flopping
on all fours to the ground. And this happens on several occasions
in the later poems. At the same time it is well to recognise that
these failures are the failures of a great ambition, of a poet who in
many other cases has achieved the 'pure flame'. In his famous
Canal sonnets, for example, we find that passionate, pure, weightless
expression:

> O unworn world enrapture me, enrapture me in a web
> Of fabulous grass and eternal voices by a beech,
> Feed the gaping need of my senses, give me ad lib
> To pray unselfconsciously with overflowing speech
> For this soul needs to be honoured with a new dress woven
> From green and blue things and arguments that cannot be proven.
>
> ('Canal Bank Walk', 150)

And so we come to the full flowing of the comic vision. At the
very centre of it is that ideal of disinterest which Kavanagh expresses
with perfect lucidity and authority in 'Intimate Parnassus'. This
might be considered as Kavanagh's *Defence of Poetry*, a brilliantly
compressed statement of poetic belief. Briefly, the poet is god-like
in his detachment and is, in the deepest sense, indestructible:

> ...The poet poor,
> Or pushed around, or to be hanged retains
> His full reality... (146)

Looking at suffering and strife, he must remain detached. Seeing
men and women going about their daily business, he must be 'sympathetic'. He must

> Count them the beautiful unbroken
> And then forget them
> As things aside from the main purpose
> Which is to be
> Passive, observing with a steady eye. (146)

In that state of passive, steady observation the poet discovers a
strong sufficiency. Here too he appreciates the nature of love and
survival because, for the man who has a 'main purpose' and lives
up to it, all things fall into sane perspective and acquire an individual meaning. In such a state, for example, the phenomenon of

evil is not seen as hideous or terrifying; it is simply 'sad'; while at the same time, seen from this divine vantage-point, it retains the capacity to be totally transfigured in the pure flame of comedy:

> ...I also found some crucial
> Documents of sad evil that may yet
> For all their ugliness and vacuous leers
> Fuel the fires of comedy...
>> ('Dear Folks', 151)

Evil does not subdue or even arrest the comic poet because his is the superb sanity of knowing what really matters. And because he knows, he wishes only the best for struggling humanity:

> ...The main thing is to continue,
> To walk Parnassus right into the sunset
> Detached in love where pygmies cannot pin you
> To the ground like Gulliver. So good luck and cheers. (151)

Here too is a new sufficiency, the happy sufficiency found in restrained serene expression:

> Making the statement is enough – there are no answers
> To any real question...
>> ('Nineteen Fifty-Four', 147)

and

> To look on is enough
> In the business of love.
>> ('Is', 154)

Now we must ask, for the comic poet, what precisely is love and what does it do? In 'The Hospital' Kavanagh tells us with all the insight of the poet-saint:

> This is what love does to things: the Rialto Bridge,
> The main gate that was bent by a heavy lorry,
> The seat at the back of a shed that was a suntrap.
> Naming these things is the love act and its pledge;
> For we must record love's mystery without claptrap,
> Snatch out of time the passionate transitory. (153)

'Love's mystery' is all around us and the poet must celebrate it. Out of that sufficiency, born of love-observation, comes the only style that matters, the style of praise:

> ...there is always the passing gift of affection
> Tossed from the windows of high charity
> In the office girl and civil servant section
> And these are no despisable commodity.
> So be reposed and praise, praise praise
> The way it happened and the way it is.
>> ('Question to Life', 164)

It is not at all surprising that Kavanagh writes about the mind of God. This is the focus of the comic vision. The attempt to understand God's mind, if rewarded with belief, is the truest source of comedy: it leads to detachment, and therefore to sanity, and therefore to the rare ability to see things as they are. That is why Kavanagh said that when he saw somebody 'important' or 'major' he was 'always in danger of bursting out laughing' (*CPr*, 17). To begin with, he finds God in woman:

> Surely my God is feminine, for Heaven
> Is the generous impulse, is contented
> With feeling praise to the good. And all
> Of these that I have known have come from women.
> While man the poet's tragic light resented
> The spirit that is Woman caressed his soul.
>
>   ('God in Woman', 147)

And again in 'Miss Universe', in 'the sensual throb/Of the explosive body, the tumultuous thighs!' he finds evidence of God's sufficiency:

> I learned, I learned – when one might be inclined
> To think, too late, you cannot recover your losses -
> I learned something of the nature of God's mind,
> Not the abstract Creator but He who caresses
> The daily and nightly earth; He who refuses
> To take failure for an answer... (158)

God and the idea of God dominate Kavanagh's poetry. I have heard some people say that Kavanagh as a man was at times extremely arrogant. This may be, for there is a poetic humility which manifests itself as social arrogance. In any case, what people call arrogance in a poet is usually a completely natural expression of his conviction. Some people like a poet to be tentative and uncertain; this is their idea of how a fine sensibility shows itself. But most poets with a conviction are neither hesitant nor uncertain. Kavanagh never was (not that it matters whether he was or not) and he was one of the most sensitive men I have known. He brooded constantly on God and in 'Having Confessed' he expresses his own conception of humility, another aspect of his comic vision:

> ...We must not anticipate
> Or awaken for a moment. God cannot catch us
> Unless we stay in the unconscious room
> Of our hearts. We must be nothing,
> Nothing that God may make us something...
>   ...Let us lie down again
> Deep in anonymous humility and God
> May find us worthy material for his hand. (149)

In other words, Kavanagh submits himself completely to the God who 'refuses to take failure for an answer'. At the deepest level of vision, Kavanagh himself refuses to take failure for an answer. And yet, paradoxically, Kavanagh did have a sense of failure, but true to character, he celebrated even that in his own inimitable way. 'If Ever You Go to Dublin Town' is a triumphant celebration of failure. In fact, it is not failure in any accepted sense of the word. It is, more accurately, a sense of not having fully accomplished what it was in him to do. But when one remembers what Kavanagh tried to do (and to a great extent actually did) one recognises the great dignity of this sense of 'failure':

> I saw his name with a hundred others
> In a book in the library
> It said he had never fully achieved
> His potentiality.
> O he was slothful
> Fol dol the di do,
> He was slothful
> I tell you.

> He knew that posterity has no use
> For anything but the soul,
> The lines that speak the passionate heart,
> The spirit that lives alone.
> O he was a lone one,
> Fol dol the di do
> Yet he lived happily
> I tell you. (144)

But there are plain, technical reasons for this sense of 'failure'. In a poem published in *Arena* (an excellent Dublin periodical now gone from the scene), not included in his *Collected Poems*, Kavanagh is quite explicit about his dilemma. The poem is called 'A Personal Problem', and it deals with something certainly not confined to Kavanagh but which is relevant to all modern Irish poetry since Yeats, and indeed to poetry throughout the world now. It is the dilemma of a poet who finds himself without a mythology. In the end, the internal world of the self needs the structure of myth to sustain it in poetry. Kavanagh never bothered to create a mythology. Indeed, the very purity of his comic vision means that the number of poems he wrote is fairly limited. He wrote about a dozen great poems. Yeats, on the other hand, sustained by a mythology gleaned from countless sources, wrote great poems in abundance. Like the body, the imagination occasionally flags; myth is a revivifying food. Kavanagh states this need in the excellent poem:

To take something as a subject, indifferent
To personal affection I have been considering
An ancient saga for my instrument
To play on without the Person suffering
From the wearing years. But I can only
Tell of my problem without solving
Anything. To rewrite a famous tale
Or perhaps to rewrite again of midnight calving
This cow sacred on a Hindu scale.
On Midsummer night.
There it is my friends. What am I to do
And the void growing more awful every hour.
I lacked a classic discipline. I grew
Uncultivated and now the soil turns sour,
Needs to be revived with a great story not my own
Of heroes enormous who do astounding deeds
Out of this world. Only thus can I attune
To despair an illness like winter alone in Leeds. [4]

There is an astonishing similarity between this poem and Yeats's
'The Circus Animals' Desertion'.[5] They are both triumphant
expressions of the sense of failure: for Yeats, because he cannot
find a theme; for Kavanagh, because he lacks a classical discipline
and needs to be revived by a power not his own. But just as evil
can fuel the fires of comedy, so can failure. The wonderful thing
is that a sensitive reader coming from a study of Kavanagh's poems
realises that here is one of the greatest modern poets whose comic
vision brought him through tragedy and suffering, whose passionate
sincerity revealed itself in an insatiable hunger for reality, who could
say:

No man need be a mediocrity if he accepts himself as God made him.
God only makes geniuses. But many men do not like God's work.
The poet teaches that every man has a purpose in life, if he would
submit and serve it, that he can sit with his feet to the fire of an eternal
passion, a valid moral entity. (*CPr*, 28)

Derek Mahon's Humane Perspective

A pervasive aspect of the poetry out of the North of Ireland from John Hewitt and Louis MacNeice onwards is a shrewd, reticent humanism. One cannot avoid the term 'Protestant' in describing this humanism because it involves the habitual workings of a conscience and/or of a consciousness which seem interchangeable. Catholicism, with its inbuilt sacramental structure of forgiveness, its absolving paternalism, offers a certainty of pardon which can have a desensitising effect on conscience because it takes, or seems to take, the consequences for the workings of the individual conscience out of the individual's hands. A system of forgiveness can help to foster a system of criminality. A crime forgiven can become a licence to commit a crime. The humanism I have in mind has little to do with forgiveness; it has everything to do with responsibility.

Humanism is a form of intelligent loneliness. The working of conscience is, by definition, a solitary activity. It dwells on the word 'human' and on that condition. It does not insult God by insisting that he should exist. It refuses to bully the Creator into His creation. It is therefore anti-Romantic, in the purely literary sense. It does not expect too much of anyone or anything. It does not brutalise another by anticipating too much of him or her. It is a condition devoid of emotional investment, a conscious renunciation of emotional capitalism. On the other hand, the dangers of agnostic constriction are immediately obvious. The humanist sets himself against a certain evil. It is the dullest, most pervasive and most accepted of all our cherished and civilised little evils: the fact that we use each other.

In other words, humanism is another kind of romanticism. Why? Because we *have* to use each other. Any two people who begin to be together must begin to use each other because they are in the grip of each other. What people call getting on with each other usually involves judicious and timely uses of the blind eye. Uses of the blind eye are usually, in such contexts, quite visionary. In the sense that I'm trying to describe it, humanism rejects this idea of use. Therefore it lays a primary emphasis on the potential of the solitary self, even the isolated self. Therefore it is romantic. Yet, because it refuses to use, it is gifted with a special detachment. Therefore, it tends to be ironic. Romantic in a special sense; ironic in a special sense.

One can search in vain in what is called Romantic Literature for a deeply developed sense of the ironic (Byron always excepted, but is Byron's poetry romantic?). You will search in vain through the literature of well known ironists for any radiant or aggressive sense of the romantic. Only the Protestant humanist has this special combination in his veins; in the veins of his imagination. Intelligent, sensitive, tough, sceptical, cautious, ironic, romantic, witty, nostalgic, reticent yet capable of outbursts at moments, constantly thoughtful, fighting against his own capacity to expect or to anticipate, conscious of the fact that he did not ask to be born, fighting his own tendency to use, yet insisting on self respect, showing concern for others but not exploiting them if at all possible (is it possible?), persisting relentlessly through the dullness of the days: this is the writer who is forced out to the edges of society. This is the writer who rejects the confusion of certain forms of involvement in the daily and nightly mess. This is the ironic romanticism of the person who knows how to refuse, the refuser who refuses to be forgiven except by himself. Never by a sacrament because he has no formula for self-forgiveness. He has not forced his God to exist because he himself never asked to exist, because existence was forced on him, not chosen by him and he has it now and he must endure it because he has nothing else. He is the result of perhaps a soporific moment of love in the dark; one can imagine him asking 'now was it love, was it love now, or was it just Black Bush, that purely erotic Protestant whiskey?'

Let us begin with Louis MacNeice's 'Prayer Before Birth'. As I see it, this is the prayer of the ironic romantic outsider who is not subject to the delusion of self pity, but who because of his detachment understands and states a valid sense of pity for all that the unborn self must endure. This poem depends very much on its rhythm, the rhythm of prayer, the prayer of the unborn, written by a man who knows something of the killing ways of the world. It is essentially a prayer to be human, to become human in the sense that it is aware of all those forces that are waiting like so many mechanical assassins to diminish one's humanity and to shrivel the potential of one's nature. This may be an appropriate moment to pay tribute to MacNeice, the humanistic source of much Ulster poetry.

I call MacNeice a source because his poetry points to the one thing that is absent from most Irish life and literature. *He is a source of alternatives*, another way of seeing, another way of experiencing. MacNeice perceives, tolerates, cherishes and celebrates *difference*. He proposes an alternative to prejudice in the North, an alternative to lethargy in the South. A humanistic alternative to piosity. This poem is a true prayer. It has the rhythm of the prayer that is said in private but has public reverberations.

> I am not yet born; O fill me
> With strength against those who would freeze my
>   humanity, would dragoon me into a lethal automaton,
>   would make me a cog in a machine, a thing with
>   one face, a thing, and against all those
>   who would dissipate my entirety, would
>   blow me like thistledown hither and
>   thither or hither and thither
>   like water held in the
>   hands would spill me.
> Let them not make me a stone and let them not spill me.
> Otherwise kill me.[1]

That is MacNeice praying for the unborn, which means most of us who flatter ourselves that we are alive.

One of the first poems by Derek Mahon, which I read many years ago in *Icarus* (a Trinity College, Dublin literary magazine), was a tribute to Louis MacNeice. It is a fluent and moving poem. Before commenting on it I would like to say something about the nature of influence, bearing in mind the influence of MacNeice on Mahon. There is an influence that is bad, a bad influence. It is born out of unquestioning adulation and encouraged by undiscriminating indifference. Such admiration is no good to anyone. It is rarely a helpful source of imitation. There is an influence that is half-way there, sloppily absorbed and turgidly reproduced. In such instances, the imagination becomes a gaping mouth. This influence is lazy. Periodicals and magazines are full of it. I think it is a peculiar poison of much Celtic Twilight poetry, for example, the fleas that Yeats talks about. And then there's an influence that is worthwhile. Plutarch on Shakespeare; Shakespeare on Shakespeare; Ibsen on Joyce; Blake on Yeats; Hazlitt on Keats; Godwin on Shelley; everybody on Eliot: these are examples of fully absorbed influences which are inseparable from growth. People often talk disparagingly about influence but it should not be so, because any true original is derivative. He is derivative from himself through others. He willingly submits himself to certain instinctively chosen influences until he emerges into himself. The thing is to see where the derivative self ends and the new original self begins. Mahon's original self begins in his tribute to Louis MacNeice. It is the first statement of this humane perspective. That word 'humane' and associated words like it, are never long absent from Mahon's idiom, his measured, courteous and decent words. And this too is the painful language of the Protestant humanist; words at war within themselves, or at least in argument with each other, ironical, loving, wild, reticent, fragile, solving. This idiomatic argument, this warring in words is evidence of conscience in action.

> Your ashes will not fly, however the rough winds burst
> Through the wild brambles and the reticent trees.
> All we may ask of you we have. The rest
> Is not for publication, will not be heard.
> Maguire, I believe, suggested a blackbird
> And over your grave a phrase from Euripides.
>
> Which suits you down to the ground, like this churchyard
> With its play of shadow, its humane perspective.
> Locked in the winter's fist, these hills are hard
> As nails, yet soft and feminine in their turn
> When fingers open and the hedges burn.
> This, you implied, is how we ought to live...
>   ('In Carrowdore Churchyard')[2]

I take the effect of perspective to mean a picture, an image that seems confused, that is confused and remains confused until you learn how to look at it, until you view it in the right direction and from the most clarifying angle and, in poetry, finding the appropriate language for that direction and that angle. It is a way of seeing inseparable from a way of saying. The slant is the word; 'In the beginning was the slant'. A certain slant of light is a certain slant of language. A humane perspective does not separate seeing from saying, or light from language, or language from humanity. There is something about skill, any skill, that seems to yearn away, or even to discipline itself away, from the human. Yeats's famous use of the phrase 'As for living our servants will do that for us'[3] comes to mind. But here I see, as sometimes elsewhere, Yeats is surprisingly simple-minded. The deepest skill is that which is most humanly convincing, not that which is most aesthetically adroit, or academically admirable. It does not easily satisfy the easy canons of mere good taste. Skill is the dance of any person's suffering; an articulate version of his own capacity for bewilderment. You don't learn living from skill; you learn skill from living, or trying to. A humane perspective recognises this; and this seems to me to be obvious in Derek Mahon's poems about human beings.

Consider for example Mahon's poem, 'My Wicked Uncle'. Everybody should have a wicked uncle. A family without an avuncular black sheep is not a family at all. How would we ever truly appreciate what we agree to call virtue if we didn't have these tipsy, reeling, benign practitioners of ludicrously happy, self-destructive vice, rippling the solid surfaces of family life? What Mahon's poem has got is a quality that comes from this humane slant of seeing his uncle in the way that is right for him. Mahon says in the poem 'That night I saw my uncle as he really was' (5). Seeing his uncle as he really was, a sort of king of innocent fibs, Mahon allows the emotion of the poem to flow in its own true channel. I would describe the emotion of this poem as one of calm, evaluative affection, un-bruised by the turbulent judgements of love or the possessive hatreds of love but with a warmly clinical recording of an amused, con-cerned sympathy.

From that wicked uncle it is instructive to turn to 'The Death of Marilyn Monroe'. From the poem of an intensely private man recalling a member of his own family in a spirit of affectionate sympathy we move to a poem about the woman who seemed to belong to the entire world, and therefore to nobody. Marilyn was a star. Viewed in her proper darkness, in the light of the attendant moon of Hollywood, she seemed to belong to anyone who looked at her. Everbody's girl. The property of eyes. The world's woman. Perhaps this was her uniqueness: this ability to belong and not belong. She was, as Mahon says, 'queen among the trash' (7), out of some bizarre modern fairy tale with a distinctly unhappy ending. Mahon captures in Marilyn something as essential as he had cap-tured in the portrait of his wicked uncle. She is caught in a pose of infinite striptease, her 'siren hair in spate' (7), a meteor, a girl, child, woman, goddess, star, wife, waif, body forever poised on the verge of disintegration. The poem is an act of appreciation, and this is what I take much of his poetry to be about – peripheral appreciation, not central love: appreciation of both potential and fragility or rather of that relationship between potential and fragility, between the promise and the vulnerability which characterised even Marilyn's smile. It reveals an essential aspect of Mahon's reality as a poet. He is a good appreciator but out on the verge. There is something in his art which is peripheral, watchful, measured, spec-tatorial, ardently uninvolved, articulately sidelined. This does not diminish his ability to appreciate others. It gives it, in fact, the authority of a certain kind of distance, a certain intellectual chastity that warms and validates his feelings:

> We are slowly learning from meteors like her
> Who have learnt how to shrivel and let live
> That when an immovable body meets an ir-
> resistible force, something has got to give. (7)

Probably the single most difficult problem for anyone seeking to get into Mahon's poetry is trying to define the quality of his voice, as it is indeed with most poetry. There are many elements in that voice. In his best poems all these elements are held in a calm and dignified balance. It is a quiet voice, not too dramatic. It is a consciously educated voice. It is learned but not pedantic. It is self aware and self mocking. It is perhaps too ironic to be noticeably passionate, and yet there is no doubt of its intensity. It is the kind of voice that craves an eloquent linguistic precision and often finds it. It is a voice of conscience, scrupulously examined, stylishly projected, rhythmically elaborated, a pleasure to hear, mysterious to think about. 'Matthew V 29-30' is a good example of what I'm trying to describe. In the Gospel of St Matthew, which is in many ways the most dramatic of the four gospels, the verses 29 and 30 from Chapter V read as follows – I'm quoting from the King James Version, a good Protestant version:

> And if thy right eye offend thee, pluck it out
> and cast it from thee: for it is profitable for
> thee that one of thy members should perish, and not
> that thy whole body should be cast into hell.

> And if thy right hand offend thee,
> cut it off, and cast it from thee: for it is profitable
> for thee that one of thy members should perish, and not
> that thy whole body should be cast into hell.

One thinks of Oedipus blinding himself out of guilt and remorse, out of conscience. Is there an implication that in deliberate self-mutilation, there lies some forlorn hope of renewal of self, of new acceptance by others? Notice in Mahon's voice, the dancing, mischievous, impish irony, the use of repetition which deepens the poem's humour, the stripping away in a comic yet sinister catalogue of bits of the self, of self-related things in the universe, until he is 'fit for human society' (71). The poem makes you ask, what does society want of yourself? What does your self want of society? What does one's self want of another self?

> Lord, mine eye offended, so I plucked it out.
>   Imagine my chagrin
> when the offence continued.
>   So I plucked out
> the other; but the offence continued.

> In the dark now, and working by touch,
>   I shaved my head.
> (The offence continued.)
>   Removed an ear,
> another, dispatched the nose.
>   The offence continued.
> Imagine my chagrin... (69)

Mahon is a true wit. There is an element of cruelty in his perception and in his precision but there is no lack of compassion. It is a complex wit: sceptical, ironic, nostalgic, funny, philosophical, mickytaking, impudent, lonely, relishing the absurd and the lyrical simultaneously. There are many poems I might cite to illustrate this. I choose a poem called 'The Mayo Tao'. I keep on thinking, when I look at the title, of a Chinese philosopher-poet living in a County Council cottage up a mucky by-road about seven miles the other side of Ballina, with all the cautious respectability of a retired referee.

> I have been working for years on
>   a four-line poem
>   about the life of a leaf.
> I think it may come out right this winter. (73)

That poem comes out right. An astonishing proportion of Mahon's poems come out right, even when he enters the most dangerous territory for the wit or the sceptical writer, that is the territory of nostalgia. Sceptical writers usually don't know how to handle this. Even MacNeice, when he tries to treat it in 'Autumn Journal' becomes loud-voiced, unnaturally loud-voiced. Even in that area when his humane perspective might be dislocated or threatened or even betrayed, Mahon is saved by his wit.

But one of the problems for this kind of writer, for an ironic, romantic, sceptical, witty, nostalgic humanist is what I shall call the problem of yourself. What are you to do with yourself? Where does 'self' stand in the poem? Where is Mahon in his poetry? I said he is a poet of the perimeter, meditating on the centre, with a mixture of amusement and pain. He is not, or he is very rarely, at the centre of his poems. He has a modesty, a kind of good manners of the imagination which nearly always prevents him from indulging in any form of Whitmanesque self-exhibitionism. So how then does he actually say things? How does the peripheral stance convey a central statement?

In different ways: and one of his principal ways is that of invoking the help of other poets, other poems. And he does this methodically and shamelessly. Immediately, therefore, we enter the indirect world. Yeats said that the poet 'never speaks directly as to somebody at the breakfast table – there is always a phantasmagoria'.[4] I think that is debatable, but I can see the point of it. There is very direct poetry in Yeats and very indirect. I want to talk about the value of imaginative indirectness, about not being candid, not being totally direct to anyone. This is a vital aspect of Mahon's humanistic stance.

First of all, from the point of view of the writer, it removes the embarrassment of having to say I, I, I or me, me, me all the time. The helpless egotism of mere selfhood, mere identity is put at a remove. And in the space created between the centre that the self would occupy and the perimeter to which the self is shifted with dignity but firmness, there arises an altruistic world, peopled by others but still paradoxically controlled by the removed self. Indirectness involves control through a deliberate act of imaginative self-abnegation. In this self-abnegation there exists not only a new order of control but also new possibilities for exciting imaginative freedom. And also, it must be admitted, a certain capacity for cunning and effective manipulation is made possible, made available. In this situation, the shadow manipulates the various substances.

By removing the self from the centre of the poem, by opting for an indirect stance, by putting other poets and other poems at the centre, by seeming to substitute a sophisticated deference for an aggressive statement, a new control, freedom and cunning imaginative power are achieved. And things can be said with a certain calm altruistic dignity which previously could only be said with perhaps an obtrusive egotism, a limited, assertive sense of self. Self is freed from self so that self may become more comprehensively articulate.

We see such a process at work in what I believe is Mahon's best poem, 'The Poet in Residence (after Corbière)'. Where is he in this poem, where is the writer in it? Nowhere; everywhere. Self denied; handing over to another writer, a feral poet, a beast-like poet, living with his Muse and his *ennui*, his boredom, in a 'one-eyed tower' (103), ordering, controlling, free, manipulating the lonely other with irony and affection. Mahon creates a truly wonderful love poem because of his mastery of indirection. Such indirection is one of the real sources of imaginative energy and power and endurance. To step aside, to empty the self, allows it to become a place of accommodation for passing ghosts who, perhaps out of gratitude for being made welcome where welcome was not expected, offer to sing of those troubles that the mere self might endure but scarcely express. 'The Poet in Residence' is an evocation of the relationship between a poet and poetry, of the bizarre comedy of dedication to what he never ultimately understands, of the arrogance of his failure as a human being, his search for an isolation, which inevitably turns into a comic prominence. This comedy involves his shocking knowledge of the futility of expressing himself and others, his desire to love equalled only by his catastrophic inability to do so, his power of expression at his ecstatic ripping asunder and destruction of that power, throwing it all in little pieces to the wind. Literally, this is what is done in the poem; he throws it all to the wind. Throwing it all to the wind may well be the best form of publication. The wind is an imaginative publisher and an inexhaustible distributor. Maybe it's a good critic as well.

'The Poet in Residence' is an exquisite and humorous use of another writer. Other writers and artists who appear as helpers, as I would call them in Mahon's work, or as mirrors, as stimulants, as media, as personae, are Brecht, Hamsun, Uccello, Nerval, Villon, Cavafy, Raftery, Beckett, Voznesensky, Rimbaud, Pasternak, Ovid, Horace and others. It is a kind of private army of conscience which he summons around him, a source of stimulation and support, an aid toward self scrutiny and self revelation. These names hover and haunt but not once do they swamp or even subdue his own voice which remains uniquely his own:

> 'I've taken my lyre and my barrel-organ
> To serenade you – ridiculous!
> Come and cry if I've made you laugh,
> Come and laugh if I've made you cry.
> Come and play at misery
> Taken from life: "Love in a Cottage"!
> It rains in my hearth, it rains fire in my heart;
> And now my fire is dead, and I have no more light...'
>
> His lamp went out; he opened the shutter.
> The sun rose; he gazed at his letter,
> Laughed and then tore it up...
>
>   The little bits of white
> Looked, in the mist, like gulls in flight. (106)

Louis MacNeice: An Irish Outsider

I was born in Belfast between the mountain and the gantries
To the hooting of lost sirens and the clang of trams:
Thence to Smoky Carrick in County Antrim
Where the bottle-neck harbour collects the mud which jams

The little boats beneath the Norman castle,
The pier shining with lumps of crystal salt;
The Scotch Quarter was a line of residential houses
But the Irish Quarter was a slum for the blind and halt...

I was the rector's son, born to the anglican order,
Banned for ever from the candles of the Irish poor;
The Chichesters knelt in marble at the end of a transept
With ruffs about their necks, their portion sure...[1]

These lines from his poem 'Carrickfergus' show that Louis MacNeice felt that in Ireland he was an outsider from birth. He was 'Banned for ever from the candles of the Irish poor'. Seán O'Casey knew poverty from his earliest days in the slums of Dublin; Patrick Kavanagh knew poverty in Monaghan and later in Dublin; and Austin Clarke wrote many poems about poverty, though his view of it tends to be that of a middle-class spectator. Yet, in their different styles, and with varying degrees of imaginative intensity, these three writers were involved in Irish society in ways that Louis MacNeice somehow never quite managed, or perhaps wished, to be. He remained an outsider to that world of seething deprivation, riotous squalor and articulate resentment so intrepidly explored by O'Casey, Kavanagh, Clarke and others. And this sense of being an outsider in Ireland is, in a deeper sense, characteristic of what we may call MacNeice's spiritual life, his developed stance as a poet. All through his poetry we encounter a man who doesn't really seem to belong anywhere, except perhaps in the fertile, mysterious, consoling and challenging land of language itself, where every fresh discovery is inextricably bound up with a new mystery. Yet even there, where a poet might reasonably be expected to feel unreasonably at home, the recurring doubts and uncertainties gnaw away at his mind and imagination. MacNeice is one of the most intelligent of all Irish poets; he is also, in his work, one of the loneliest. And he has, apart from a few loyal followers among the poets of Ulster, such as Longley, Mahon, Heaney, Ormsby, Hewitt and Muldoon, as well as the distinguished critics, Terence Brown and Edna Longley, been largely ignored in Ireland, particularly in the Republic. He is still the outsider, still 'banned', not only from the 'Irish poor', but from the anthologies which help to educate the vast majority of Irish children. It is a shame, because MacNeice is an excellent poet, a skilful crafts- man, a shrewd critic of both literature and society, a thinker who makes complex thoughts lucid and shapely, a considerable dramatist, a disciplined classicist, an assured translator and an attractive person- ality. He achieved all this while remaining a loner. Even his early education in England helped to put him firmly in this position. Here is a moving picture of the Irish boy in that state of sophisticated exile from which he never really returned.

> I went to school in Dorset, the world of parents
> Contracted into a puppet world of sons
> Far from the mill girls, the smell of porter, the salt-mines
> And the soldiers with their guns.
>
> ('Carrickfergus', 70)

To some extent, every poet is an outsider, almost by definition. But it is also true to say that many poets believe they have an audience, however reserved or limited, of their own, a coherent and patient community of sympathetic listeners. This kind of audience helps to deepen and direct a poet's imaginative energy. Kavanagh said, 'I have my friends, my public'.[2] Yeats's poetry pre-supposes a chosen, gifted, discriminating audience. Even the hermetic Austin Clarke, labouring away in the satirical solitude of a Dublin suburb, could count on a ready audience to snap up his stinging limited editions. These poets, and many others, find their audience to a considerable extent, though by no means completely, in the Irish capital, Dublin. (When I use the term 'audience', I am not referring merely to University students of literature whose reasons for reading poetry sometimes have precious little to do with love of the thing.) Yeats may have scoffed at 'the daily spite of this unmannerly town';[3] the same town was 'malignant Dublin'[4] to Kavanagh; and Clarke never ceased to satirise various aspects of Dublin life. But nevertheless, all three poets were *listened* to in Dublin; and all three derived a paradoxical sustenance from the city they castigated. They learned to thrive on enmity, to flourish in a climate of spontaneous envy and disparagement. But Dublin did not listen to MacNeice; it still doesn't. And MacNeice knew it. His poem 'Dublin' (in the sequence 'The Closing Album') acknowledges the fact that Ireland's capital city will not have him 'alive or dead'. Despite this, however, or perhaps because of it, MacNeice has a certain detached affection, the casual, steady, isolated sympathy of the outsider, for the city of Yeats, Joyce, O'Casey, Clarke – the city that ignores him. The following lines are not only an eloquent description of Dublin; they are also a revelation of MacNeice's poetic position. In MacNeice's case, description is self-revelation:

This was never my town,
I was not born nor bred
Nor schooled here and she will not
Have me alive or dead
But yet she holds my mind
With her seedy elegance,
With her gentle veils of rain
And all her ghosts that walk
And all that hide behind
Her Georgian façades –
The catcalls and the pain,
The glamour of her squalor,
The bravado of her talk.

The lights jig in the river
With a concertina movement
And the sun comes up in the morning
Like barley-sugar on the water
And the mist on the Wicklow hills
Is close, as close
As the peasantry were to the landlord,
As the Irish to the Anglo-Irish,
As the killer is close one moment
To the man he kills,
Or as the moment itself
Is close to the next moment.

She is not an Irish town
And she is not English,
Historic with guns and vermin
And the cold renown
Of a fragment of Church latin
Of an oratorical phrase.
But O the days are soft,
Soft enough to forget
The lesson better learnt
The bullet on the wet
Streets, the crooked deal,
The steel behind the laugh,
The Four Courts burnt.

Fort of the Dane,
Garrison of the Saxon,
Augustan capital
Of a Gaelic nation,
Appropriating all
The alien brought,
You give me time for thought
And by a juggler's trick

> You poise the toppling hour –
> O greyness run to flower,
> Grey stone, grey water
> And brick upon grey brick. (163-64)

'She will not have me alive or dead'. MacNeice might have made the same charge against many Irish poets and critics. And yet this being ignored may have goaded MacNeice into contemplation, into trying to see exactly what had helped to shape him as a poet. He learned to look clearly and critically at himself; and he achieved the hard lucidity of the loner. He writes:

> Speaking for myself, I should say that the following things, among others, had conditioned my poetry – having been brought up in the North of Ireland, having a father who was a clergyman; the fact that my mother died when I was little; repression from the age of six to nine; inferiority complex on grounds of physique and class-consciousness; lack of a social life until I was grown up; late puberty; ignorance of music (which could have been a substitute for poetry); inability to ride horses or practise successfully most of the sports which satisfy a sense of rhythm; an adolescent liking for the role of 'enfant terrible'; shyness in the company of young women until I was 20; a liking (now dead) for metaphysics; marriage and divorce; Birmingham; an indolent pleasure in gardens and wild landscapes;…a liking for animals; an interest in dress.[5]

This reads like a somewhat quirky list of influences; in fact, the influences are clearly perceived and accurately stated. One can appreciate how his 'inferiority complex' due to 'class-consciousness' may have driven him towards his interest in Communism in the 1930s; one can see how his 'ignorance of music' may have led him to try to create, often with startling success, a poetry remarkable for its rich musicality, its rhythmical assurance and subtlety: his confessed 'liking for metaphysics' helped him to work towards a poetry that is often complex but clear in its thoughts; the solitary name 'Birmingham' brings home to us the fact that MacNeice celebrates and criticises the life of cities such as London, Dublin and Belfast with rare eloquence and insight; and even the final 'liking for animals' and 'interest in dress' point towards a poetry involved with ordinary human activities and feelings. MacNeice sees the poet as a spokesman for ordinary people. He believes that poetry should always be in touch with what he calls 'the spontaneous colouring of ordinary speech'.[6]

The clarity of MacNeice's self-knowledge, the precise presentation of influences, the candid statements concerning his views of language in poetry – all this suggests a poet who is honest, unpretentious, undeceived, cultivated, perceptive, relishing the activity and bustle of the ordinary world. And MacNeice is a truly 'worldly' poet in this sense: he looks closely at society, at people, at his roots, at his present situation, at the complex, changing state of the world in which he has to live. And he moves through that world on his own, alert, watchful, scrupulously recording what he sees and feels. To this extent, he is not a poet of the fascinating past, or the perplexing future; he is neither conventional historian nor aspiring prophet; he is much more the poet of the swirling, urgent present. Many Irish poets are deeply concerned with the past, finding in Ireland's turbulent history images and personalities that, when dramatised and charged with imagination, help to shed light on current problems. Here, as in so many other respects, MacNeice is an outsider. He is a superb chronicler of the contemporary. His most famous poem, 'Autumn Journal', is proof of this. It is a brilliant, sweeping, comprehensive poem.

In a prefatory note to 'Autumn Journal' in *The Collected Poems of Louis MacNeice* (a note not included in the first edition of the book), the poet stresses that he is writing what he calls a 'Journal', and adds that 'In a journal or a personal letter a man writes what he feels at the moment; to attempt scientific truthfulness would be, paradoxically, dishonest...It is the nature of this poem to be neither final nor balanced...Poetry in my opinion must be honest before anything else and I refuse to be "objective" or clear-cut at the cost of honesty' (101).

That, briefly, is a statement of the poet of conscience refusing to surrender to the aesthetic stylist in himself. This is the logic of MacNeice's position as an outsider. He clings to his individual moral honesty with an unrelenting grip even as he is deeply aware of its artistic limitations and defects. He knows that there are overstatements and inconsistencies in his poem; but he leaves them there, in their earned place in the work, because they are valid aspects of his vision of contemporary reality. The poem was written between August 1938 and early 1939; and it is steeped in a grim awareness of the coming war. In the midst of this awareness, MacNeice turns, significantly, to Ireland and broods, with the peculiar intensity of the outsider he is, on the violence and lunacy of the land of his birth. Even though this passage was written in a way which, according to MacNeice himself, was neither 'final nor balanced', the picture of violence, futility, self-deception, prejudice and chronic unemployment is as true now as when MacNeice wrote it in the 1930s. Because MacNeice honestly describes contemporary Ireland, he is hair-raisingly pertinent half-a-century later. It may be that if a

poet has the courage to be passionately true to the passing moment
he will be true to all time:

> Why do we like being Irish? Partly because
> It gives us a hold on the sentimental English
> As members of a world that never was,
> Baptised with fairy water;
> And partly because Ireland is small enough
> To be still thought of with a family feeling,
> And because the waves are rough
> That split her from a more commercial culture;
> And because one feels that here at least one can
> Do local work which is not at the world's mercy
> And that on this tiny stage with luck a man
> Might see the end of one particular action.
> It is self-deception of course;
> There is no immunity in this island either;
> A cart that is drawn by somebody else's horse
> And carrying goods to somebody else's market.
> The bombs in the turnip sack, the sniper from the roof,
> Griffith, Connolly, Collins, where have they brought us?
> Ourselves alone! Let the round tower stand aloof
> In a world of bursting mortar!
> Let the school-children fumble their sums
> In a half-dead language;
> Let the censor be busy on the books; pull down the Georgian slums;
> Let the games be played in Gaelic.
> Let them grow beet-sugar; let them build
> A factory in every hamlet;
> Let them pigeon-hole the souls of the killed
> Into sheep and goats, patriots and traitors.
> And the North, where I was a boy,
> Is still the North, veneered with the grime of Glasgow,
> Thousands of men whom nobody will employ
> Standing at the corners, coughing... (132-33)

All through 'Autumn Journal', we feel the impact of MacNeice's
compulsive honesty. The poem has all the excitement of a long,
detailed, lively letter from a friend whose thoughts are worthy of
respect and whose perceptions are unfailingly stimulating. Excessive
self-consciousness in poetry frequently has a deadening effect on the
poem's language because the tone tends to become portentous,
laboured and self-important. But MacNeice, reaching for the vitality
inherent in 'the spontaneous colouring of ordinary speech', and determined to speak to his reader as if he were writing him a spontaneous letter, creates a poetry that is natural, chatty and gripping.
Themes of extraordinary importance fill the day's ordinary talk:

Today was a beautiful day, the sky was a brilliant
Blue for the first time for weeks and weeks
But posters flapping on the railings tell the fluttered
World that Hitler speaks, that Hitler speaks
And we cannot take it in and we go to our daily
Jobs to the dull refrain of the caption 'War'
Buzzing around us as from hidden insects
And we think 'This must be wrong, it has happened before,
Just like this before, we must be dreaming;
It was long ago these flies
Buzzed like this, so why are they still bombarding
The ears if not the eyes?'
And we laugh it off and go round town in the evening
And this, we say, is on me;
Something out of the usual, a Pimm's Number One, a Picon –
But did you see
The latest? (108)

Inevitably, this deliberate chattiness leads to weaknesses in the poem.
Just as diaries, journals and personal letters are often a mixture of
the trivial and the serious, the irrelevant and the significant, so
'Autumn Journal' contains lines, even whole passages, which add
little or nothing to the poem as a whole. But this, as already stated,
was deliberate on MacNeice's part. These lines and passages, therefore, are most fairly criticised when seen in the context of a flawed,
conscious design, and not as weak or slight moments of which the
poet is unaware.

MacNeice's stubborn honesty helps to account for his strengths
and weaknesses as a poet. He is a celebrant and critic of urban life;
he has, therefore, a keen eye for the characters that abound in cities
(see 'The Mixer', for example, in which he effectively compares a
man to a Latin word, 'often spoken but no longer heard' [205]);
he has a profound respect for the integrity of the individual and a
vehement hatred for the forces which violate that respect (see 'Prayer
Before Birth' [193-94]); his exploration of time concentrates, for the
most part, on the present so that even his most personal poetry,
his love-poetry, for example, deals with the present fleetingness,
or the fleeting presence of love. Paradoxically, this concentration
on the present moment seems to rid him (for the moment) of the
burden of time:

Time was away and somewhere else,
There were two glasses and two chairs
And two people with the one pulse
(Somebody stopped the moving stairs):
Time was away and somewhere else...

Time was away and she was here
And life no longer what it was,
The bell was silent in the air
And all the room one glow because
Time was away and she was here.
                              ('Meeting Point', 167-68)

MacNeice's love-poems are among his best. The more one reads them, the more haunting they become.

These are some of MacNeice's strong points as a poet. If one must point to a weakness in his work, one must concede, I think, that it is closely connected with his concept of the poet as spokesman.[7] Many of MacNeice's poems have a kind of sophisticated literalness which tends to limit his work to one meaning, to deny it the musical, mysterious echoes and reverberations one finds in Blake and Yeats, for example. And since this is a direct consequence of MacNeice's determination to be 'honest', it may be more accurate to describe this 'weakness' in his work as the inevitable limitation of his strength, the necessary consequence of the flaw in his declared artistic intention.

As the years went by, MacNeice became increasingly conscious of this limitation. Accompanying his dissatisfaction with the literal utterance is a growing longing for a symbolic one. The poet is not only a spokesman; he is also an explorer. He is not only a representative voice; he is also a medium for many voices. His job is to find a style and a method that will do justice to all these functions. MacNeice, while retaining his basic view of the poet as spokesman, ('I have grouped the poet with ordinary men and opposed him to the mystic proper. I do not withdraw from this position'),[8] becomes increasingly aware of the fact that language itself is symbolic and will not, when imaginatively handled, permit itself to be restricted to mere literalism. Writing about characters, situations and occurrences in fiction, MacNeice says that 'these, if they are recognised at all by the reader as having anything to do with his own experience (and I take 'experience' here to include potential experience), will at once acquire a wider reference. They will stand for something not themselves; in other words, they will be symbols'.[9]

In his later poetry, MacNeice moves more and more deeply into a symbolic richness and resonance. I shall give one example; it is 'Charon', a late poem. Here the literal is enriched by the mythological; the poem is rooted in concrete reality but it also suggests strange worlds, mysterious possibilities. London and the Thames mingle with Virgil and Dante. Charon, son of Erebus (Darkness) and Nyx

(Night), ferries the dead across the river Styx to their final abode
in Hades. Here we find MacNeice writing from a very deep level
of his being; he is no longer a mere spokesman for others; he is
exploring the dark underworld of his mortal self. Perhaps the irony
of all this is that the poet who writes uncompromisingly of his own
experience, in this symbolic way, becomes in the end a more enduring
spokesman for others than the poet who consciously tries to speak
on behalf of others. MacNeice's poetic self included both kinds of
poet; or rather, the literalist was forced, or forced himself to become
a symbolist; reluctantly, the symbolist emerged as the one capable
of the more complex utterance. I am not suggesting a poetic schizo-
phrenia in MacNeice; I am talking about a slow development. Here
is the poem, 'Charon'. It presents MacNeice the outsider at his
most lonely and compelling:

> The conductor's hands were black with money:
> Hold on to your ticket, he said, the inspector's
> Mind is black with suspicion, and hold on to
> That dissolving map. We moved through London,
> We could see the pigeons through the glass but failed
> To hear their rumours of wars, we could see
> The lost dog barking but never knew
> That his bark was as shrill as a cock crowing,
> We just jogged on, at each request
> Stop there was a crowd of aggressively vacant
> Faces, we just jogged on, eternity
> Gave itself airs in revolving lights
> And then we came to the Thames and all
> The bridges were down, the further shore
> Was lost in fog, so we asked the conductor
> What we should do. He said: Take the ferry
> Faute de mieux. We flicked the flashlight
> And there was the ferryman just as Virgil
> And Dante had seen him. He looked at us coldly
> And his eyes were dead and his hands on the oar
> Were black with obols and varicose veins
> Marbled his calves and he said to us coldly:
> If you want to die you will have to pay for it. (530)

MacNeice's *Collected Poems* comprise almost six hundred pages of
skilled, musical and immensely enjoyable poetry. It may well be
that his very honesty led him to become the outsider he remained
to the end. One thing is certain though: he deserves a more attentive,
critical readership. To read through his published poems is to encounter a voice speaking for intelligent, questing, somewhat bewildered
people in our modern world that remains unquestionably wonderful
and is increasingly threatened.

George Moore's Lonely Voices:
A Study of His Short Stories

1

In his introduction to *Celibate Lives*, George Moore has an imaginary conversation in which, with a characteristically light touch, he reveals something of his attitude to the short story. When his imaginary protagonist asks Moore if he is for or against adventures, he replies that he does not deal in adventures 'but in soul cries'.[1] Here, Moore gets to the very core of what has preoccupied Irish short story writers ever since his time – the problem of man's loneliness. Frank O'Connor, in his extremely perceptive study of the short story, *The Lonely Voice* writes: 'There is in the short story at its most characteristic something we do not often find in the novel – an intense awareness of human loneliness. Indeed, it might be truer to say that while we often read a familiar novel again for companionship, we approach the short story in a very different mood. It is more akin to the mood of Pascal's saying: 'le silence éternel des ces espaces infinis m'effraie'.[2] It is not unfair to say that George Moore gave Irish short story writers that theme of human loneliness which has so fascinated their imagination. It is in every story of *Dubliners*, and that remarkable collection ends with a lyrical affirmation of the fact that man is essentially alone. Joyce, in fact, takes Gabriel Conroy to the very threshold of the loneliness that is unspeakable – the loneliness of death.

> His soul had approached that region where dwell the vast hosts of the dead. He was conscious of, but could not apprehend, their wayward and flickering existence. His own identity was fading out into a grey impalpable world: the solid world itself, which these dead had one time reared and lived in, was dissolving and dwindling.[3]

Frank O'Connor, Seán O'Faoláin, Liam O'Flaherty, Mary Lavin, and Benedict Kiely continually and skilfully explore the dark pit of loneliness. The same preoccupation is evident in the work of writers such as Edna O'Brien, James Plunkett, and John McGahern. The fact that several of these writers frequently examine this problem in comic terms is a measure of their skill – laughter is seen as the sunny emphasis of a desolate fact. Moore is, of course, a fine comic writer, and it was Moore who first pointed out to modern Irish writers the fact that the best short stories consist of brief but profound and luminous insights into the lives of those who haunt the

fringes of society, drab figures who live anonymously and suffer
quietly. I would like to examine *Celibate Lives*, *The Untilled Field*,
and *A Story-Teller's Holiday* in an effort to show the various ways
in which Moore examined the problem of loneliness; how he found
a form that later Irish writers tried to perfect; I shall try also to
evaluate his importance in the distinguished tradition of the Irish
short story.

Celibate Lives would have been more accurately entitled *Lonely
Lives* because in this collection of stories one is struck not so much
by the celibacy of any of the characters, but by the loneliness that
is their typical condition. The five stories in the volume have for
titles the proper names of the main characters concerned, and Moore
subjects each of these people to a penetrating and sustained scrutiny.
The opening story, 'Wilfrid Holmes', concerns a typically casual
outcast, the 'fool' of the Holmes family, the one who refuses to work,
and therefore mars the respectability which his relatives esteem so
much. Wilfrid is a childlike figure who, in his timid and harmless
way, plays at being scholar, musician, composer, and journalist,
living all the time on a small allowance from his aunt. The crisis in
his life comes when the allowance fails to arrive, and he experiences
that moment of bitter self-awareness, of implacable self confrontation,
which so many of Joyce's characters also experience in *Dubliners*.
Wilfrid sees himself for the outcast he is. He understands that he
cannot understand, and that he cannot be understood:

> Nobody would understand that he could not earn his living. Nobody
> had ever understood this except his mother, and nobody ever would.
> He laid no blame on anybody; he did not understand it himself...But
> he could not earn his living, and, worst of all, he could not tell why...
> Nobody would understand – he did not understand. A frightened look
> came into his face, for he saw in that instant a lonely figure, a confessed
> failure, amid sad shrubberies and dismal woods. (*CL*, 13-14)

In Joyce's finest short story, 'The Dead', Gabriel Conroy experiences a similar moment of harrowing self-vision:

> He saw himself as a ludicrous figure, acting as a penny-boy for his aunts,
> a nervous, well-meaning sentimentalist, orating to vulgarians and idealising
> his own clownish lusts, the pitiable fatuous fellow he had caught a glimpse
> of in the mirror.[4]

In both Moore and Joyce, one of the chief effects of a fully realised
loneliness is the brutal moment of self-knowledge that is merciless
and complete. Though Moore's story ends on a comparatively happy
note, we have seen Wilfrid Holmes stripped bare as a tree in winter
down to his essential timidity and mediocrity, a black sheep without

talent or resource, a devoted nonentity, a pariah committed to a life of quiet absurdity.

The loneliness of 'Priscilla and Emily Lofft' is that of a woman who has lost her sister. Emily had known Priscilla so intimately that 'Priscilla had never seemed another being to her, but her second self, her shadow, her ghost, each akin to the other as the sound and its echo' (*CL*, 29). Alone in the house after Priscilla's death, Emily realises her loneliness:

> ...sitting on the little rep sofa, her eyes brimming with occasional tears, she bethought herself of the life that awaited her without Priscilla, alone in the world, without parents or relations. Aunt Clara was gone; a few distant cousins there were, dispersed over the world; a few neighbours, a few friends, scattered through Dublin; but nobody whom she could love. Lonely evenings...' (*CL*, 32-33)

Out of Emily's loneliness springs her responsibility to the dead Priscilla. Priscilla had died trying to tell something to Emily, and had managed to write the words 'in the garden' before she expired. Later, in the garden, Emily discovers a French novel which Priscilla had been reading – the story of an unfaithful wife with two lovers; This was the closest Priscilla had ever come to an emotional experience. Following her dying wishes, Emily destroys the book, and having fulfilled her responsibility to the dead, is thereafter, as it were, free to be lonely among the living:

> ...she was free to leave this dusty old house and the dusty conventions in which half her life had been spent. She was free to return to Aix and to live like other English spinsters on a small income, travelling whither she listed, from one boarding-house to another, seeking – Does anybody do more than to seek and to find, mayhap, something? (*CL*, 42-43)

An important aspect of Moore's genius is that he continually sees loneliness as an integral part of ordinary life. Patrick Kavanagh speaks in his long poem, *The Great Hunger*, about 'the weak, washy way of true tragedy',[5] and goes on to portray the wretchedness of the humdrum life of his central character, Patrick Maguire. In Moore's stories, one finds a similar kind of perception. One of his most agonising pictures of loneliness is his story of Albert Nobbs, a waiter in a Dublin hotel, a woman who, in order to survive during her youth, dressed as a man and so managed to make a living. With a very daring stroke, Moore creates a situation in which Albert's secret is revealed to another woman, also disguised as a man. This other person, Hubert Page, explains that she found happiness by leaving her brutal husband and her children and by setting up

house with a girl. She thus plants in Albert's mind the possibility
of a similar solution to her problem. Page agrees to keep Albert's
secret, and leaves. Albert dreams of happiness and becomes involved
in a farcical courtship with a girl, Helen Dawes, a colourful, vulgar
girl who ruthlessly exploits Albert, while she has an affair with a
scullion in the hotel. The courtship ends ludicrously and for a
while Albert is heart-broken. She recovers her spirits somewhat,
but then becomes ill and dies. Her secret is an open book to the
ready mockers of Dublin. Page, the other disguised woman, returns,
and hearing of Albert's death, decides to go home to the husband
and children she had abandoned fifteen years previously.

Moore handles here a theme which, in the hands of a less skilled
writer, could easily degenerate into a burlesque of incredible disguise
and sensational disclosure. Think of it! Two women disguised as
men find themselves in the same bed, and when one of them is
bitten by a very persistent flea, the secret is out! But Moore completely avoids the attractive comic distortions of caricature, and
instead describes, with wonderfully compassionate insight, Albert
Nobbs's daily indignities, the small revolting brutalities of an insensitive world, and above all, the constant loneliness of the 'per-
hapser', Moore's name for Albert Nobbs, who could hardly claim
to be either man or woman. Albert's life had been

> ...a mere drifting, it seemed to her, from one hotel to another, without
> friends; meeting, it is true, sometimes men and women who seemed
> willing to be friendly. But her secret forced her to live apart from men
> as well as women; the clothes she wore smothered the woman in her;
> she no longer thought and felt as she used to when she wore petticoats,
> and she didn't think and feel like a man though she wore trousers. What
> was she? Nothing, neither man nor woman, so small wonder she was
> lonely. (*CL*, 64)

An outcast from both sexes, Albert fails miserably with the girl,
Helen Dawes. In despair, she walks the streets of Dublin, finally
picking up a street-walker. But she fails even with the street-walker,
who simply walks off with a friend. This is the depth of Albert's
desolation and it is very movingly described by Moore. Albert's
being is a chaos of grief:

> The street-walkers have friends, and when they meet them their troubles
> are over for the night; but my chances have gone by me; and, checking
> herself in the midst of the irrelevant question, whether it were better
> to be casual, as they were, or to have a husband that you could not get
> rid of, she plunged into her own grief, and walked sobbing through street
> after street, taking no heed of where she was going. (*CL*, 85)

Humbert Wolfe says that 'George Moore has the widest human sympathy of any English novelist'.[6] An extravagant claim, surely, yet when one considers the compassionate accuracy with which Moore traces the pathetic course of Albert Nobbs's life through its long years of deprivation and failure, right up to the last, lonely moments, portrayed in precisely the right kind of intense under-statement, one can at least appreciate, if not wholly agree with, Wolfe's enthusiastic judgment. A brilliant structural device was Moore's decision *not* to end the story at that point when Albert dies, but to bring back the other disguised woman, Hubert Page, who, seeing the circumstances of Albert's death, decides to return to her own abandoned family. Page's desire to finally choose that domestic stability for which Albert so long and vainly yearned merely emphasises the pity of Albert's death – an essentially lost creature whose life began in bastardy and ended in anonymity.

Moore understood that loneliness manifests itself in several ways. In the case of Wilfrid Holmes, it appeared as childish eccentricity; with Emily Lofft, it meant an almost visionary awareness of her dead sister and a final resolution to leave the house where they had lived together; and it involved Albert Nobbs in what turned out to be an absurd quest for happiness. In the longest story in *Celibate Lives*, entitled 'Henrietta Marr', Moore examines what is best de-scribed as the predatory energy of loneliness. Etta Marr is a woman with whom several men fall in love, who is attracted to men, but who is unable to give herself sexually. Her dilemma makes her attractive and treacherous, lovable and phoney. Moore traces her career through five relationships, skilfully drawing a deepening sense of Etta's brilliant superficiality. Her inability to give herself makes her a patient, resolute flirt with a desire to have power over men. Once she acquires the power, however, she runs away from the possibility of any lasting attachment, so that she becomes a kind of professional hit-and-run lover, eager for triumph, afraid of the prize, yet always compelled to re-commence her conquest. In the end, she is rejected by the man she seems to want to marry, and kills herself.

Moore once wrote that 'in the midst of our deepest emotions, we are acting a comedy with ourselves' (*CL*, 37). Etta Marr's basic inability to give herself involves her in a black comedy of loneliness. Her first lover is an English painter, Ralph Hoskin, who actually dies of a broken heart. Etta knows this, yet later, she tells another lover, Morton Mitchell, that Ralph had been slowly poisoned by his mistress whom Etta very much disliked. Moore, with his gift for understatement, merely hints at Etta's private fantasies of self-justification, and simply allows other characters in the story to suggest very briefly that Etta may be somewhat unbalanced, mentally. Further, she turns her fear to advantage, so that her sexual coldness becomes a demonstrable virtue, and her own personal deficiency an agent of her control over others. Moore is saying, I believe, that beauty that is lonely for Etta's reason is necessarily predatory and false. Etta is the essentially passionless woman who cannot fail to inspire passion in others, the fraud who attracts what is most genuine in men. This is not to say that her lovers are not aware of her falsehood. Morton Mitchell, her third lover, sees through Etta when she is at her most beautiful, during a ball given by the Comte de Malmédy:

> ...as Etta went upstairs, three or four steps in front of the Comte, Morton saw her so clearly that the thought struck him that he had never seen her before. She appeared in that instant as a toy, a trivial toy made of coloured glass, and he wondered why he had been attracted by this bit of coloured glass.
> He laughed at his folly and went home, certain that he could lose her without pain... (*CL*, 160)

Morton, of course, is wrong, and falsehood continues to fascinate him until, and after, Etta leaves him for the Comte. At the end, when Etta is using her charms on an English clergyman, the Comte rejects her. When I said that Moore sees loneliness as predatory, I meant that it cuts both ways. Etta's rejection of Hoskin and Mitchell led to the death of one man and the unhappiness of the other; the Comte's rejection of Etta is directly responsible for her sudden death. In a bitterly ironic way, Etta, at the end, changes places with her first lover who, losing her, lost the will to live. Moore's story of this mutual ravaging process is told with admirable subtlety and deliberation. Albert Nobbs had dreamed of companionship and could not achieve it; Etta Marr is several times offered companionship but will not accept it, and when she requests it, she is refused. Because of the cruel ironies of her life and death, she is one of the loneliest of George Moore's lonely voices.

All the main characters in *Celibate Lives* opt out of the bustle of daily life in one way or another, and Moore, in a subtle but adamant way, repeats that sexual inadequacy is one of the truest sources of loneliness. Moore makes this point, not in an overt or brutal manner as certain modern novelists do, but through gradual implication, thereby creating a profound and far-reaching sense of the human complexity of the problem. In the final story, 'Sarah

Gwynn', we meet a young woman who retires to a convent to spend her life in prayer for the prostitute who helped her when she was in dire need. Again, Moore is here treating a theme which would have been a disaster in the hands of a less sophisticated writer, but just as he avoided burlesque in 'Albert Nobbs', so does he escape sentimentality in 'Sarah Gwynn'.

Sarah is 'a tiny, thread-paper girl in a straw hat, an alpaca jacket, and a thin skirt that did not hide her broken boots, a starveling' (*CL*, 178-79), a parlourmaid in the service of Dr O'Reardon. Very soon, she proves herself a paragon of efficiency, 'the parlourmaid that every doctor desires and never finds' (*CL*, 183), but after a year of diligent and careful service, she informs the doctor that she is leaving because, she says, the gardener wants to marry her. O'Reardon presses her for further explanation, and Sarah tells him the story of her life; how after she had left her home in the North of Ireland to run away to Dublin, she almost starved but for the kindness of Phyllis Hoey, a factory-worker by day and a prostitute at night. Phyllis had asked Sarah to go on the streets with her, but Sarah, with help from Phyllis, had gone instead to a convent in Wales which she left after a few years to return to Dublin, go into the service of Doctor O'Reardon, and resume her search for Phyllis. The story ends with Sarah's decision to enter another convent where she can pray for the woman who had been kind to her.

Moore's insight into the mind of the self-effacing and distant Sarah is extremely penetrating. When Sarah takes up the narrative, going into a long monologue about her own life, we see deeply into a person whose hardship is equalled only by her courage. Moore had a gift fairly rare among short story writers and novelists – he could create totally authentic female characters. Esther Waters is his finest achievement in this respect, but Sarah Gwynn is also a triumphant creation. Moore puts in her mouth a completely appropriate language. Speaking of Phyllis's suggestion that she become a whore, she says,

> Phyllis didn't try to persuade me; she said that every girl must do the best she can for herself. She had often heard of girls marrying in the end off the streets, but she didn't want to say a word that might lead me where I didn't want to go. She said she quite understood, but there wouldn't be enough money for both of us if I didn't go, and in the end I might have been pushed into it, for I'm no better than Phyllis; and there never was a kinder soul, and maybe it's kindness that counts in the end. (*CL*, 192)

'Sarah Gwynn' is a moving conclusion to a moving book. Her calm, resolute withdrawal from life follows a pattern typical also of the

other main characters. *Celibate Lives* proves that loneliness always
has its origin in the heart but can lead practically anywhere; 'Sarah
Gwynn' shows that it can sometimes lead to a kind of peace.

2

Whatever loneliness and deprivation are in *The Untilled Field* are
attributed by Moore to the stultifying influence of the Roman
Catholic Church in Ireland. Irish writers from Moore to Edna O'Brien
have noted this and have very scrupulously and insistently pointed
it out. Behind Irish puritanism and repression stretches a long,
dark history of methodical English tyranny and futile Irish protest
that helps to account for the emotional and moral climate of *The
Untilled Field*. This collection of short stories is essentially a scrutiny
of spiritual inertia just as *Dubliners* is an exposition of various kinds
of paralysis. In the penultimate story, 'The Wild Goose', Moore
very succinctly describes how, in Ireland, inspiration degenerated
into stagnation and passionate Christianity became pious inhibition.
He speaks through the mouth of Ned Carmady whose political
ambitions for Ireland have been thwarted by a puritanical wife and
a meddling priest:

> For two centuries little else existed but Christ in Ireland; Ireland breathed
> Christ, saw and heard Christ during the fifth and sixth centuries. Christ
> was everywhere – above, beneath, within and without – Patrick's own
> words...Ireland dozed long centuries in the happy aspiration of Christ,
> the living God, till suddenly God, remembering that happiness could
> not be allowed to last for ever, sent the Danes up the estuaries and rivers
> to burn and to pillage. And then, as if God's heart had softened, Brian
> Boru came and defeated the Danes. God, indeed, seemed to have wished
> to do something with Ireland in the tenth century, for the Cross of
> Cong, the Tara brooch, and Cormac's chapel are works of art; but he
> changed his mind, and ever since Ireland sinks deeper, struggling all
> the while to free herself, but held back by the parish priest; were another
> Saint Patrick to appear she would not listen. [7]

The lamentable change in Christianity from an inspired love of
creation to a resolute distrust of life is the central theme of *The
Untilled Field*. Other pathetic features follow from this: the atmosphere
of unrelieved poverty and squalor; the frustration of all ideals; the
suppression of individual thinking; the hysterical fear of sex as the
supreme evil of which man is capable; the confusion of servility
with obedience, furtive inhibition with virtuous self-denial, caution
with wisdom; the fear of full expression and hence the distrust of
the artist – all these things are examined by Moore with considerable skill and subtlety. Co-existing with this theme of stagnation is

the theme of escape – especially to America, the land of promise where it seems possible to fulfil these aspirations so tragically stifled in Ireland. In 'Home Sickness', Moore not only points out how unquestioned clerical authority throttles all genuine vitality, but also effectively contrasts Irish sluggishness with American competence. Ironically, James Bryden returns from America to recover his health, falls in love with Margaret Dirken, but is horrified to find everybody pathetically submissive to the power of the priest:

> ...he listened in mixed anger and wonderment to the priest, who was scolding his parishioners, speaking to them by name, saying that he had heard there was dancing going on in their homes. Worse than that, he said he had seen boys and girls loitering about the road, and the talk that went on was of one kind – love. He said that newspapers containing love stories were finding their way into the people's houses, stories about love, in which there was nothing elevating or ennobling. The people listened, accepting the priest's opinion without question. And their pathetic submission was the submission of a primitive people clinging to religious authority, and Bryden contrasted the weakness and incompetence of the people about him with the modern restlessness and cold energy of the people he left behind. (*UF*, 34)

Because of this claustrophobic world with the priest at its centre, Bryden leaves Ireland and Margaret Dirken behind him, deliberately choosing the noisy bar-room in the Bowery slum to the intolerable repression of the Irish village. But, like all the chief characters in *Celibate Lives*, Bryden is an essentially lonely man, his loneliness deriving from his inability to forget the life he was compelled to reject. In the end, the rejected world becomes more real than the chosen one:

> There is an unchanging, silent life within every man that none knows but himself, and his unchanging silent life was his memory of Margaret Dirken. The bar-room was forgotten and all that concerned it, and the things he saw most clearly were the green hillside, and the bog lake and the rushes about it, and the greater lake in the distance, and behind it the blue line of wandering hills. (*UF*, 39)

If Moore had insisted that every Irish priest was despotic and narrow-minded, his stories would have degenerated into sledge-hammer polemic. But he is careful to set one priest's generosity against another's meanness, one's tolerance against another's inhumanity. In 'Patchwork', there is a calm but effective contrast between an old priest's warmth and a young one's repressive pettiness. Moore is here examining a national dilemma from within, and fairly presenting both sides of the story. The only trouble is, one feels, that the views of the young priest will prevail:

'Pleasure,' said Father Tom. 'Drinking and dancing, hugging and kissing
each other about the lanes.'
    'You said dancing, – now, I can see no harm in it.'
    'There's no harm in dancing, but it leads to harm. If they only went
back with their parents after the dance, but they linger in the lanes.'
    'It was raining the other night, and I felt sorry, and I said, "Well,
the boys and girls will have to stop at home tonight, there will be no
courting tonight." If you don't let them walk about the lanes and make
their own marriages, they marry for money. These walks at eventide
represent all the aspiration that may come into their lives. After they
get married, the work of the world grinds all the poetry out of them.'
    'Walking under the moon,' said Father Tom, 'with their arms round
one another's waist, sitting for hours saying stupid things to each other –
that isn't my idea of poetry. The Irish find poetry in other things than sex.'
    'Mankind,' said Father John, 'is the same all the world over. The
Irish aren't different from other races; do not think it. Woman represents
all the poetry that the ordinary man is capable of appreciating.' (*UF*, 62)

Consistently, throughout *The Untilled Field*, there is this balance
between tyranny and tolerance, brutality and benevolence. One of
Moore's most sympathetically-drawn characters is old Father Mac
Turnan who, fearing for the future of Catholicism, writes a letter
to the Pope in which he requests that the law of priestly celibacy
be abolished. In this way, he calculates that all the priests of Ireland
could become the fathers of thousands of Catholics, thereby ensuring
the stability of that religion. Moore creates a strong picture of the
old priest's naïveté and simple goodness and, during an interview
with his Bishop concerning the letter to Rome, we are made aware
of Mac Turnan's essential, customary loneliness, hidden under his
concern for his poor parishioners:

    'A car will take you back, Father Mac Turnan. I will see to that. I
    must have some exact information about your poor people. We must do
    something for them.'
    Father Mac Turnan and the Bishop were talking together when the
    car came to take Father Mac Turnan home, and the Bishop said:
    'Father Mac Turnan, you have borne the loneliness of your parish
    a long while.'
    'Loneliness is only a matter of habit. I think, your Grace, I'm better
    suited to the place than I am for any other.' (*UF*, 116)

Mac Turnan is a lonely dreamer with the compassionate aim of
helping the poor people of his parish. He has the impractical but
magnificent idea of building a little theatre in his western wilderness
– a play-house in the waste. All his hopes centre on the extraordinary
venture which, of course, fails – failure is Mac Turnan's daily bread.
The local peasantry appreciate both his generous character and his
odd ambition:

> 'It was indeed, sir, a quare idea, but you see he's a quare man. He
> has been always thinking of something to do good, and it is said that
> he thinks too much. Father James is a very quare man, your honour.'
> (*UF*, 129)

But the dominant impression left by Moore's priests is one of
pious brutality. They insist not merely on guiding the people, but
on completely ruling their lives. So they cajole, demote, bully,
arrange marriages, orate from the pulpit, control all social events,
and manipulate private destinies according to their own will. To
resist this will is to be expelled from society, and the individual
who shows courage becomes an outcast branded with shame. Julia
Cahill, in 'Julia Cahill's Curse', an extremely beautiful girl with a
mind of her own, refuses to allow the priest, Father Madden, to
arrange her marriage with a farmer. As a result, the priest expels
her from society and, in the end, she is compelled to go to America,
but not before she puts a curse on the people. As a result, the little
society becomes 'the loneliest parish in Ireland' (*UF*, 135). The
narrator of the story, looking at the land cursed by this outcast
Venus, describes its peculiar desolation. Julia Cahill's loneliness,
caused by the priest who hated her individuality, is the source of
the loneliness afflicting the land. The priest's expulsion of beauty
has impoverished the very soil of Ireland:

> I noticed that though the land was good, there seemed to be few people
> on it, and what was more significant than the untilled fields were the
> ruins, for they were not the cold ruins of twenty, or thirty, or forty years
> ago when the people were evicted and their village turned into pasture
> – the ruins I saw were the ruins of cabins that had been lately abandoned...
> (*UF*, 135)

It is precisely this point that Moore drives home again and again
– the priestly determination to smother or expel any manifestation
of the individual dissenting will. There are two other outstanding
examples towards the end of the book – one concerning a politician,
the other an artist. Ned Carmady, in 'The Wild Goose', an Irish-
American with little interest in religion apart from his belief in the
corruption of most of its practitioners, thinks that he is the man
that Ireland needs and initially encouraged by his wife, plunges
into politics, but falls into disfavour as soon as it is recognised that
he is anti-clerical, and that he desires a new spiritual and political
order in Ireland. His wife is Ellen Cronin, a puritan who dreams
of heroism and shuns reality. As his marriage grows thinner, the
priest applies pressure, and Carmady, knowing that all his political
hopes are now as dead as his marriage is cold, hoists his sail and

leaves, like one of the 'wild geese' – Irish soldiers who fled the country after the siege of Limerick in the seventeenth century. With Moore, exile is the recognition of failure in Ireland as well as the possibility of achievement elsewhere, and Carmady's departure is as much a desire for freedom as it is a gesture of disgust:

> ...he did not feel he was a free soul until the outlines of Howth began to melt into the grey drift of evening. There was a little mist on the water, and he stood watching the waves tossing in the mist, thinking it were well done that he had left home. If he had stayed he would have come to accept all the base moral coinage in circulation; and he stood watching the green waves tossing in the mist, at one moment ashamed of what he had done, at the next overjoyed that he had done it. (*UF*, 221)

The other illustration of how the individual dissenting will is outlawed is seen in the last story of the book, 'Fugitives'. John Rodney, a young sculptor, is hired by a priest, Father McCabe, to do a Mother and child for McCabe's new church. Rodney gets McCabe's cousin, Lucy Delaney, to pose in the nude for him; McCabe discovers this and, after Rodney's sculpture is destroyed by Lucy's two young brothers, Rodney decides to leave Ireland for good. There is no place for the artist in a society where creative originality is frowned on, and sensuousness is equated with sin:

> The wrecking of his studio had broken the last link that bound him to Ireland. 'There is no place in Ireland for an artist,' he said, 'nor yet for a poor man who would live his life in his own way. The rich leave Ireland for pleasure, and the young fellow who would escape from the priest puts it differently. "Off with me coat," he says, "to earn five pounds that'll take me out of Ireland."' Thank God he was going! (*UF*, 233)

'Fugitives' ends with an ironic exposition of the priestly faith in bad art and bad taste, since bad statues are 'further removed from perilous nature' (*UF*, 245). By making the political idealist and the creative artist victims of those shoddy values, Moore reveals the shady weaknesses and implacable mediocrity of Ireland as he knew it. There have been many changes in Irish society (and many for the better) since Moore's day, but *The Untilled Field* is still a monument in the history of the Irish short story. Its influence on Joyce, O'Connor, and O'Faoláin is, I would say, profound. *Dubliners* is, in many ways, like a more sophisticated and more cleverly-organised version of *The Untilled Field*. The two themes of paralysis and escape are common to both books, although Moore is more optimistic insofar as in his stories the characters' desire for escape is frequently realised whereas in *Dubliners* it is usually thwarted. Moore was not being immodest when he claimed that '*The Untilled Field* was a landmark in Anglo-Irish literature, a new departure',

(*UF*, xiii) although we may disagree with his opinion of the extent of its influence on Synge. In *The Untilled Field*, Moore began to examine a certain sickness at the very heart of Irish society which Joyce later examined at far greater depth. Moore's young sculptor, John Rodney, is remarkably like Joyce's Stephen Dedalus in his deliberate choice of exile, but he lacks Stephen's lofty ambition to forge in the smithy of his soul 'the uncreated conscience of my race'.[8] Joyce regarded *Dubliners* as 'a chapter in the moral history' of Ireland and the Irish people. In this, he was quite right, but *Dubliners* is the second chapter of that moral history. *The Untilled Field* is the first.

3

One of the more regrettable aspects of Moore's career as a short story writer is that he did not continue in the realistic vein of *The Untilled Field*. The stories in that collection are neatly chiselled, and their critical comments on life in general and Irish life in particular are made in a cleancut, incisive manner which makes a strong and enduring impact on the reader's mind. One would have expected Moore, therefore, to continue in this manner, but instead, he turned his back on the contemporary scene and returned in *A Story-Teller's Holiday* to the colourful primitive world of early Ireland. Even the title indicates a new slackness in Moore and, although *A Story-Teller's Holiday* contains some very fine stories, the collection as a whole lacks the urgency and passion of *The Untilled Field*. It may be that Moore was reacting against the puritanism which he examined so penetratingly in *The Untilled Field* because the first volume of *A Story-Teller's Holiday* (revised version, 1928) deals almost completely, either in comic or tragic terms, with the theme of temptation. Early Irish Christianity was infinitely less inhibited, and far more expressive, than the modern version, and Moore must have taken great delight in portraying piety enlivened by abandon and in showing how devotion is animated by a vigorous sex-life. As well as that, *A Story-Teller's Holiday* enabled Moore to explore the nature of the *form* of the short story, and this he does with obvious relish and delight in his own experimentation. Ernest Longworth says in the preface that 'it is the business of every considerable writer to produce at least one joyous book', and he describes the stories in this book as 'spontaneous inventions, with here and there an oddment of folk-lore, and in the rich, Anglo-Irish idiom they carry a fragrance of newly-upturned earth'.[9] *A Story-Teller's Holiday* is experimental in two senses; it is an experiment in the communication of joy, and also in the very nature of the short story itself. Ernest Longworth

calls it 'a dialogue between the original and the acquired self'
(*STH I*, viii), but it would be more accurate to describe it as an
attempt to show the differences between primitive and sophisticated
storytelling. To do this, Moore introduces Alec Trusselby, the *shanachie* or traditional story-teller from Westport, who, at his best, narrates
with something approaching the crude, colourful energy that one
finds in Old Irish epics such as *Táin Bó Cúailgne*. Alec is the
superbly articulate primitive, the Connemara Homer delighting in
outrageous events, flamboyant characters and extravagant language
spiced with vivid image and metaphor. He is a born story-teller,
nothing else seems to matter to him, and he successfully commun-
icates his own profound delight in the world evoked by his primitive imagination. He is, in short, Moore's 'original self' against which
Moore puts his 'acquired self', the educated, sophisticated writer
who tells stories in a crisp, modern idiom which, if it lacks the expan-
sive energy of Trusselby's language, has yet an urbane precision and
telling restraint that make it a completely appropriate vehicle for the
sophisticated story-teller. Much of the delight of *A Story-Teller's
Holiday* springs from the balance which Moore creates between the
primitive and the sophisticated. The opening of the book is marred
by dull gossip, slack reminiscence, a conscious 'artiness', and ponderous philosophising, but when he actually gets down to dealing with
the theme of temptation from both the primitive and sophisticated
points of view, we find ourselves, as if by magic, in a vanished Ireland where the tragedy and the comedy of temptation are revealed in
a rich, lively language. Moore's monks and nuns form a panorama of
bawdy innocents who might have been created by an Irish Boccaccio.
Their thoughts aspire to heaven, but they are very much of the earth.
They create temptation on earth that they may resist it and therefore
gain a higher place in heaven. The question they ask of life seems to
be – if we do not know how far is far enough, then how can we be
expected to know when we are going too far? And unless we know
that, how do we know that we are overcoming temptation? Such
an attitude, with its infinite capacity for showing that amusing and
sometimes outrageous double-think which even today one frequently
finds in Irish life, gave Moore, equipped with a dynamic sense of
mischief, ample scope for exploring the humorous potential of a
world in which monks went to bed with nuns to measure the nuns'
power of attraction against their own power of resistance, and by
so doing, to discover precisely the nature of the evils and the im-
perfections of this world, and consequently to aspire more ardently
to the perfection of the next.

The second volume of *A Story-Teller's Holiday* deals mainly with the love story of Ulick and Soracha, the bastard nobleman and the beautiful nun who ran away together and, after many adventures, finally came to grief. Moore here sustains the method of story-telling he used in the first volume, and both Moore and Trusselby tell different parts of the story, so that when the reader is beginning to feel that Moore's sophisticated method and idiom are wearing thin, he is jolted into a new awareness by the sudden advent of Trusselby's primitive energy. At odd moments throughout the tale, Moore halts the narrative to discuss it with Trusselby, so that we never lose sight of the fact that Moore is consciously experimenting with the form of the story.

The love story itself is skilfully and movingly told, but the most impressive thing in it is the fate of Ulick's old harper, Tadhg O'Dorachy, who, after Ulick and Soracha are dead, lives on, marries a young woman and, after a life completely devoid of love-making, dies watching his wife in her nakedness. Significantly, this part of the story is told by the Westport shanachie, Trusselby: it is Moore's final act of faith in the primitive. As he gaily says to Alec – 'You have exceeded me in invention. The Ballinrobe cock is outdone, and the crow is to the Westport rooster!' (*STH II*, 223).

One cannot argue that loneliness is consistently portrayed in *A Story-Teller's Holiday*, and yet the most memorable section of that great love story deals with the loneliness of Tadhg O'Dorachy, the harper, when he is making his journey back to Ireland from Scotland where he had been a slave. Moore describes O'Dorachy's loneliness and hardship at great length, thus preparing us for the pathos of his death. On this journey, we are aware not only of the man's loneliness, but of the loneliness of Ireland itself. Tadhg has only one companion during his suffering – a goose named Maria! Moore, with a wonderfully assured touch, avoids sentimentality in his portrait of the relationship between the harper and the goose. In fact, one of the most moving parts of the story is Tadhg's reaction to Maria's death:

> We were alike and lonely and good to each other. And his grief became so intense that he thought he must die of it, and leaning over the rocks among which he had found a seat he wept upon them for his goose and for himself until he could weep no more. And then he wandered without heed or care whither he was going, not awakening out of the stupor of his grief till the sound of rooks in the branches caught his ear and he said: Wherever there are rooks there is a house, for like poor Maria they are lonely away from the homes of men. And wandering round the rookery he asked himself how it was that so many of the creatures

of the earth had given up their freedom to dwell with men. Mayhap,
he said, it is because we have souls and they have not; maybe it is our
souls that draw them to us. (*STH II*, 152)

Yet, despite its many merits, *A Story-Teller's Holiday* is a retro-
grade step for Moore. It has very little of the formal compactness
and concentration of *The Untilled Field*; there are long patches of
loose, slack writing, with the result that we occasionally tend to lose
interest in the narrative. The lack of contemporary interest is another
defect, and while his treatment of the theme of temptation and
calculated resistance is extremely amusing, it tends to become rather
repetitive. One must conclude that Moore should have continued
to cast his cold eye on contemporary Ireland rather than exploring
the monkish and nunnish pranks of a much earlier time.

Nevertheless, Moore's importance as a short-story writer is considerable. He has had a deep influence on the Irish short story
and, in fact, consciously intended to do this. He considered *The
Untilled Field*, he said, as 'a book written in the beginning out of
no desire of self-expression, but in the hope of furnishing the young
Irish of the future with models' (*UF*, ix). This statement, with its
emphasis on artistic impersonality and formal experiment, immediately
reminds one of Joyce, whose prose is distinguished by precisely
these two qualities. Moore had a thematic and formal influence on
Joyce. Just as Moore in *The Untilled Field* chose to depict the inhibitions and frustrations of rural Ireland, so Joyce in *Dubliners*
chose to describe Catholic Ireland, particularly Catholic Dublin, in
all its pious mediocrity, claustrophobic middle-class respectability,
garrulous sentimentality, and superstitious religiosity. Though Moore's
world is, for the most part, rural, and Joyce's urban, there are distinct similarities between them. If we compare, for example, Moore's
'The Clerk's Quest' with Joyce's 'A Little Cloud', we see their
portraits of two essentially timid men. Moore's clerk is thus described:

> For thirty years Edward Dempsey had worked low down in the list of
> clerks in the firm of Quin and Wee. He did his work so well that he
> seemed born to it...He was interested only in his desk...
>
> An obscure, clandestine, taciturn, little man occupying in life only
> the space necessary to bend over a desk, and whose conical head leaned
> to one side as if in token of his humility. (*UF*, 147)

Joyce's Little Chandler is similarly timid and anonymous:

> He was called Little Chandler because, though he was but slightly under
> the average stature, he gave one the idea of being a little man. His hands
> were white and small and his manners were refined. He took the greatest
> care of his fair silken hair and moustache, and used perfume discreetly
> on his handkerchief. [10]

Both these little men suddenly undergo profound changes in their lives and both exchange anonymous timidity for outlandish romanticism. Though, in the end, Moore's character dies of starvation while Joyce's, characteristically, simply stays where he is, one is struck by the formal and thematic similarities between the stories. *Dubliners* shows evidence of far greater craftsmanship and is much more expertly organised, but it would be difficult to deny Joyce's debt to Moore.

Moore was especially aware of the complexity of the perennial Irish problem of exile. In an essay called 'Irish Literature', Frank O'Connor writes that it is doubtful 'if Irish literature has produced a better short story than "Home Sickness" '.[11] O'Connor himself wrote constantly about exile in its various forms, and one of Liam O'Flaherty's finest short stories, 'Going Into Exile',[12] deals very directly with that bleak Irish fact. 'Home Sickness' and 'Going Into Exile' are two of the most moving Irish short stories, because exile is as much a part of Irish life as birth and love and death. Both Moore and O'Flaherty fully realised this.

On the whole, Irish prose is more distinguished for its short stories than for its novels (despite *Ulysses, Finnegans Wake,* Flann O'Brien's *At Swim-Two-Birds,* and Michael Farrell's *Thy Tears Might Cease*). A very distinct Irish short story tradition exists, and today that tradition is being extended by writers such as Brian Friel, Benedict Kiely, Patrick Boyle, John Montague, John McGahern, James Plunkett, Edna O'Brien, and others. It is not at all certain that these writers have read Moore's stories, but it must be conceded that Moore is a foundation stone of that tradition. As a man, Moore could be arrogant and treacherous; he could sting like a scorpion. But while we may deplore the fact that Moore frequently betrayed his friends through caricature, behaving like some eloquent Iscariot of the Irish literary scene, we must recognise that he remained true to himself as an artist. Letting aside his novels, his contribution to the Irish short story is excellent proof of that.

The Heroic Ideal in Yeats's Cuchulain Plays

Yeats was not the first Irish poet to realise that ancient Gaelic saga could inspire heroic poetry in English. In the nineteenth century, such writers as de Vere, Todhunter, and Ferguson[1] had drawn on that vast, neglected saga material and had produced solid, if not very exciting poetry; their Victorian reticence and sophisticated timidity had prevented them from exploring the more violent or shocking aspects of the sagas, and these poets provide an illuminating contrast with Yeats's more full-blooded and intensely personal use of myth. In order to express the diverse facets of what may be considered his heroic ideal, Yeats went to the aristocratic Ulster cycle of tales and from these, chose Cuchulain, the Red Branch hero. He wrote five plays about Cuchulain. We cannot say that these five plays make a strict unity; in fact, the first play, *On Baile's Strand* (1904), does not deal with Cuchulain's birth or boyhood or early manhood, but ends with his death. Nevertheless, the five plays, each a distinct dramatic and poetic entity, present five different views of Cuchulain; taken together, they constitute a profound study of a developing heroic personality. Birgit Bjersby has brilliantly shown how the plays correspond to crucial moments in Yeats's own life;[2] that is, she views myth as a vehicle for the portrayal of the poet's many-sided personality. So it is, but such a view does not prevent us from examining the plays as an expression of an heroic ideal which includes violent self-assertion, a power of reconciliation, moments of disillusion, remorse and loneliness, and in the end, an identification of the mythic hero with the struggles of his modern counterparts. Yeats, in short, shows the extraordinary imaginative resilience and flexibility of myth. By using one consistent symbolic figure, Cuchulain, over a period of almost forty years, Yeats was able to express the complexities, even the contradictions of his heroic ideal as it changed and developed during that time. I shall go through the plays to try to show how Yeats, tenaciously depicting a solitary figure in different situations, presents a unique and many-sided ideal of heroism.

In *On Baile's Strand*, Cuchulain fights and kills an arrogant but noble young stranger, and then, discovering that he has slain his own son, he fights the sea. Cuchulain is, in a sense, forced into fighting the young man because he has to observe his oath of obedience to Conchobar who, as High King, succeeds in his plan to harness Cuchulain's passionate energy in the service of the kingdom.

There is a tension between Cuchulain's wildness, his violent, amorous nature, capable of erupting capriciously, and Conchobar's desire for secure and stable government, untroubled by the explosive whims of the hero who 'lives like a bird's flight from tree to tree'.[3] There is an ironic and rather squalid parallel to this tension between king and hero in the relationship between the Fool and the Blind Man, who act also as a kind of grotesque chorus to the main action. The High King asserts that Cuchulain needs his – Conchobar's – wisdom, just as Conchobar needs Cuchulain's 'might of hand and burning heart' (260); united, they would be formidable. Similarly, on a lower level, the Blind Man needs the Fool's vision, and the Fool is futile without the Blind Man's cunning. Cuchulain at first refuses to take the oath, but he is finally persuaded. In other words, he compromises his own heroic vision, and the play's conclusion shows that, for the hero, compromise is disaster. Left to himself, Cuchulain would not fight the young man at all but be generous and friendly towards him; yet, because he has taken the oath of obedience, he must observe not his own will, but Conchobar's. And so, doing combat to ensure the security of the kingdom for Conchobar's sons, Cuchulain kills his own son. The bitter irony is further deepened when Cuchulain discovers the truth of his action, not from Conchobar or those other kings who had urged him to fight the young man, but from the wandering talk of the Fool who, with a certain weird inanity, echoing what he has heard the Blind Man say, unwittingly reveals to Cuchulain exactly what he had done:

> BLIND MAN: None knew whose son he was.
> CUCHULAIN: None knew! Did you know, old listener at doors?
> BLIND MAN: No, no; I knew nothing.
> FOOL: He said a while ago that he heard Aoife boast that she'd never but the one lover, and he the only man that had overcome her in battle. (*Pause*)
> BLIND MAN: Somebody is trembling, Fool! The bench is shaking. Why are you trembling? Is Cuchulain going to hurt us? It was not I who told you, Cuchulain.
> FOOL: It is Cuchulain who is trembling. It is Cuchulain who is shaking the bench.
> BLIND MAN: It is his own son he has slain. (276)

Yeats sustains this irony to the end by presenting Cuchulain's fight with the sea through the Fool's eyes. In that final scene, Cuchulain is hopelessly heroic, suffering the disaster which, for the hero, is the inevitable result of compromise. And yet this mad, magnificent, utterly hopeless gesture is typical of one who would always

> dance or hunt or quarrel or make love
> Wherever and whenever I've a mind to. (255)

In *The Green Helmet* (1910), Cuchulain plays a role almost opposite to that of *On Baile's Strand*. Instead of being partly subdued by authority through being bound to it, Cuchulain here asserts himself as a conciliatory hero. Reconciliation presupposes discord and the central theme of *The Green Helmet* is the imposition of harmony on chaos. The instrument of this imposition is Cuchulain; the creator of discord is the Red Man; the chaotic elements are the other heroes, Conall and Laegaire, the heroes' wives, the charioteers, the stable boys and the scullions. The farcical plot hinges around the problem of who is to honour the debt owing to the Red Man, that is, a hero's head. This is worked out in a noisy, wrangling atmosphere. We can see a new bitterness in this play, a bitterness springing from Yeats's frustrating experiences in trying to establish a National Theatre, from the spectacle of a people riotously rejecting its own dramatic masterpieces, and above all perhaps, from the death of Ireland's most poetic dramatist, John Millington Synge. Yeats had discovered Synge; he admired him for his 'complete absorption in his own dream', for the fact that he was 'too confident for self-assertion',[4] for his simplicity, profundity and passionate dedication to the drama. Synge had enriched Ireland by expressing it; Ireland had rejected Synge; and so, in *The Green Helmet*, Ireland is bitterly described as a land where

> neighbour wars on neighbour, and why there is no man knows,
> And if a man is lucky, all wish his luck away,
> And take his good name from him between a day and a day. (225)

Ireland becomes 'an unlucky country that was made when the Devil spat', and 'a house that has fallen on shame and disgrace' (227). It had rejected Synge because he had tried to tell the truth, and so in *The Green Helmet* we find:

> Such hatred has each for each
> They have taken the hunting-horns to drown one another's speech
> For fear the truth may prevail. (234)

Discord piles on discord, quarrel follows quarrel. It is the world of 'The Second Coming':

> Things fall apart; the centre cannot hold;
> Mere anarchy is loosed upon the world...[5]

Yet, though disorder is bitterly portrayed, the ultimate impression of *The Green Helmet* is not one of bitterness but of a gay reconciliation. On at least three occasions, Cuchulain restores order.[6] In addition, only he has the courage to honour the debt owing to the Red Man – 'I will give him my head' (242) – and it is precisely this calm willingness to honour the debt through self-immolation that establishes Cuchulain in heroic superiority. The Red Man turns out to be 'the Rector of this land'; he had consciously created chaos so as to discover somebody who could impose order on it, deliberately stirring up trouble so that the very confusion might produce the conciliatory hero, who could then be honoured for his gaiety, tolerance, generosity and daring. Only Cuchulain completely fulfils this image, and only he deserves the appropriate immortality:

> And I choose the laughing lip
> That shall not turn from laughing, whatever rise or fall;
> That heart that grows no bitterer although betrayed by all;
> The hand that loves to scatter; the life like a gambler's throw;
> And these things I make prosper, till a day come that I know,
> When heart and mind shall darken that the weak may end the strong,
> And the long-remembering harpers have matter for their song. (243)

The general trend of Yeats's poetry is from an ornate pre-Raphaelite sensuousness to dynamic austerity. Similarly, his drama moves from the vague, shadowy world of such plays as *The Land of Heart's Desire* (1894) to the intensely compressed dramatic lyricism of his later work. It is precisely this quality of intense concentration that distinguishes the third Cuchulain play, *At the Hawk's Well* (1917). Cuchulain is here the heroic seeker after immortality, ironically thwarted at the moment he comes nearest his desire, but ultimately asserting his heroic personality.

At the Hawk's Well is a Noh play, and in order to appreciate it fully, we must look at this fascinating Japanese dramatic form, rooted in one of the world's oldest dramatic traditions. As Ernest Fenollosa says, it is 'as primitive, as intense, and almost as beautiful as the ancient Greek drama at Athens',[7] and, unlike the Greek drama, it is still alive and flourishing, ' having been transmitted almost unchanged from one perfected form reached in Kioto in the fifteenth century'.[8] It is interesting to us here in so far as it helps us to understand *At the Hawk's Well*. Certain aspects of the Noh appealed very strongly to Yeats.

Firstly, the Noh makes constant use of allusion and suggestion. The art of allusion is essential to this form. As Ezra Pound says:

> It is a symbolic stage, a drama of masks...It is not, like our theatre, a place where every fineness and subtlety must give way; where every fineness of word or word-cadence is sacrificed to the 'broad effect';

where the paint must be put on with a broom. It is a stage where every
subsidiary art is bent precisely upon holding the faintest shade of a
difference; where the poet may even be silent while the gestures con-
secrated by four centuries of usage show meaning.[9]

It is important to remember that the Noh is an *oriental* dramatic
phenomenon; it is as pointless to criticise it according to our western
dramatic principles as it is unreal to criticise O'Casey's *Juno and
the Paycock* or Miller's *Death of a Salesman* according to the principles set forth in Aristotle's *Poetics*. Pound and Fenollosa stress
this point: 'the Noh abounds in dramatic situations, perhaps too
subtle and fragile for our western stage, but none the less intensely
dramatic'.[10] This subtle, intense fragility is largely achieved through
the use of words, music, dancing, masks, song and a chorus. We
must remember that the words are only one part of this art; they
are 'fused with the music and with the ceremonial dancing'.[11] The
music is 'simple melody, hardly more than a chat, accompanied by
drums and flutes',[12] and the dance

> is full of meaning, representing divine situations and emotions, artistically,
> with restraint and with the chastening of a conventional beauty, which
> makes every posture of the whole body – head, trunk, hands and feet
> – harmonious in line, and all the transitions from posture to posture
> balanced and graceful in line.[13]

The use of the mask also attracted Yeats, as did the chorus, with
its function of poetical comment, carrying the mind 'beyond what
the action exhibits to the core of the spiritual meaning'.[14] When we
consider that 'in no other drama does the supernatural play so great,
so intimate a part',[15] we begin to understand why this ancient form
so fascinated Yeats. And finally, the Noh possessed the quality
towards which Yeats himself, both in poetry and drama, moves with
industrious certainty and lifelong deliberation:

> The beauty and power of Noh lie in the concentration. All elements –
> costume, verse and music – unite to produce a single clarified impres-
> sion. Each drama embodies some primary human relation or emotion;
> and the poetic sweetness or poignancy of this is carried to its highest
> degree by carefully excluding all such obtrusive elements as a mimetic
> realism or vulgar sensation might demand.[16]

Yeats aims at this intense allusive concentration in *At the Hawk's
Well*. As in the Noh, the plot is slight. Cuchulain, seeking immortality,
comes to the well where an old man, who has kept a vain vigil for
fifty years, still watches the well, hoping for the faintest sign of the
miraculous water. Finally, the rare moment comes; the water plashes;
but, ironically, the old man is asleep and Cuchulain, fascinated and
deceived by the hawk-woman's dance, turns his back on the glittering

water. Later, released from the fascination of the dance, Cuchulain, accepting the fact that he has not achieved his aim, relishes the prospect of heroic self-assertion in battle against the hawk-woman and 'the fierce women of the hills'. The play ends with the musicians' song which is concerned with disillusion, recklessness and indolence; although its conclusion strikes a bitter note, it also celebrates Cuchulain's heroic folly. He, on an impulse, a mere rumour, had set out in search of the miraculous water of immortality. The essence of the heroic search is a vital faith in the reckless gesture and is rooted, not in a flippant unawareness of the meaning of mortality, but in a deliberate choice, made with the full consciousness of its nature and implications:

> Folly alone I cherish,
> I choose it for my share;
> Being but a mouthful of air,
> I am content to perish;
> I am but a mouthful of sweet air. (219)

That this recognition of the heroic position has also a disillusioned note does not diminish its impact; it serves rather to increase it because it shows that the hero is aware of the factors that obstruct or imperil the full attainment of his ideal: hatred, laziness, aimlessness. For the hero, immortality is found, not in a lifetime of secure mediocrity, but in one brief and self-assertive brilliance. That is why the last *spoken* sentence of the play comes from Cuchulain; it is a curt assertion of the heroic personality:

> He comes! Cuchulain, son of Sualtim, comes! (218)

The outstanding quality of *At the Hawk's Well* is precisely that of the Japanese Noh – a marvellous dramatic concentration. But Yeats adds to this his own incomparable lyrical intensity, and so the final product is a compressed drama, a small play containing large issues, a lyrical proof of the harmonious fusion of the Japanese form with the Irish myth. It presents a more complex Cuchulain, one who, in the pursuit of his ideal, experiences misgivings and recognises obstacles, but whose heroic resolution is deepened and intensified by such experience and recognition.

In only one of the five plays does the heroic emphasis shift from Cuchulain to another character, and that is in *The Only Jealousy of Emer* (1919). Yeats writes that this play is filled with 'those little known convictions about the nature and history of a woman's beauty';[17] he might have added that it deals even more fully with the nature and consequences of a woman's heroism. That woman is Emer, Cuchulain's wife, a paragon of domestic stability, decent, calm, resourceful,

who rescues Cuchulain from Fand, the ideal, inhuman beauty, by re-
nouncing his love for ever. In this play, Cuchulain is almost entirely
passive, a rather subdued figure, afflicted by loneliness, the tyranny
of memory and 'intricacies of blind remorse'. Three women desire
him: wife, mistress, and the Woman of the Sidhe, Fand. The latter's
appeal is very strong; her beauty can rescue him from the scourge
of memory:

> at my kiss
> Memory on the moment vanishes:
> Nothing but beauty can remain. (292)

She has almost snared Cuchulain when Emer retrieves him in
the only way possible: she renounces all claim to his love. The
irony of her heroic renunciation is that the death of her hope makes
possible Cuchulain's new lease of life with her rival, Eithne Inguba,
Cuchulain's mistress. Emer is the only true heroic woman in Yeats's
Cuchulain plays; her heroism is manifest not in self-assertion but
in self-effacement, and her most heroic moment is her moment of
greatest personal loss. She retrieves Cuchulain by losing him for ever.

Cuchulain is superseded by Emer in *The Only Jealousy*, and his
memories bring him suffering. In the final play, *The Death of Cuchulain*, the hero is slaughtered by the Blind Man of *On Baile's Strand*.
It would appear, at first glance, that Yeats's heroic ideal is therefore
very far from being idealistic, but in fact *The Death of Cuchulain*
proves that his ideal withstands the squalid thought and the treacherous act. Granted, he dies at the hands of a blind old butcher, a
Judas before his time – 'If I brought Cuchulain's head in a bag, I
would be given twelve pennies' (702) – but the play concludes with
a lyrical affirmation of the value of the heroic life; through music,
dance and song, the hero of ancient myth and the heroes of modern
times become identified, their separate identities, divided from each
other over countless generations, indissolubly fused in the unifying
fire of heroism.

> Are those things that men adore and loathe
> Their sole reality?
> What stood in the Post Office
> With Pearse and Connolly?
> What comes out of the mountain
> Where men first shed their blood?
> Who thought Cuchulain till it seemed
> He stood where they had stood?
>
> No body like his body
> Has modern woman borne,
> But an old man looking on life

Imagines it in scorn.
A statue's there to mark the place,
By Oliver Sheppard done. (704-705)

I have tried to show that the strength of Yeats's heroic ideal, as
expounded in these plays, derives not from a blind self-assertion
on the part of Cuchulain, but from the knowledge that the man
who lives heroically meets dangerous obstacles on all sides; he is
heroic because he encounters these and overcomes them. He makes
a deliberate choice and is aware of consequence; his actions are
based on this free choice so that what may seem pointless folly to
less adventurous eyes is in fact the sane expression of a deliberate
decision. Yeats believed that 'The great virtues, the great joys, the
great privations come in the myths, and, as it were, take mankind
between their naked arms, and without putting off their divinity'.[18]
The Cuchulain plays, as we have seen, abound in the great virtues
of courage, loyalty and generosity, the great joys of friendship, love
and conquest, the great privations of defeat, renunciation and death.
At the very heart of all these is the complex figure of Cuchulain,
whose life and death, subtly and profoundly portrayed by Yeats,
express what has almost disappeared from modern life and literature
– an heroic ideal.

Austin Clarke and the Epic Poem

In his autobiography, *Twice Round the Black Church*, Austin Clarke expresses his admiration of Douglas Hyde's attempts to revive the old Irish literary tradition. Clarke tells how Hyde

> ...spoke of the aims and ideals of the language revival...Those plain words changed me in a few seconds. The hands of our lost despised centuries were laid on me.[1]

At the beginning of his career, Clarke turned to the sagas of those 'lost centuries' for inspiration. He made four attempts to write an epic poem; three had Gaelic origins and one was inspired by a verse from the Pentateuch. It will be seen how unsuccessful his excursion into Oriental mythology is in comparison with the poems based on Irish sagas; how even these latter poems fall short of his epic aim; and how he finally abandoned epic poetry for lyrical and satirical verse which is rooted for the most part, not in the exciting sagas of those 'lost centuries' but in the complexities of modern life.

The epic strain in Clarke's work may be traced through four poems: *The Vengeance of Fionn, The Fires of Baal, The Sword of the West*, and *The Cattledrive in Connaught*. Clarke was first inspired to write epic poetry after reading Herbert Trench's poem *Deirdre Wed*. He had also studied Samuel Ferguson's epic work but had been disappointed by the caution and rather ponderous moralising quite frequently found in Ferguson's poetry.[2] Clarke writes that *Deirdre Wed*, however, 'captivated me when I was young,'[3] and, in an essay on Herbert Trench, he describes it as 'the most original and strongest long narrative poem in modern Irish literature.'[4] To Clarke, this poem was 'a strange furious voice from the remote past' to which he 'instantly became a captive'.[5] So fascinated was he by the epic of this 'neglected Irish poet' that he chose it as his model and 'imitated it in that first long poem', *The Vengeance of Fionn*.

Clarke's debt to Trench is considerable. Several aspects of *The Vengeance of Fionn* stem directly from *Deirdre Wed*. There are at least four major ways in which Clarke's poem is indebted to Trench's work. Firstly, Trench takes for theme the great love story of the Ulster cycle of tales; Clarke treats its counterpart in the Fenian cycle. Secondly, Clarke's unusual but effective treatment of time owes much to Trench. The narrative in *The Vengeance of Fionn* does not follow a strict chronological order. Clarke succeeds in creating in his poem a curiously timeless atmosphere appropriate to the birth, development and consummation of Naoise's and Deirdre's love.

The chronological pattern of *Deirdre Wed* is as follows: it begins in the first century, sways back to a 'century more remote but unknown,'[6] leaps forward to the sixth century and achieves a cyclic completeness by reverting at its conclusion, to the first century. Clarke imitates Trench's time-pattern faithfully and effectively. In his introductory argument to *The Vengeance of Fionn*, he writes that 'the poem begins in the middle age of Diarmaid and Gráinne, and changes rapidly, visionally, to their youth and love, so that the reader has an awareness of the past – ideal in itself, yet further idealised by memory – in the present'.[7] This reversal of the natural order of time is economically done. At the very beginning, the aged Fionn sees Diarmaid and Gráinne in middle age:

> ...he saw the troubled births
> And child-cares in her face, upon her lips
> Languored, as of old, sad autumn light;
> Thereafter, darker, prouder with his age
> Diarmaid standing near. (*VF*, 3)

The poem, in moving forward, goes quickly backwards in time to the ecstasy of youthful love. Diarmaid's avowals are strengthened by the contrast with the middle-aged portrait of himself and Gráinne at the beginning of the poem; his passionate words are a blend of unconscious irony and deep sincerity:

> What have the old, the tired, to do with love,
> To pilfer pleasure and dote and think they dream?
> O it is for youth, only for arrogant youth,
> To love and love! (*VF*, 45)

Like Trench, Clarke achieves a cyclic effect by concluding his poem with a young woman's description of the ageing Gráinne, thus enclosing the love story in a frame of years, but showing also how the myth applies to lovers in all places, at all points in time. Placing the legendary couple at a distance has the paradoxical effect of making their story more strikingly immediate:

> 'And I saw poor Gráinne in the sunlight
> Wrinkled and ugly. I do not think she slept.
> My mother says that she was beautiful,
> Proud, white and a queen's daughter long ago,
> And that they were great lovers in the old days –
> Before she was married – and lived in hilly woods
> Until they wearied.
> I do not want to grow so old like her.
> O it is best to be young and dance and laugh

And sing all day and comb my sleepy hair
In the startime, and never, never grow old.'
                              'O shiny dew,
    O little wild bird of the air,
    Youth only is wisdom and it is love.' (*VF*, 55-56)

The third respect in which Clarke closely resembles Trench is
in his dramatic handling of the narrative. It is significant that both
poets turned to the stage later in their respective careers. Trench
produced an epic drama, *Napoleon*, which was successfully staged,[8]
and Clarke's *Collected Plays* (1963) are, after Yeats's dramatic work,
the most impressive body of verse-plays in Anglo-Irish literature.
In both *The Vengeance of Fionn* and *Deirdre Wed*, there is a constant use of voices to achieve dramatic effect. Trench presents the
action through the voices of three old bards, Fintan, Urmael and
Cir. We hear not only the bards' voices, but also the fairly constant, tense dialogue of the lovers. The result of this is that
Trench considerably compresses the action, and the tight narrative
sweeps on to a dramatic conclusion.

Clarke likewise relies heavily on voices, dialogue and what read
like stage directions to further his narrative. Two sections of the
poem are completely in dialogue, section III and section VII, the
poem's conclusion. The absence of any linking narrative heightens
the dramatic impact, and for this reason Clarke's conclusion is more
impressive than Trench's. Both poets aim at a subtle, indirect and
dramatic presentation of the story. Related to this is the fact that
Clarke, like Trench, uses a number of different metres to suggest
the rapid stir and change of events; in both poems, the metrical
variety conveys the atmosphere of uncertainty and pursuit through
which the lovers move.

The fourth important way in which Clarke follows Trench is in
the sheer verbal exuberance of his poem. When he first read *Deirdre
Wed*, he was delighted to discover 'a mad discordancy, like fifes,
drums, brasses,' instead of what he calls 'the muted music of the
Celtic twilight'. Trench's poem excited him 'with the concussion
of fine words',[9] and in *The Vengeance of Fionn* Clarke aims at the
verbal dynamism that animates *Deirdre Wed*. Here, for example, is
Clarke's depiction of the tumult and confusion which follows
Fionn's discovery that Gráinne has fled with Diarmaid:

                              Arose uproar
    Of running men and sobs of women cowed
    In shadowy corners – through tapestries night airs
    Whistled and waned – outside the torches tore
    The night with windy flame – the frightened mares

> And foals whinnied – hounds bayed their hunger – at last
> With shouts and tossing torchlights, swept in a blast
> Through clouds of dark stampeded dust, lash-urged
> The stallions screamed, the shuddering chariots creaked
> Madder than mountain oakboughs stormfully wreaked
> And the parched axles rumbling in the naves
> Grew hot as when their hammered bronze was forged
> Loud on the hissing anvils, stripped of flame.
> So down the roads of Temair the Fianna came
> Charioteered in thundering; bloodhounds
> Sniffed, fanged the wind and then in mighty bounds
> Sprang at the throat of night... (*VF*, 32-33)

Despite the fact that Clarke imitates Trench in other less important ways,[10] *The Vengeance of Fionn* is a remarkable beginning to his career, a successful poem in its own right. When Clarke says that 'In returning to Irish mythology, our poets experienced an emotion which was unknown to English poets, an emotion which gives their work its peculiar intensity',[11] he is in fact describing the special character of his own poem. *The Vengeance of Fionn* is really an epic fragment of sustained lyrical intensity – an intensity due directly to the fact that Clarke, like Ferguson and Yeats, was 'not exploring a borrowed mythology, but one which belonged to [his] country, survived in its oral tradition, and in the very names of its hills, rivers and plains'.[12] For his second attempt at an epic poem, however, Clarke abandoned Gaelic sources to explore a 'borrowed mythology'. The result is at once unfortunate and profitable: unfortunate in that Clarke is here frequently at sea; profitable in that this digression confirmed him in his subsequent choice of subject-matter.

The Fires of Baal is an extension of the following verse from the Pentateuch:

> And the Lord spake unto Moses that self-same day, saying 'Get thee up into this mountain Abarim, unto Mount Nebo, which is in the land of Moab, that is over against Jericho; and behold the land of Canaan, which I give unto the children of Israel for a possession; and die in the mount whither thou goest up, and be gathered unto thy people'.[13]

Apparently considering it necessary to justify his departure from Gaelic saga, Clarke holds that there is an Eastern tradition in Irish literature from Moore's *Lalla Rookh* onwards (*FB*, 31), but in fact the tradition, if one dare give it so strong a name, is very slight indeed.[14] In all fairness, one cannot say that *The Fires of Baal* is a substantial addition to that dubious tradition or to any other. The entire poem depends on a single event – the death of Moses.

There is therefore very little action, and, in a desperate attempt to compensate for this, Clarke indulges in long, exotically sensuous descriptions of a remote Eastern way of life with which he is painfully unfamiliar. The poem's stagnant atmosphere is further emphasised by the flatulent rhetoric which Clarke uses to portray the sensuous Orient. In *The Vengeance of Fionn*, Clarke had written intimately and authoritatively of the Irish countryside, depicting its richness, desolation and bewildering changes of mood with a masterly touch, but the Eastern world he evokes in *The Fires of Baal* – despite its Nubian eunuchs and harlots, its pagan temples and moon-edged scimitars, its fruity atmosphere of grapes, apricots, sloes and orchards of crimson pomegranate – remains a mere tapestry glittering with false brilliance. It is a poor poem. Tottering under its burden of adjectives, it depends for its effect on vague imagery and feeble Miltonic echoes:

> Multitudes
> Glimmering through the darkness slowly moved
> With voices of lamentation and of hate,
> Across vast ultimate plains until night passed
> And sworded cries of desolating angels
> Swept down tumultuous light; and mighty kingdoms
> Unpeopled, dropped in flame and flaming lit
> The black abyss... (*FB*, 28-29)

The poem is nevertheless valuable for two reasons. The first is that it makes a gallant attempt to portray the loneliness of Moses, the wanderer tired and solitary near the end of his days, but still bearing his responsibility towards his people. In a striking way, this portrayal of Moses reminds one of Clarke's later position; detached from his people, the poet broods on their plight with the compassion of Moses, but with the added bitterness of his own heart:

> He watched with dazzled eyes the lonely sun
> Westering swiftly through white mountain clouds,
> Below the richer skies, until the drouth
> And hunger of his peoples wandering
> For generations through the desert sands
> Stormed with fierce unassuageable pangs
> Upon his heart, and shaken with the grief
> And sudden joy of that far Promised Land,
> Shading his eyes, half blind with aged tears
> He gazed upon the plain. (*FB*, 22)

Secondly, the poem is valuable because it showed Clarke that, whatever his hopes were of writing a successful epic on a theme taken from Irish mythology, he was for the most part out of his depth when dealing with the mythology of the East. His imagination

is more at home in Leinster and Connaught than in Sodom and
Gomorrah, dwelling more profitably on Cuchulain than on Moses,
on the plains of Emain Macha than on the Promised Land. It is
not surprising to find that his next attempt at an epic poem plunges
into the most hectic and exciting of our ancient sagas – the Ulster
cycle of tales.

The Sword of the West, written in 1921, the same year as *The
Fires of Baal*, is by far Clarke's longest poem and is divided into
two books, *Concobar* and *The Death of Cuchullin*, which, as Clarke
writes, 'form the introduction and the conclusion of a poem
embracing the entire Cuchullin saga, and the wars of the western
and northern kingdoms for supremacy'.[15] The poem is an attempt
to reproduce in English verse the barbaric splendour and passionate extravagance of the ancient world; in this respect, it will be
seen that it is not entirely successful since, as will be shown,
Clarke's imagination is often repelled by what is violent or grotesque
in the sagas. This is ironic, since he criticised Ferguson's Victorian
timidity and inhibition in handling the ancient material.[16] What we
get in *The Sword of the West*, in fact, is a lyrical evasion of the
starkness and brutality of the original. In his foreword to the poem,
Clarke makes two significant statements which help to explain this
evasion. 'Poetry is incantation,' he writes, and adds that 'it is well
that the mythological world should remain clouded and that the
fords are deep' (*SW*). The poem's sustained exuberant lyricism,
with its rich assonantal patterns and internal rhyming schemes,
stems directly from the belief inherent in the first statement. The
second statement explains the vagueness which enshrouds the heroic
world as it is here recreated by Clarke. Action, and especially violent
action, is swamped under the incantatory lyricism, and the poem
leaves an impression of incongruity arising from the fact that it is
essentially a lyrical treatment of epic material.

Concobar deals mainly with the causes of, and preparations for
the war between the western and northern kingdoms. As in *The
Vengeance of Fionn*, Clarke shows his skill in his handling of time.
Deftly and effectively, he weaves into the narrative, which deals
with the present, certain important events out of the past which
combine to make the present what it is. For example, after giving
an impressive description of Concobar's kingdom, with its rich
grasslands, plains, forests and pastures, he achieves a powerful
contrast by immediately knitting into the narrative a brief account
of the event which caused an overpowering weakness to descend
on the men of Ulster at the most crucial moments in their lives:

> The plain of Emain Macha – named from her
> Who stood, a goddess, tall and virginal,
> In sudden sunlight once, her hair unbound
> Like yellow brass upon her ample breasts
> Before stern Duvthach as he watched his goats
> Upon wild crags above a crooked glen –
> Where scarce a magpie came or late green buds
> Upon the thorns – and for a summer kept
> His jealous bed until in place of spears,
> Braggart with mead, he mouthed abundant praise
> Of her long supple body and its speed,
> Thence dragged through mocking clans before the King,
> And she, grey-smiled, unwomancd by her love,
> Though heavy-burdened in her womb, outran
> The uncharioted mares of Concobar
> And fainting beyond the thudded dust, brought forth
> Unshapen twins and from the mountain-clouds
> A druid voice across the plains called down
> The curse of Dana on the sombre clans:
> In their most perilous hour at rath or ford,
> The weakness of women in first childbed. (*SW*, 5-6)

As in *The Vengeance of Fionn*, the past illuminates the present. The purpose of the first book of *The Sword of the West* is to create the tense atmosphere of war, and so Clarke depicts past events that help to create and sustain this climate. Concobar's wily acquisition of the throne; the imposing litany of Red Branch heroes; the deposition of Fergus; the growing tension between the two kingdoms, sharpened by the menacing roar of Concobar's shield which 'Thrice muttered kingly danger to the land' (*SW*, 8) – all these things, neatly knit into the narrative, build up the battle-climate. The atmosphere is further heightened by a curt, retrospective account of the battle of Moytura, including some fine descriptions of conflicts between individual gods. Here, for example, is how Goibniu slays Ruadan:

>   Goibniu heard
> Uproar of windy battle, and raining sparks
> Blackened his swearing skin...
>   Far off like torches
> He saw the eye of Ruadan; a spear
> Pierced deeply through his jagged breasting wolf-skins
> And tore the tender pap. Backward he staggered,
> Fearfully swaying like a charioteer
> Drunken with speed between the plunging stallions
> And roar of earth, then forging his great arm
> He grasped his sword and with a heaving groan
> Cleft the great Fomor through the groin. (*SW*, 38-39)

The atmosphere is further intensified by Clarke's movingly
detailed portrayal of the Irish countryside where every river, hill
and glen is linked with some violence, love or heroism. Places are
images of passion:

> Bare mountain gaps where Doirche, the usurper,
> Mated fierce loves between his spears – the sea
> Narrow beyond the lower glens, cantreds
> Beyond Sliav Mish, where the thick sunset fumes
> Smouldering from topmost crags down hidden glens
> Meave, the Half-Red, crouched with lonely broods
> Of blackening spears and the dark waterish bogs,
> No man had wandered, where Fearcu, the Hounded,
> Ruled monstrous clans; wild sally glens that hid
> Clan Ernain, the raths of Temair and southward
> A mighty kingdom of black ocean'd mountains
> Where Curoi sat in thunder. (*SW*, 4)

The book closes in a pent-up atmosphere of imminent battle in
which Concobar's royal shield 'Thrice thundered hidden danger
to the King' (*SW*, 47), and there is a brief mention of Cuchulain
whose most heroic stand is brought about by the events described
in Book One. It is at this point, when the atmosphere of imminent
war is most intense, that Cuchulain is first mentioned:

>   ...he comes from darkness, a torch
> Of war, his strength a thousand sworded clans
> Blazing the marching kingdoms with renown
> Twice-named the Hound of Ulad. (*SW*, 46)

Precisely the same merits and defects emerge in Book Two of
The Sword of the West. The major weakness is that Clarke avoids a
direct or detailed portrayal of that event which the book's title, *The
Death of Cuchullin*, would lead one to believe is its central event.
The poem works with a certain laboured power towards this climax,
but then, as if his imagination were repelled by the rather gruesome
account of the hero's death as given in various versions of the saga,[17]
Clarke, with lyrical agility, side-steps the central issue and, instead,
the hero's death is indirectly reported:

>   As the jaded horses
> Drank and the clan tore ravenous bread, they heard
> A woman crying by the waters: 'He is dead,
> My Hound is dead!' (*SW*, 90)

and

>   But darker ocean clouds
> Rolled downward, hiding the remoter sunset,
> And a cry rose, as when some royal hound
> Is slain. (*SW*, 94)

It is interesting to compare Clarke's indirect conclusion with Yeats's effective use of the same device in *On Baile's Strand*. At the end of Yeats's play, Cuchulain's fight with the sea is graphically described by the Fool and the Blind Man; the hypnotic effect of the repeated phrases creates a dramatic picture of the hero's last futile but magnificent gesture as he fights the waves:

> FOOL. There, he is down! He is up again. He is going out in the deep water. There is a big wave. It has gone over him. I cannot see him now. He has killed kings and giants, but the waves have mastered him, the waves have mastered him!
>
> BLIND MAN. Come here, fool!
>
> FOOL. The waves have mastered him.
>
> BLIND MAN. Come here!
>
> FOOL. The waves have mastered him.
>
> BLIND MAN Come here, I say.
>
> FOOL (*Coming towards him, but looking backwards towards the door*). What is it?
>
> BLIND MAN. There will be nobody in the houses. Come this way; come quickly! The ovens will be full. We will put our hands into the ovens.[18]

The Fool's almost incredulous realisation that the hero has been vanquished by the sea, and the Blind Man's sharply repeated injunction, prompted by his self-interest and cunning sense of exploitation, combine to produce a strong dramatic effect. By contrast, Clarke's use of the same device is rather weak. Yeats uses it to create a powerful climax, but with Clarke it is another manifestation of a curiously evasive attitude towards his material. It is this unwillingness to recreate the heroic world in its complete savage splendour and brutality, combined with a gushing lyricism which tends to stifle whatever action there is, that prevents the poem from reaching the epic heights that Clarke had aimed at. In an occasional descriptive moment, he presents glimpses of the heroic world, as in this portrait of Cuchulain:

> But menacing he rose into the glooms
> Of breaking smoke and raftered light, the horns
> Of his great helmet loud with storm, his torques
> Of hammered gold began to slowly burn
> Resounding, and like a woman terrified,
> His massive sword fell with a piercing cry.

Cuchulain's resolution to defend Ulster is striking also:

> Now war
> Reels with fierce clans and I, alone, defend
> These smouldering lands until the desolate end. (*SW*, 82)

Such moments, however, are all too rare, and, because of its evasions, the poem flags to an unconvincing conclusion. Yet *The*

Sword of the West justifies Clarke's return to Irish mythology, and his final and most successful attempt at epic poetry continues his exploration of the Ulster cycle. In 1925, he produced *The Cattle-drive in Connaught*, which is 'based on *The Pillow Talk at Cruachan*, the prologue to the *Táin Bó Cuailgne*, the great prose epic of the wars between the northern and western kingdoms'.[19] The pity is that Clarke deals only with the prologue to the epic. Yet this is consistent with his general attitude; he presents the part rather than the whole, the vivid segment rather than the turbulent totality.

The argument of the poem is brief: 'How Maeve of Connaught disputed with her husband at an unreasonable hour, in the comfort of the royal bed, regarding their respective possessions. How the cattle were driven in and counted. How a plenipotentiary was sent to Ulster to negotiate for the Brown Bull, and a good deal of ale was consumed' (*CC*, 42). From the beginning of the narrative when

> Queen Maeve sat up in bed and shook once more
> Her snoring husband (*CC*, 43)

the poem moves at a lively pace. The action is swift and forceful; Clarke the dramatist strengthens Clarke the poet, and the earthy dialogue builds up an atmosphere of colourful extravagance and boisterous vitality that distinguishes the characters of the poems. Maeve will not have her ambition thwarted:

> She called the royal messenger,
>   'Go, go,
> MacRoth, with drovers, stable boys and food,
> Hurry into his lands and know a queen
> Follows your wind. Promise him what you will
> So that you get the bull, nay fifty bloods
> To stock his field or, if he would, the best
> Of acreage in Connaught that has yielded
> The sea no tribute. We give powers to you
> For peace and war. If he is filled with greed
> As such small farmers are, promise him more
> Than a foolish head can hold and pinch the bargain
> In the black o' the nail, or name the dreaded will
> And majesty of the west, for empty or full
> I will not sleep until I have that bull.' (*CC*, 56-57)

Clarke captures the atmosphere of wrangling and disunity leading to war, and the conflict of personal passions set against and seeming to grow out of the wild landscape. Dara, the Ulsterman, 'bull-headed, blood-eyed', refuses to give the Brown Bull to Maeve's emissary and

> The Connaught man
> Replied –
> 'The new green writhe is peeled
> For breaking. Dara, you have scorned the will
> That holds wide Connaught and the windy flock
> Of islands but the armies of Red Maeve
> Shall bare these plains with hooks of fire and take
> The Bull.' –
> And turning at the crowded door
> Of parting flung his sword upon the floor. (*CC*, 62)

In this poem, more than in any of the three others, Clarke comes near the grotesque, violent world of the original Gaelic epic.[20] Ironically, just when he appears to be on the point of writing a good epic poem, he turns away from heroic saga. This development is, I suggest, inevitable, since, as has been pointed out, his imagination is repelled by violence and, unlike Yeats, he puts very little of his personal experiences into the sagas. In a short poem, 'The Tales of Ireland', Clarke declares his intention to leave behind the epic world that had so fascinated his youthful imagination:

> The thousand tales of Ireland sink: I leave
> Unfinished what I had begun nor count
> As gain the youthful frenzy of those years;
> For I remember my own passing breath,
> Man's violence and all the despair of brain
> That wind and river took in Glenasmole.[21]

This 'unfinished' quality is the ultimate impression left by Clarke's epic poetry. Later, his imagination sought the more congenial atmosphere of the mid-Irish world which, as Padraic Colum observes, is the Ireland between the heroic legends and the present-day folk-songs.[22] Later still, Clarke became an uncompromising satirist of modern Irish life. The hesitant epic poet has been transformed into a chillingly skilled satirist, who relentlessly probes and reveals the servilities and hypocrisies of a self-righteous Catholicism. Clarke has moved far from his early preoccupation with the Irish epic tradition; yet he has not forgotten it completely. In one of his late poems, 'Forget Me Not,' he refers briefly to Cuchulain:

> The moon
> Eclipsed: I stood on the Rock of Cashel, saw dimly
> Carved on the royal arch of Cormac's Chapel
> Sign of the Sagittary, turned my back
> On all that Celtic Romanesque; thinking
> Of older story and legend, how Cuchullain,
> Half man, half god-son, tamed the elemental
> Coursers: dear comrades: how at his death
> The Gray of Macha laid her mane upon his breast
> And wept.[23]

Clarke's epic poetry, therefore, is not by any means his best work. As the poet Padraic Fallon points out, it was as if Clarke 'had to keep the distances of mythology between himself and the world.' [24] Yeats used mythology to express and illuminate the diverse facets of his complex personality; Clarke, on the contrary, conceals himself behind it, and it is only after four attempts at an epic poem that he begins to take his stand as an impassioned observer and critic of modern life. Nevertheless, his epic poetry is important as a heroic introduction to a body of satire which, for technical skill and incisive comment, must be among the most impressive of this century.

Satire in Flann O'Brien's *The Poor Mouth*

The book I want to deal with, *The Poor Mouth* (*An Béal Bocht*)[1] is a masterpiece, for many reasons. The first reason is that its author, Flann O'Brien, has a mastery of the Irish language. (He has an equal mastery of English, but that's another story.) Secondly, he writes with a wide and deep knowledge of the Irish tradition. Thirdly, his satirical genius is equal to that of Swift, and, like Swift, Flann O'Brien[2] is a savage moralist with a hatred of hypocrisy and a fiercely articulate awareness of evil.

It is only fair that I should admit that my own Irish is nothing to write home about; yet, as I re-read this book, I was able to appreciate the skill, the comic agility, the lacerating fury with which Flann O'Brien could invest the Irish language.

Why is *The Poor Mouth* such an angry book? What is it hitting at?

The book's plot, if it can be called such, is straight-forward. The hero, Bónapart Ó Cúnasa, is born into the Gaeltacht area of Corca Dorcha. Also in the house are Bónapart's mother, an old man called An Seanduine Liath, and many pigs, sheep and cattle. Bónapart's father is in prison, or, as the Old Man says, 'Tá sé sa chrúiscín' (He is in the jug). Bónapart grows up, has a number of adventures which seem more like nightmares, and at the end of the book, he is imprisoned for twenty-nine years, having been found guilty of murdering a man in Galway, and stealing his gold. Bónapart understands nothing of his trial. Just before he enters prison he meets his father, or somebody whom he takes to be his father, for the first time. The encounter is over almost as soon as it began. And that is the end of the book.

The plot may be skeletal, but the satire is merciless. The title gives us a clue. An Béal Bocht is, of course, the poor mouth, the assumption and emphasis of poverty in order to gain a more advantageous position. The poor mouth is the slave's weapon, the instrument of the whining opportunist. There are at least two great pieces of Irish writing concerning poverty – Patrick Kavanagh's poem *The Great Hunger* and *The Poor Mouth*. Kavanagh's long poem is tragic; Flann O'Brien's novel is at once funny and bitter. Here, he describes the bad smell (of pigs and humans together) in Bónapart's house:

> In my youth we always had a bad smell in our house. Sometimes it was so bad that I asked my mother to send me to school, even though

I could not walk correctly. Passers-by neither stopped nor even walked when in the vicinity of our house but raced past the door and never ceased until they were half a mile from the bad smell. There was another house two hundred yards down the road from us and one day when our smell was extremely bad the folks there cleared out, went to America and never returned. It was stated that they told people in that place that Ireland was a fine country but that the air was too strong there. Alas! there was never any air in our house.[3]

This is Bónapart's stinking home. He lives literally with the pigs and is almost indistinguishable from them. (Later in the novel, when he becomes a father, he thinks his own son is a little pig.) Inside the house, all is stinking congestion. Outside, is the endless downpour of hostile heaven. It never stops raining in Corca Dorcha, as though heaven had nothing but complete contempt for those with the béal bocht. There are times in this book when the reader himself feels absolutely drenched through to the skin, and indeed beneath the skin.

This drenched, battered, foul, stinking place is the home of the fiorGaels. This is the well of purest Gaelic, somewhat defiled. Yet Flann O'Brien is not attacking the language. (His own Irish shows how long and hard and lovingly he must have worked to achieve such precision.) No, he is attacking certain uses of the language, and certain attitudes which seem almost synonymous with those *uses*. In doing this, he employs, with a great deal of effective repetition, certain phrases picked from other writers. For example, many of us will remember the phrase 'Ní bheidh ár leithéidí arís ann' (Our likes won't be there again). This phrase is used by Tomás Ó Crohan in his book *An tOileánach* (*The Islandman*, 1929, English translation 1937). Heroic Fenian literature is full of this kind of epic self-commemoration and self-assertion. Oisín and Fionn would speak like that. But Flann O'Brien uses the phrase when he speaks of the death of a pig – a particularly foul-smelling and ever-swelling and swilling pig, Ambrós. This is Bónapart praying for the dead pig, God rest his grunt:

> Ambrose was an odd pig and I do not think that his like will be there again. Good luck to him if he be alive in another world today! [4] (28)

The poison of the béal bocht penetrates everything. It even pollutes the language itself. At one stage in the book, a gentleman from Dublin is collecting Gaelic phrases on a recorder from the people of Corca Dorcha. In doing this, he spends a lot of money on whiskey to get the people talking. One night, he gives drink to a gathering of locals in a house (the typical condescending bribe of the insensitive

outsider) but the whiskey fails to loosen the tongues of the sons of
Corca Dorcha. Suddenly, somebody stumbles into the house, falls
on the floor drunk, and unleashes a flood of what seems like talk,
which, however, is quite unintelligible. According to the gentleman
from Dublin, good Irish should be difficult, but the best Irish should
be unintelligible. Perfection is another name for the incomprehensible.
Well, in this case, the gentleman has perfection well recorded
because what he manages to collect is the squealing of a rambling
pig. Delighted with his treasure, the gentleman leaves Corca Dorcha
to seek proper academic recognition for his labours. Flann O'Brien
is here hitting at everything from self-delusion to acquisitive con-
descension to academic pretentiousness. It is as if he were saying
– there is nothing wrong with language, Irish or otherwise; but
there is something very wrong with those who use it, or rather *abuse*
it, who change it from an instrument of possible illumination to
something which can inspire loathing and disgust. Language can
help us to tell what we know of the truth; it can also be the weapon
of liars, frauds and opportunists.

One senses in Flann O'Brien a great reverence for language, and
a great hatred for those who abuse it, those who tell the profitable
lie.

This love of verbal precision is the expression of an essentially
moral imagination. Cliché is not only the truth worn dull by repetition; it can also be a form of immoral evasion, a refusal to exercise
the mind at a moment when it should be exercised, even to one's
own discomfort or distress. Cliché is also a form of imaginative
fatigue, the unthinking use of listless formula to fill a blank space.

By taking the clichés of *other* writers, and by repeatedly inserting
them into his own vivid, animated narrative, Flann O'Brien achieves
unfailing satiric and comic effects. He mocks evasion; he parodies
inertia. And in showing the verbal tiredness of others, he proves
his own tremendous exuberance. The language of *The Poor Mouth*
is remarkable for its substained energy. There is nothing flabby or
soft about it. It has an intellectual cut and keenness, a constant
hitting of the satirical bull's-eye, a stabbing accuracy, that simply
cannot fail to delight any mind which recognises that a respect for
language is a respect for life itself. Unless we try, with all our hearts
and minds, to say what we mean, we do not mean what we say.
That is what I mean by 'respect'.

Flann O'Brien shows no mercy whatever to those who lack this
respect. In one of the most memorable chapters of his book, there
is a Grand Feis in Corca Dorcha, and it is opened by an t-Uactarán

himself, who gives an 'oráid' – a big speech. This is a fine example
of inflated pomposity and self-importance, a windy exercise in self-
delusion, a substitution of chauvinism for intelligence, an outburst
of rhetorical drivel. It is also wickedly funny:

> – Gaels! he said, it delights my Gaelic heart to be here today speaking
> Gaelic with you at this Gaelic feis in the centre of the Gaeltacht. May I
> state that I am a Gael. I'm Gaelic from the crown of my head to the
> soles of my feet – Gaelic front and back, above and below. Likewise,
> you are all truly Gaelic. We are all Gaelic Gaels of Gaelic lineage. He
> who is Gaelic, will be Gaelic evermore. I myself have spoken not a word
> except Gaelic since the day I was born – just like you – and every sen-
> tence I've ever uttered has been on the subject of Gaelic. If we're truly
> Gaelic, we must constantly discuss the question of the Gaelic revival
> and the question of Gaelicism. There is no use in having Gaelic, if we
> converse in it on non-Gaelic topics. He who speaks Gaelic but fails to
> discuss the language question is not truly Gaelic in his heart; such
> conduct is of no benefit to Gaelicism because he only jeers at Gaelic
> and reviles the Gaels. There is nothing in this life so nice and so Gaelic
> as truly true Gaelic Gaels who speak in true Gaelic Gaelic about the
> truly Gaelic language. I hereby declare this feis to be Gaelically open!
> Up the Gaels! Long live the Gaelic tongue!
>   When this noble Gael sat down on his Gaelic backside, a great tumult
> and hand-clapping arose throughout the assembly.[5] (54-55)

It is at this feis too that our hero Bónapart gets drunk for the
first time. Flann O'Brien's account of Bónapart's hangover must
be one of the funniest and most accurate descriptions of that un-
promising state ever written. There is simply no questioning the
authority of this description:

> If the bare truth be told, I did not prosper very well. My senses went
> astray, evidently. Misadventure fell on my misfortune, a further mis-
> adventure fell on that misadventure and before long the misadventures
> were falling thickly on the first misfortune and on myself. Then a shower
> of misfortunes fell on the misadventures, heavy misadventures fell on
> the misfortunes after that and finally one great brown misadventure
> came upon everything, quenching the light and stopping the course of
> life. I did not feel anything for a long while; I did not see anything,
> neither did I hear a sound. Unknown to me, the earth was revolving
> on its course through the firmament. It was a week before I felt that a
> stir of life was still within me and a fortnight before I was completely
> certain that I was alive. A half-year went by before I had recovered fully
> from the ill-health which that night's business had bestowed on me,
> God give us all grace! I did not notice the second day of the feis.[6] (60-61)

There is of course a note of exaggeration in that, and exaggeration
is one of Flann O'Brien's most effective satiric devices. It might
be more accurate of me to use the word 'distortion' rather than the
word 'exaggeration'. The passage dealing with those whom Flann

O'Brien calls the fiorGaels is, quite obviously, distorted; nobody would ever speak like that. Yet, in the language of certain people whose commitment borders on fanaticism, there is an element, a seed, of precisely this bloated verbal absurdity. What the accomplished satirist does is to take that element, that seed, which is of course only part of a total picture, and, by sheer style, make the part appear as though it were the complete thing. By the deft use of this kind of emphasis, the satirist draws our contemptuous attention to the element which he himself abhors. This, if you like, is the morality of his mockery, the ethical point of his distortion. The satirist is the enemy of the phoncy element which probably, to some degree at least, exists in all of us. His target is the pretentious and the ridiculous, his weapon is mockery, his aim is the spotlighting, and if possible, the eradication of the pompous and the hypocritical.

Exaggeration and distortion are probably the most characteristic features of the writing from beginning to end of this book. The very setting of the novel is a distortion, although a delightful one. From his house, reeking of pigs, the baby Bónapart can see Donegal, Galway and Kerry – a spectacle hardly available to any other house in Ireland. The food is dreadful. The weather is worse. It's hard to tell which of the two is dirtier – the people or the pigs. It is a world of unrelieved stupidity, filth, superstition and congestion. Fate is totally malignant and every circumstance is moronically accepted as part of God's will. And at the back of it all lies the origin and product of *an béal bocht* – poverty. At bottom Flann O'Brien is showing us the sad, ravaging mental attitudes that result from severe physical poverty – materialism, opportunism, suspicion, the closed mind, incestuous stupidity, the lack of definite identity (everybody in the area is called Jams O'Donnell), the prevalence of brutality and thievery, and the strange, predominant sense of evil and oppression. Listening to that list, you might think this is a gloomy book, a modern anatomy of melancholy and malaise. It is, on the contrary, packed with laughter, full of its own special gaiety, even when it describes one of those figures of total poverty that lie scattered not only through Irish history, but are buried in the consciousness of the race:

> There was a man in this townland at one time and he was named Sitric O'Sanassa. He had the best hunting, a generous heart and every other good quality which earn praise and respect at all times. But alas! there was another report abroad concerning him which was neither good nor fortunate. He possessed the very best poverty, hunger and distress also. He was generous and open-handed and he never possessed the smallest object which he did not share with the neighbours; nevertheless, I can

never remember him during my time possessing the least thing, even the quantity of little potatoes needful to keep body and soul joined together. In Corkadoragha, where every human being was sunk in poverty, we always regarded him as a recipient of alms and compassion. The gentlemen from Dublin who came in motors to inspect the paupers praised him for his Gaelic poverty and stated that they never saw any-one who appeared so truly Gaelic. One of the gentlemen broke a little bottle of water which Sitric had, because, said he, it spoiled the effect. There was no one in Ireland comparable to O'Sanassa in the excellence of his poverty; the amount of famine which was delineated in his person. He had neither pig nor cup nor any household goods. In the depths of winter I often saw him on the hillside fighting and competing with a stray dog, both contending for a narrow hard bone and the same snorting and angry barking issuing from them both. He had no cabin either, nor any acquaintance with shelter or kitchen heat. He had excavated a hole with his two hands in the middle of the countryside and over its mouth he had placed old sacks and branches of trees as well as any useful object that might provide shelter against the water which came down on the countryside every night. Strangers passing by thought that he was a badger in the earth when they perceived the heavy breathing which came from the recesses of the hole as well as the wild appearance of the habitation in general.[7] (88-89)

I am not happy, however, to call this book a satirical fantasy, and leave it at that. There is, in fact, in the work a strong *tragic* aware-ness of those powerful forces which can victimise man. Throughout the book, the elements lash down on the heads of everybody, man and beast alike. What strikes the reader is the *relentless* nature of this oppression, the fierce tireless energy of its tyranny. Flann O'Brien sees man as a sort of target for the fury of nature. Now I realise that this, like the picture of poverty, is a necessary part of his satirical picture, but I can't help feeling that this black vision sometimes transcends the satirical purpose it so brilliantly serves, and achieves at certain moments a real tragic intensity. And Flann O'Brien's language reflects this occasional strange hovering between the satirical and the tragic.

Nevertheless, the novel, as a whole, stays in the mind for its comic vigour, for its devastation of various Holy Cows, for its mocking onslaught on attitudes that are usually either mindless or slavish, or both. It is the work of a highly civilised mind, angered and appalled by certain aspects of the life and literature it is most deeply involved with. It is also the work of that most driven kind of moralist – the writer for whom the precise use of language is evidence of the mind's capacity for intellectual passion, the heart's capacity for sincerity. Behind it all is love of lucidity and candour, as well as this constant recognition of the mystery of life. The irreverence that abounds in the novel springs from the deepest possible respect for both life and language. This is one reason for its enormous emotional range: it is funny, sad, bitter, outrageous, bleak, insulting – and totally unforgettable. It is searingly honest, and it should be read, if possible, by everybody. *The Poor Mouth* may be about various kinds of poverty, but for the reader it is an immensely rich experience.

The Little Monasteries: Frank O'Connor as Poet

Frank O'Connor's fame as a writer of short stories has somewhat overshadowed his achievement as a poet. It was as a poet, in fact, that he began his writing career, and he produced a number of original poems. Then he turned to the short story form and dedicated the greater part of his energy to that. But once a poet, always a poet, practising or otherwise, and while O'Connor created several masterpieces in his chosen form, he also continued his service to poetry, mainly by way of translation. His *Kings, Lords, & Commons* is a monumental work, containing excellent poems, the most impressive of which seems to me to be the translation of Brian Merriman's long poem, *The Midnight Court*, vibrant with a kind of visionary bawdiness and uproarious spiritual gusto, perfectly capturing the curious mixture of verbal licence and emotional inhibition, of audacity and frustration, that Merriman discovered in eighteenth-century Gaelic Ireland. O'Connor's uncanny insight into the poetry of that time and that society enabled him to bring a remote eighteenth-century poet right into the heart of our times, portraying both the frustration and the ebullience with a vitality of language that Merriman himself would have loved. Here, for example, is one of these sexually frustrated young women,

> Heartsick, bitter, dour and wan,
> Unable to sleep for want of a man...[1]

compelled to lie in a lukewarm bed, desperately revealing her vain stratagems to get a man. It is frantic, funny and sad:

> Every night when I went to bed
> I'd a stocking of apples beneath my head;
> I fasted three canonical hours
> To try and come round the heavenly powers;
> I washed my shift where the stream ran deep
> To hear a lover's voice in sleep;
> Often I swept the woodstack bare,
> Burned bits of my frock, my nails, my hair,
> Up the chimney stuck the flail,
> Slept with a spade without avail;
> Hid my wool in the lime-kiln late
> And my distaff behind the churchyard gate;...
> But 'twas all no good and I'm broken-hearted
> For here I'm back at the place I started;
> And this is the cause of all my tears
> I am fast in the rope of the rushing years,
> With age and need in lessening span,
> And death beyond, and no hopes of a man...[2]

From beginning to end the poem bristles with this sort of vitality, giving the urbane couplet which Merriman took from contemporary English poetry a shock of earthy realism. *Kings, Lords, & Commons* is full of such treasures; it is fair to say that in many cases O'Connor created completely new poems, as Ezra Pound does in his translations from the Chinese. In 1963 O'Connor produced his last book of poems, *The Little Monasteries*. It contains twenty poems, all of which may be looked on as new creations, obviously the work of a dedicated poet and a scrupulous craftsman. This small collection of poems contains some of Frank O'Connor's finest work.

The book falls neatly into three thematic divisions. It is concerned with nature, poets and love. The forms are in many cases simple but effective, the rhythms frequently predictable but always strong, the idiom an impressive blend of a modern conversational tone and a unique kind of passionate formality. Above all the poems are intensely dramatic in mood, tone and structure. O'Connor came more and more to believe in the concentrated urgency and intensity of the dramatic lyric. When he read poetry aloud, he made it a dramatic experience, scorning the sophisticated timidity and urbane spinelessness of so many contemporary poetry-readers. He shamelessly and delightedly wrung the last shred of drama from every poem he read, and, in most cases, he communicated both the drama and the delight to his audience. In *The Little Monasteries* we shall see how effectively he explores and develops the dramatic lyric.

Only the first two poems deal directly with nature. 'The Seasons' is exquisitely wrought, rich in vowel music, and immediately striking for its precision and fullness of detail. It opens with a description of autumn, marvellously portraying the curious mixture of fatigue and superfluity characteristic of that season. Every line is concrete and evocative, making a conscious but judicious use of alliteration; notice how the word 'fall', used both as noun and verb, opens and closes the stanza, so that what we get is a bursting picture of ripe fullness enclosed in a framework of finality. The unmistakable feeling of autumn fills those lines:

> Fall is no man's travelling time;
> Tasks are heavy; husbandmen
> Heed the low light, lingering less.
> Lightly their young drop from the deer,
> Dandled in the faded fern;
> Fiercely the stag stalks from the hill,
> Hearing the herd in clamorous call;
> Cobbled the mast in windless woods,
> Weary the corn upon its canes,
> > Colouring the brown earth.

> Endless the thorns that foul the fence
> Which frames the hollow of some house;
> The hard dry ground is filled with fruit,
> And by the fort, hard from their height,
>   Hazelnuts break and fall.[3]

The other three seasons are described with the same delicacy and detail. 'The Seasons' is purely objective in its appreciation of nature. 'In the Country' is similarly appreciative, but the poet intrudes to tell us that though he is willing to praise the singing birds, he is also happy about his own capacity for expression. The result of this sense of excellence within and outside himself is to make him ask the source of all excellence not to be too hard on him when the hour for judging poets is at hand, suggesting, perhaps, that the final fruit of any human perfection is the realisation of its ultimate inadequacy:

> A hedge of trees is all around;
>   The blackbird 's praise I shall not hide;
> Above my book so smoothly lined
>   The birds are singing far and wide.
>
> In a green cloak of bushy boughs
>   The cuckoo pipes his melodies –
> Be good to me, God, on Judgment Day! –
>   How well I write beneath the trees! (9)

In the second section there are several poems dealing with various kinds of poets. It begins with a four-line poem in which an old poet prays and gives thanks to God for continued inspiration:

> God be praised who ne'er forgets me
>   In my art so high and cold
> And still sheds upon my verses
>   All the magic of red gold.
>   ('The Old Poet', 70)

Nobody knew better than O'Connor with what intensity poets were feared and loved in ancient Ireland, and, in 'The Thirsty Poet', he records a poet's gratitude to a king's daughter because she slaked his thirst. This is the diametrical opposite of James Stephens's poem in which he denounces a 'whey-faced slut' of a woman for refusing him a drink. Stephens satirises meanness; O'Connor celebrates generosity:

> Blessings on King Donal's daughter,
>   Gracious Ethna, good indeed,
> Who, when I had cased the township
>   For rat poison,

> Sent me two and thirty wry-necked
> Harnessed hauliers'
> Load of mead. (11)

'The Angry Poet' (13), on the contrary, displays a vicious spirit; the poet is here in a bitter rage and he condemns the targets of his anger – the hound, the lackey, the master and his wife – to a lifetime of foul intimacy. It is in 'The Ex-Poet', however, that the real O'Connor emerges. He is here dealing with one of these lonely voices, those solitary people that fill his short stories. The ex-poet is such a figure, a drab spiritual pariah on the fringe of society, moving anonymously towards a casual oblivion. This is an area where O'Connor's compassionate imagination is most penetrating and active, and, with terrifying bareness, he presents the fate of the lonely outcast.

> No woman now shall be his mate,
> No son nor daughter share his fate,
> No thigh beside his thigh repose –
> Solitary the ex-poet goes. (12)

It is in the third section of the book, the love-poetry, that O'Connor is at his best. The range of these poems is far wider, the theme is obsessively explored from various angles and, above all, their essentially *dramatic* character is always compelling. In all the poems, except one, 'The Nun of Beare', it is the man or the ghost of the man who speaks, usually dramatising his loss. The poems range from the facetious to the profound, from the realistic to the supernatural. O'Connor is true to all tones, discovering an appropriate idiom and form for the prevailing mood.

In *The Little Monasteries*, O'Connor produces some love-poems which must surely be among the best in Irish literature. There is no trace of embarrassment, no sense of unbearable intimacy, no sentimental overstatement, or romantic distortion of the reality. He saves it by irony, passion and sometimes even a spirit of mischief as in, for example, 'Advice to Lovers', where the counsel is one of jovial indifference, which gives the lover who possesses it a gay resilience to practically everything. The cheeky metre is in tune both with the gumption of the man who offers the advice and the audacity of the lover who would accept it:

> The way to get on with a girl
>   Is to drift like a man in a mist,
> Happy enough to be caught,
>   Happy to be dismissed.

> Glad to be out of her way,
>   Glad to rejoin her in bed,
> Equally grieved or gay
>   To learn that she's living or dead. (15)

The supernatural element enters in 'The Dead Lover', in which O'Connor compresses a fifty-verse ninth-century poem into nineteen austerely hewn stanzas. It tells how Fohad, leader of a band of mercenaries, elopes with the wife of another mercenary chief. He is killed in battle, but returns to keep his tryst. This is one of the most dramatic of all the poems. Fohad's ghost addresses the girl with shattering directness:

> Silence, girl! What can you say?
> My thoughts are not of you, they stray;
> I think of nothing else tonight
> Except the battlefield and fight.
>
> My headless body tossed aside
> Lies on the slope whereon I died,
> And in that heap my head you see
> Near those of men who died with me.
>
> A lovers' tryst is waste of breath
> Beside the final tryst with death,
> And so the lovers' tryst we made
> I can keep only as a shade... (16)

With dramatic simplicity O'Connor portrays the lover's ghost looking back on his own dead body, thinking of the fight and of his love:

> I am not the first in body's heat
> Who found some outland woman sweet,
> And though our parting tryst be drear
> It was your love that brought me here.
>
> It was for love alone I came,
> Leaving my gentle wife in shame:
> Had I but known what would befall
> How gladly would I have shunned it all... (16)

He confesses his love for her, at the same time pointing out how futile is her love for him:

> Why should you spend a night of dread
> Alone among the unburied dead?... (17)

He must part with her because the dawn, which severs mortal from immortal, is near. The sundering is complete:

> From human things I must take flight
> After my men with the first light;
> Already the night's end has come;
> Do not stay here, back to your home!... (18)

He tells her to raise a 'great tomb' above him that he may be remembered and praised, and the poem closes with a heartbreaking statement about lonely descent into the grave:

> Now my pierced body must descend
> To torture where the fiends attend;
> Worldly love is a foolish thing
> Beside the worship of Heaven's king.
>
> It is the blackbird! Once again
> He calls at dawn to living men;
> My voice, my face are of the dead.
> Silence! What is there to be said? (18)

There is a deft partial reversal in 'On the Death of His Wife' in which the living man mourns the dead woman. We are plunged at the beginning into a mood of desolation and loss which is sustained throughout:

> I parted from my life last night,
> A woman's body sunk in clay:
> The tender bosom that I loved
> Wrapped in a sheet they took away... (19)

The dark mood of lamentation in this poem is continually offset by other poems of a much lighter tone, wavering between seriousness and flippancy. And so in 'Women' we meet a lover who appears to be wryly amused by his own lack of prejudice towards women:

> No fanaticism I share
> For blue or black in someone's eye
> Or the colour of her hair... (21)

In fact, the only criticism one can make of this man is that he has no criticism to make of women; his fault is that he sees no fault:

> And all may hear what I would say
> In women, such is my disgrace,
> I never found a thing astray... (22)

The point of the poem, however, is not that he is indiscriminate through ignorance, but that he is tolerant through knowledge. As he neatly and rather glibly lists for us those qualities which he insists he does not require in women, we realise that he is deeply aware of feminine merits and defects. In stating his acceptance of the many limitations of women, he reveals himself as an acute observer of their attractions. The uncritical liberal is in fact a scrupulous connoisseur:

I don't require them cold or warm;
    Widows have knowledge and good sense
But there is still a certain charm
    In a young girl's inexperience.

I like them in church, demure and slow,
    Solem without, relaxed at home;
I like them full of push and go
    When love has left me overcome.

I find no fault in them, by God,
    But being old and gone to waste
Who still are girls at forty odd –
    And every man may suit his taste. (22-23)

It is difficult to realise with what industry and tenacity O'Connor worked at these poems. His finest love-poem, 'The Nun of Beare', was written and re-written over a period of at least thirty years. It first appeared in *The Oxford Book of Modern Verse*, edited by Yeats, in 1936, and the finished version is in *The Little Monasteries*. What strikes one most of all about the changes in the poem over the years is the way in which O'Connor insisted on dramatising it more and more. In the *Oxford Book*, it is a straightforward lyric; in *The Little Monasteries*, it is a dramatic poem with voices. O'Connor had for many years accepted the view of the editors of the original Old Irish poem, Kuno Meyer and Gerard Murphy, but as time passed, he became convinced that

> it is really a series of lyrics from a lost eighth century romance which was edited in the tenth or eleventh century to give it a fictitious homogeneity, and that this rehandling is largely responsible for its formless appearance...
>
>   The heroine of the romance would seem to have been originally the Goddess of Munster, though the story teller did not know this. All he knew was the tradition of the various marriages she had celebrated with the Munster Kings, and he regarded her as an Irish Mary Magdalen. This is how she appears in the first lyric. Then Saint Cummine, 'whose knowledge of the byways of sexual behaviour is entitled to rank beside Kinsey's', in the words of one Irish scholar, is brought to deal with her. It is clear that at the crisis of the story, The Nun challenged Christ to spend the night with her, and after He appeared, was converted and reconciled to the idea of old age.[4]

The dominating voices in the final version of the poem are the Nun and Cummine. The poem is charged with the pathos filling the memories of this archetypal lover who sadly contrasts the excitement of her youth with her present uneventful life as an ageing spiritual recluse:

> I, the old woman of Beare,
>   Who wore dresses ever-new
> Have so lost the shape I wore
>   Even an old one will not do.
>
> And my hands as you can see
>   Are but bony wasted things,
> Hands that once would grasp the hand
>   Clasp the royal neck of kings... (28)

Cummine's interjections are relatively quiet, and towards the end the old woman has moments when she harrowingly realises the truth of her position:

> Floodtide!
>   And the ebb with hurrying fall;
> I have seen many, ebb and flow,
>   Ay, and now I know them all... (32)

In complete contrast to the old woman of Beare is Eve, in the poem of that name. Whereas the old woman yearns for youthful excitement, Eve is full of remorse for her mistake in Eden. The two poems present a dramatic contrast between the old woman's indomitable lust for life, and the original mother of men yelping about the consequences of her sin. Of the two, the old woman of Beare is by far the more admirable. Despite her consciousness of lost beauty and her sense of being ravaged by time, she is remarkable for a serene note of reconciliation in her thoughts, for her spirit of goodwill towards her many lovers, and for the sad last remnants of desire. Whereas, in the case of Eve, it is easy enough to see not only how she became the first unfortunate mother of humanity, but also how she must have been the world's first nagging wife:

> Dreadful was the choice I made,
>   I who was once a mighty queen;
> Dreadful, too, the price I paid
>   Woe, my hand is still unclean!
>
> I plucked the apple from the spray,
>   Because of greed I could not rule;
> Even until their final day
>   Women still will play the fool.
>
> Ice would not be anywhere,
>   Wild white winter would not be;
> There would be no hell, no fear
>   And no sorrow but for me. (38)

I have tried to give some idea of the variety and vitality of this poetry which O'Connor rescued and translated from distant centuries.

With the exception of four, all the poems in *The Little Monasteries* come from the period between the seventh and the twelfth centuries. O'Connor was that rare, happy combination – a brilliant creative writer and a scrupulous scholar. In *Kings, Lords, & Commons* and *The Little Monasteries*, O'Connor has given us a body of poems which brilliantly re-create personalities and situations of an ancient world and, more important still, help to order and illuminate the world in which we live.

Liam O'Flaherty: The Unchained Storm

It would be a mistake, I think, to lump Liam O'Flaherty with those other distinguished writers such as Frank O'Connor, Seán O'Faoláin, Mary Lavin and others, and say, with convenient finality, that O'Flaherty, like these, makes his own special contribution to the Irish short story tradition. He does, of course. And yet I must admit, at the outset, that it seems to me to be inaccurate to limit the scope and depth of O'Flaherty's art by pinning on him the label 'short story writer'. It seems more precise to me to say that he is a poet in prose, who chose the short story as a medium. It follows that while his stories may be considered purely as stories, it is also helpful to look on many of them as poems in prose, poems of a peculiarly explosive, energetic and echoing nature.

I choose the word 'energetic' deliberately. His stories are, for the most part, energetic responses to infinitely varied spectacles of energy. It is energy that obsesses him, that most draws his astonishing capacity for wonder and admiration into full play. There are times when O'Flaherty writes as though he were Adam opening his eyes on creation for the first time. Forms of boringness and dulling familiarity seem not to exist for him; when they do, he attacks them savagely. He seems attuned to the astounding energies of life itself; and this is why his prose frequently has the intensity and strong momentum of a poetry whose primary impulse is wonder, admiration and praise. It follows that what most repels O'Flaherty is death, all forms of death – inertia, boredom, emotional pettiness and fatigue. And it must be admitted that he is not at his best when dealing with what are for him forms of emotional death; some of his worst writing, 'The Wedding',[1] for example, shows him floundering, bewildered and jabbering, among various forms of human ugliness and distortion. In stories like 'The Wedding' O'Flaherty tries to compensate for a fatal uncertainty of perception with fake lyricism and strident melodrama. The reason is, I think, that there is singularly little energy in the story; and where there is no form of energy to wonder at, O'Flaherty's prose relies on a kind of blind, simplistic swiping that might be insulting if it weren't so ridiculous. Saddest of all, in such stories, O'Flaherty seems to have no critical awareness of his flaws. Indeed, it seems that for O'Flaherty, the critic has little or no existence. It is well to remember, though, that while this lack of critical awareness can lead to writing of not easily equalled atrocity, it is also connected with O'Flaherty's highest and most uninhibitedly ecstatic flights, the splendid ferocity of his lyricism. All in all, therefore, one is glad to accept him as he is.

Not many of O'Flaherty's stories are as bad as 'The Wedding'. For the most part, he writes with a vehemently sustained skill. Even when he is well below his best, he still writes grippingly. Because he writes out of excitement and wonder, he usually stirs excitement and wonder in his readers. It is precisely this capacity for primal excitement that helps us to understand the poetic qualities of O'Flaherty's prose.

In an issue of *The Irish Statesman*[2] there was a letter from Liam O'Flaherty, headed 'National Energy'. The letter was in reply to an essay entitled 'Leaders of Indian Nationalism' which had appeared in the issue of 4 October 1924. O'Flaherty was intensely moved by what he called the 'vitality and force and passion and stinging truth of that essay, the surging rhythm of the prose, the ferocity of expression'. The essay had been in praise of peace, of 'quiet culture'. To O'Flaherty, this didn't really matter, because 'in literature it is the method and the manner that counts, the manner of expressing the passion that is within the heart'.

There follows a passage in the letter which I would like to quote in full because it is an eloquent statement of O'Flaherty's great love and great theme – energy. It is equally eloquent about his loathing for fraud, corruption, usury and sluggishness. In fact, this passage may be used as a condensed statement of O'Flaherty's aesthetics.

> But the human race has not advanced from savagery to culture on the feeble crutches of philosophy. What epics have there been written about the disputations of scholars? Did Homer write of philosophy or of the hunting of wild boars and the savage wars waged around stone-walled cities? Did Shakespeare live in the days of twenty per cent. interest on oil stocks and the loathsome mouthings of Ramsay MacDonalds at Geneva about Leagues of Nations that are based on fraud, corruption, and the usury of slim-fingered, cultured bankers? Did he not live in the days when piratical adventurers carried the standards of Britain across the oceans and the continents? Did he not live in the days when his race was emerging, with bloodshot eyes, lean, hungry, virile, savage, from the savagery of feudalism into the struggle for Empire ?
>
> In Ireland, to my mind, we have reached that point in the progress of our race, the point which marked the appearance of Shakespeare in English literature. Let us not be ashamed that gunshots are heard in our streets. Let us rather be glad. For force is, after all, the opposite of sluggishness. It is an intensity of movement, of motion. And motion is the opposite of death.

O'Flaherty concludes his letter by contrasting Irish culture with Indian culture which he sees as 'a culture of sweet, beautiful words

and of slim fingers, slim, long, aristocratic fingers that are effete
and on their death-bed'. Irish culture, on the other hand, 'is the
wild tumult of the unchained storm, the tumult of the army on
the march, clashing its cymbals, rioting with excess of energy'. I
do not think that I would accept this as an accurate description of
Irish culture as a whole or even at that point in time. As a way of
appreciating O'Flaherty's own work, however, it seems to me to
be helpful. I would like, therefore, to consider some of the stories
under the following headings: Nature; Wild Creatures; Humans. In
many stories these themes fuse with each other. I shall try to do
justice to this fusion while pointing out the poetic qualities of the
writing.

More than any other natural image, the image of the sea pounds
and roars through O'Flaherty's work. 'In literature, it is the method
and the manner that counts'. O'Flaherty's 'manner' of presenting
the sea in a story like 'The Landing', for example, is both distinctive
and effective. He creates a cosmic drama around the efforts of
fishermen in a curragh to land safely during a storm, watched by
their relatives and friends on the shore. O'Flaherty convincingly
connects the tumult of the natural world with the confusion and
terror of minds forced to witness such a spectacle. As O'Flaherty
presents it, it is a massive, terrifying music filling sea, sky and every
witnessing mind. He deftly gives us the 'horrid distinctness' of
sounds becoming mental visions on the threshold of madness. The
effectiveness of this passage, as of so many other similar passages,
is that the storm is no mere hullaballoo of nature; it is inseparable
from a tortured human drama, a wild music of minds on the brink
of disintegration. Rhythm and images combine perfectly to dramatise
the sense of being simultaneously together and isolated. Prose is
heightened to the point of poetry:

> The crashing of the waves against the cliffs to the east was drowning
> the wind. The wind came steadily, like the rushing of a great cataract
> heard at a great distance, but the noises of the sea were continually
> changing, rising and falling, with the stupendous modulations of an
> orchestra played by giants. Each sound boomed or hissed or crashed
> with a horrid distinctness. It stood apart from the other sounds that
> followed and preceded it as menacing and overwhelming as the visions
> that crowd on a disordered mind, each standing apart from the others
> in crazy independence. (*SLO*, 35)

Of O'Flaherty's sea-stories, it is those in which the sea is inseparable from the drama, human and inhuman, that best succeed.
'The Rockfish' and 'The Oar' are good examples. Less successful are
the stories in which the sea is not convincingly evoked, or seems

incidental to the drama. In 'The Struggle',[3] for example, two drunken men have a fight in a boat; in the end they drown. The violence is strongly presented, but O'Flaherty fails to dramatise it convincingly; after the initial shock, the violence is tedious. The fact that it takes place in a boat on the sea makes little difference to the story which in the end strikes one as having a sordid and mechanical character. At such moments, one regrets the absence in O'Flaherty of an intellectual questioning of his own themes; instead of this questioning one gets the sense of a deadpan satisfaction with the fact that he is actally treating violence in a way that is complacent, unmoved. Stories like 'The Struggle' have the subtlety of a hammer-blow.

It is worth noting at this stage that the deadpan presentation of violence is often the mask for melodrama and sentimentality. Any critical appraisal of O'Flaherty's stories must acknowledge these faults before his merits can be properly appreciated. There are many examples in his stories of melodrama and sentimentality. Here, however, I am merely making the point that under the obsession with violence and bravado, in which self-congratulation masquerades as detachment, one can hear, if one listens carefully, the hearbeat of the softie, the romantic slob. This soft writing happens more when O'Flaherty is dealing with human beings than wild animals or birds. An excellent example of this is his treatment of mother-hood in 'The Outcast', which deals with the death of a girl and her child after an encounter with a brutal priest, and 'The Cow's Death', which tells how a cow leaps to her death into the sea when she sees the body of her calf on the rocks below. In 'The Outcast', almost nothing is credible. From the grotesquely exaggerated picture of the priest at the beginning to the girl's final leap into the lake (laughing 'madly, wildly, loudly' [*IP*, 94], mind you, as she does so) with the child in her arms, we are in a world of vivid incredibility. In 'The Cow's Death', however, which presents a situation that would appear to pose a far greater problem of stylistic treatment, O'Flaherty is infinitely more convincing. Although at the beginning of the story he hovers on the edge of sentimentality, his narrative proceeds at a swift, relentless pace, matching the cow's increasingly frantic, self-wounding, and finally self-destroying quest for her calf. A primal impulse is captured in a primal style. From a comparison of these two stories, it would seem that there are times when O'Flaherty's imagination is more at home among the beasts in their fertile and dangerous world than among humans in their world of confused and tangled emotions.

And yet, even poor stories like 'The Struggle' indicate one of O'Flaherty's major concerns – the struggle of men and women with the natural world of sea and land. When he avoids exaggeration and distortion, his treatment of this fundamental and eternal struggle can be intensely moving. 'Spring Sowing', which deals with the first day of the first spring sowing of a young peasant and his wife, must surely be one of O'Flaherty's finest creations. The young couple, still in the first joy of marriage, face their struggle with the land. As the story unfolds, so do the characters of the couple, and so do not only their lives on this particular spring day but also their lives in future years. In this struggle with the land, the young woman becomes afraid of the 'pitiless, cruel earth, the peasant's slave master, that would keep her chained to hard work and poverty all her life until she would sink again into its bosom. Her short-lived love was gone' (*SLO*, 4). But she also discovers 'a strange joy' which overpowers 'that other feeling of dread' (*SLO*, 5). The young man discovers that he is capable of struggling successfully with the earth. The final sentences of the story beautifully portray a picture of that struggle – its hardship, its rewards, its devouring endlessness:

> They stood for a few moments in silence, looking at the work they had done. All her dissatisfaction and weariness vanished from Mary's mind with the delicious feeling of comfort that overcame her at having done this work with her husband. They had done it together. They had planted seeds in the earth. The next day and the next and all their lives, when spring came they would have to bend their backs and do it until their hands and bones got twisted with rheumatism. But night would always bring sleep and forgetfulness. (*SLO*, 8)

My main effort in this essay is to try to define or describe what constitutes the poetry of O'Flaherty's prose. It is, as I have said, connected with his response to energy, and to a lesser extent with the workings of his imagination when it is freed from the need to disentangle the emotional complexities of people. That is why, I believe, his best stories are about wild creatures, and why the distinctive O'Flaherty poetry occurs most of all in those stories. This poetry has in it a genuine epic throb, an unpolluted primitive wonder, a strong purity of narrative line which, by reason of its very strength, is more like verse than prose. I am convinced in fact that 'Wild Stallions' falls naturally into verse. If we listen to its rhythms, the varying cool impassioned flow of its sympathies, its unfolding of anticipation, conflict and resolution, we find ourselves in the company not of a modern writer of short stories but of a bardic teller of tales, a narrator for whom the disclosure of marvels is as natural and inevitable as the ear for the rhythms of city-talk is natural to James Joyce. Here is the opening of 'Wild Stallions':

> As he stood over his grazing herd,
> on a hillock near the northern wall
> of his lofty mountain glen,
> the golden stallion's mane and tail
> looked almost white in the radiant light of dawn.
> At the centre of his forehead,
> a small star shone like a jewel.[4]

This beautiful rhythm is maintained right through the story which has a fierce sexual pulse. The final clash of the two wild stallions, which will decide the sexual supremacy for which they struggle to the death, shows O'Flaherty's poetry in full epic flight:

> Neighing hoarsely in his throat,
> the invader cantered forward slowly
> with his head bowed. The golden stallion
> stood his ground on widespread legs,
> mustering the last remnants of his strength,
> until the enemy swerved at close quarters
> to deliver a broadside.
> Then he rose and brought his forelegs down
> with great force.
> Struck above the kidneys,
> the grey uttered a shrill cry and fell.
> While rolling away, a second blow on the spine
> made him groan and shudder from head to tail.
> With his glazed eyes wide open,
> he turned over on his back,
> swung his neck from side to side
> and snapped his jaws without known purpose
> in the urgent agony of death. (PR, 87)

It is worth noting here that 'Wild Stallions' is an excellent example of the crisp, definite way in which O'Flaherty often manages to finish his stories. He rarely lingers indulgently in the drama he has created, or dallies complacently in lyrical climax. The ending of 'Wild Stallions' is as clean as the cut of the sharpest axe. The golden stallion, a maimed victor pursued by wild predators, is briefly defended by his mares but

> Then two of the mountain lions
> broke through the circle
> and brought him down. (PR, 88)

In 'Wild Stallions' both stallions die. The wild swan, in the story of that name, loses his mate and, after a struggle, finds a new one, and brings her back to his nest. This particular ending pulses with the promise of new life, but two sentences are enough to express the full glory of that promise:

> The two great white birds walked round the nest, flapping their wings and uttering harsh cries of joy. Then they began to prepare the place for their brood. (*SLO*, 415)

Contemplating his wild creatures, O'Flaherty's language is precise, confident, unstrained. These stories are visions of energies at work. Human eyes, conditioned by the civilized strictures of necessary moralities, may see such energies as cruel or barbaric. To O'Flaherty, however, these energies are the truest and deepest manifestations of reality. Of the hawk, in the story of that name, and of the wild swan, he uses the phrase 'brute soul' (*SLO*, 349), to express his concept of that energy. This belief in a kind of brute spirituality or spiritual brutishness is a primary reason why these stories are immediately and permanently compelling. If it is possible to speak of a soul in action (and I believe it is), then O'Flaherty must be commended for his vision of the 'brute soul' of the hawk in action as natural as it is superb:

> The hawk waited until the songbird had almost reached the limit of his climb. Then he took aim and stooped. With his wings half-closed, he raked like a meteor from the clouds. The lark's warbling changed to a shriek of terror as he heard the fierce rush of the charging hawk. Then he swerved aside, just in time to avoid the full force of the blow. Half-stunned, he folded his wings and plunged headlong towards the earth, leaving behind a flutter of feathers that had been torn from his tail by the claws of his enemy.
>
> When he missed his mark, the hawk at once opened wide his wings and canted them to stay his rush. He circled once more above his falling prey, took aim, and stooped again. This time the lark did nothing to avoid the kill. He died the instant he was struck; his inert wings unfolded. With his head dangling from his limp throat, through which his lovely song had just been pouring, he came tumbling down, convoyed by the closely circling hawk. He struck earth on a patch of soft brown sand, beside a shining stream.
>
> The hawk stood for a few moments over his kill, with his lewd purple tongue lolling from his open beak and his blackbarred breast heaving from the effort of pursuit. Then he secured the carcase in his claws, took wing, and flew off to the cliff where his mate was hatching on a broad ledge, beneath a massive tawny-gold rock that rose, over-arching, to the summit. (*SLO*, 348)

It is very important to remember that O'Flaherty sees himself as presenting the workings of a 'brute soul'. This is one reason why these stories are totally devoid of sentimentality. They are packed with the pressure of the author's love and admiration for his creatures or, as I prefer to call them, his visions of living energy. Not all these visions concern struggle and conflict, maiming and killing. One of the purest moments of tenderness I know occurs in 'The Wild Goat's Kid' in which a wild goat encourages her new-born kid to stand, to face the world, to live:

> How she manoeuvred to make him stand ! She breathed on him to warm him. She raised him gently with her forehead, uttering strange, soft sounds to encourage him. Then he stood up, trembling, staggering, swaying on his curiously long legs. She became very excited, rushing around him, bleating nervously, afraid that he should fall again. He fell. She was in agony. Bitter wails came from her distended jaws and she crunched her teeth. But she renewed her efforts, urging the kid to rise, to rise and live...to live, live, live. (*SLO*, 100)

I believe that this impulse 'to live, live, live' is what O'Flaherty most admires in his wild creatures and what he would most like human beings to do. It is his deepest passion. As such, it helps to explain the intensely simplistic quality of most of his stories dealing with people and their relationships with each other. It is not enough to say that O'Flaherty deals mainly with peasants and peasants are rather simple-minded and simple-hearted folk. Nor is it enough to say that O'Flaherty is a sort of emotional fundamentalist, one who is, quite simply, not interested in the more elusive shades of emotional subtlety but is content to prowl among the apparently sharply-defined blacks and whites of the heart. No, I think it is fair to say that the main fault of most of his stories about human relationships – their simplistic intensities, their hammering unawareness of the heart's subtler uncertainties – is due, paradoxically, to what is most admirable in this writer, his almost messianic wish that his human characters embody and manifest the magnificent energy of his wild creatures. Therefore, when he describes a beautiful woman, he sees her in terms of a snake and a young tree. Red Barbara, in the story of that name, is splendid but she is more of a wild, idealised creation than a credible human being:

> She had a small head, like a snake, but with no malice or subtlety in her large, sleepy, blue eyes. She had long, golden eyelashes and pretty little teeth like a young girl. Her hair was red-gold. Her limbs were long and supple. She walked with a long raking stride, almost sideways, for her slim body swayed voluptuously, like a young tree swaying in the wind. And when she rested she appeared half asleep, without thought; as if she knew she was only made for love and must always wait for and suffer admiration or caresses. Her lips were always half open, her lashes drooped and her little ears, peeping from beneath her red-gold hair, seemed to be perpetually listening for words of admiration. (*SLO*, 190-91)

The problem is this. O'Flaherty loves the free, the flawless, the ecstatically abandoned, the amoral exultant spirit, but, confronted with human beings in all their weaknesses and failings, he drives himself into a necessarily simplistic position by his compulsion, understandable as a result of his love for perfect embodiments of energy, to create characters who tend to be either too flawless or too flawed. Either way, a certain distortion takes place. In spite of this, I would like to say that O'Flaherty's heart, if not his head, is nearly always in the right place. After all, he does love freedom, and he would like his people to be free. In his ironic, and often bitterly comic *A Tourist's Guide To Ireland*, he attacks many of the enemies of Irish freedom, which, in his eyes, is freedom from 'priests, politicians, ignorance and various other diseases'. In the following passage, he paints for the tourist a picture of pious scavengers:

> He'll see other orders of religious clergy who make it their business to go around the country on missions terrorising the unfortunate lower classes with threats of fire and brimstone in the hereafter, while in their train march countless vendors of statues, medals, scapulars and *agnus deis*, which are used by the ignorant in the place of medicine. He'll find other orders that live simply by begging. And on every side, among all orders, he'll find a rapid accumulation of property, which threatens to turn the whole country into a clerical kingdom. He'll meet nuns, also accumulating property. He'll meet Christian Brothers, who are in the teaching business, midway between the secular clergy and the religious orders. And he'll finish up, if he is any way sensitive, by getting an impression of Ireland, as a beautiful sad-faced country that is being rapidly covered by a black rash.[5]

The same clergy are portrayed as the enemies of freedom in several O'Flaherty stories. In 'The Child of God', a priest banishes the young artist, Peter, from the community. In 'The Fairy Goose', the priest is a black harbinger of fear. In 'The Outcast', the priest is largely responsible for the deaths of the girl and her child. In all three cases, O'Flaherty is making a strong, humane point; but it must be admitted that in no case is he fully successful in creating a totally credible priest figure.

O'Flaherty's love of freedom finds its most convincing artistic expression in those stories dealing with tramps and tinkers. 'The Tramp', for example, works as a story because the central figure's love of freedom gives him a Synge-like volubility in his talk, makes him a patient, discriminating listener, and above all, perhaps, endows him with a capacity for swift, decisive action which is firmly and acceptably contrasted with the slavish indecisiveness of Deignan to whom the tramp has been kind and generous and whom he has tried to persuade to set out on the exciting road to freedom. At the end, the tramp moves forward into freedom but Deignan remains behind, petrified by indecision.

Among the other enemies of freedom whom O'Flaherty loathes are the single-minded money-makers, the usurers, the gombeen men, the unscrupulous dealers, the mercenary opportunists, callous and tireless. In *A Tourist's Guide To Ireland*, he savages the greedy publican and his mean, sordid house:

> Here one must eat like a hermit in the desert, in order that the parish priest may have abundance for his table. Here one must drink, standing up like a cab-horse at a drinking trough, black beverages that remind us of the death that is the common destiny of us all. And one must drink quickly, on an empty stomach, drink after drink, diluted and weakened, so that the publican may rake in quickly, with little labour, enough money to make his sons priests, doctors, lawyers and politicians, and then to build a new church or repair an old one, as a duty to God and to save his immortal soul in payment for all the robbery he has committed.[6]

Throughout the stories, O'Flaherty is bitterly critical of the effects of greed and ruthless ambition on people. What he deplores most of all are the dehumanizing effects on people of the slavish dedication to the making of money. One of the most powerful examples of this is 'Two Lovely Beasts' in which Colm Derrane determines to rise in the world by purchasing two promising calves. Very soon, he becomes 'as ruthless towards his family as he was tender towards the calves' (*SLO*, 212). At the end of the story, he is 'cold and resolute and ruthless' (*SLO*, 227). The pursuit of money has robbed him of his warm humanity. A new, implacable ugliness has taken hold of him.

Conversely, the man who lives free from the tyrannies of money-making is for O'Flaherty a natural aristocrat, a sort of male version of Red Barbara. The tinker in 'The Tent' is a good example. He is a 'slim, tall, graceful man, with a beautiful head poised gracefully on a brown neck, and great black lashes falling down over his half-closed eyes, just like a woman'. He is one of those who are 'cut off from the mass of society yet living at their expense' (*SLO*, 81). Clearly, he has O'Flaherty's unqualified admiration and approval. The tinker is as near as one gets to a human version of one of O'Flaherty's wild creatures.

This is at once his appeal and his limitation. Once we accept the limitation, the appeal becomes more convincing. This remark, in fact, applies to most of O'Flaherty's stories about people.

One final point. It seems to me a pity that O'Flaherty did not attempt more stories in the comic vein of 'The Post Office' (*SLO*).

It is funny because it is, for the most part, understated. The creation of comedy shows O'Flaherty capable of an effective reticence in his writing.

O'Flaherty probably has more faults than any of the other outstanding Irish writers of short stories. But, with the exception of Joyce, he also rises to greater heights. His failures as a writer are directly connected with his ecstatic successes. He is a poet who has chosen to tell stories. He is capable of the most sustained imaginative intensity; and he can sink into the most deplorable depths of melodrama. At times, his writing seems to have the pure energy of a natural force. 'Ours', he claimed in that letter to *The Irish States man* in 1924, 'Ours is the wild tumult of the unchained storm'. O'Flaherty's imaginative energy reminds one at times of 'the unchained storm'. It can be rough and wild and whirling but it can also be profoundly exhilarating.

Seán O'Casey's Journey into Joy

There is an intriguing tendency common to some of the most interesting Irish writers. Looking at the artistic careers of these writers, we might describe this tendency as a journey into joy. Naturally, the different writers offer different manifestations of this tendency. What I have in mind is the transfiguration of experience, through language, into works of art, which, because their livingness derives from their attempt to understand and express the nature of suffering, become, in themselves, images of joy. One can, of course, use different words or terms to describe this transfiguration. Yeats called it 'tragic joy'.[1] He also called it 'gaiety':

> Gaiety transfiguring all that dread,
> All men have aimed at, found and lost;
> Black-out: Heaven blazing into the head...
> ('Lapis Lazuli')[2]

Joyce's greatest work, *Ulysses*, ends with the most affirmative word in the English language. Yes. Yes to life. Yes, particularly, when so many have said no. And Patrick Kavanagh says that the true mark of a poet is his gaiety. So

> ...all true poems laugh inwardly
> Out of grief-born intensity...
> ...suffering soars in summer air –
> The millstone has become a star...
> ('Prelude')[3]

That, I believe is what genuine art is all about. Millstones becoming stars. In Seán O'Casey's own words – 'Life cannot believe in death... though the purple of joy at times changes to a black hue of sorrow, there remain the crimson and gold bordering every horizon'.[4] O'Casey loved colour with all his heart; and his heart was the colour of hope. To him, the drama is a song of life, a song he never tired of singing. Let us look now at some of his encounters at different stages of his journey into joy.

Seán O'Casey was a proud man – fiercely, at times bitterly so. He was proud of his work, of his thought, of his politics, of his opinions. Most importantly, he was proud of the *humanity* of people. 'Man,' says O'Casey, 'is, at least, as kind, kindlier in fact, than God is preached to be, for man isn't responsible for most of the major disasters periodically afflicting the comfort and security of his own kind. Famine comes from Him...His hand shakes a city or a town,

and an earthquake levels the town or the city into a huge, tumbled-
down funeral pile...a bursting-out volcano buries a village...Pest-
ilence, too, like the swift epidemic of 1919 that laid low in less than
a year double the number of lives that were lost within four years
of a bitter and bloody world-wide war...We have no reason whatever to be ashamed of our humanity; we have many good reasons
to be proud of it'.[5]

Whatever one thinks of that passage, there is no doubting the
emotional honesty of the man who wrote it. I wish to link the final
joy of O'Casey's art with this belief in the value of people. I do
not think that O'Casey is a very deep or a very subtle thinker. He
is not an intellectual; he is a celebrant. The deepest impulse of
the celebrant is to praise. Most of all, O'Casey celebrates people.
Because his celebration is sincere, his criticism is often bitter. When
he attacks modern writers such as Kafka, Eliot, Orwell, Huxley,
Genet and Camus, it is because they are 'clogged with a sense of
sin, and frown upon any inclination of the heart to sing'.[6] How
deeply or how superficially O'Casey understood these writers is
hardly for me to say. I simply do not know. But I do know that he
deplored what he called the 'despairs of the American beats and the
European wailers'[7] and that this intense deploring of wailing despair
is also a measure of his capacity for celebrating what he calls 'the
greatness of life; its stresses and its joys'.[8] I offer the following
passage as an example of the impassioned meditation of a celebrant,
that is, a man whose faith compels him to sing a song of praise:

> Man is the only life on earth that can see its form and love its grandeur;
> he has enriched the world, for without him it would have no meaning
> and look dead; it would be dead. He has ennobled the star we stand
> on; exceptional souls give things exceptional beauty. When Christ saw
> the lilies of the field, he said to those around him, 'I say unto you that
> even Solomon in all his glory was not arrayed like one of these'; he
> gave the blossoms an eternal beauty; and when Shakespeare looking at
> another flower in an English field, said, 'Daffodils that come before
> the swallow dares, and take the winds of March with beauty', he gave
> these flowers a loveliness and a courage unrecognised before.[9]

It is the logic of O'Casey's celebration that, to him, the people
are the theatre. One of his most fiery essays begins with that sentence.
'The people are the theatre'. And he continues:

> Nature sets the scene, and the man plays his part through the changing
> scenes of seed-time and harvest, in the cold days when the frost comes
> and the keen winds blow. It is from the things manifested in the people's
> life – their love, joy, hatred, malice, envy, generosity, passion, courage,
> and fear – that the truest playwrights weave their sombre and gay patterns

of action and dialogue. Every art is rooted in the life of the people – what they see, do, how they hear, all they touch and taste; how they live, love, and go to the grave. The question for all artists is this: Is the colour and form of what has been taken from their life done well or done badly? [10]

Before we accuse him of what O'Casey himself calls 'Bolshevist blathering', let us see if this is true of O'Casey's work. To read through his plays – or better still to see them – is to become increasingly aware of O'Casey's reverence for life, his respect and affection for those who add to it, usually by their gaiety, and his savage scorn for those who diminish it, usually by their callous application of the heartless standards of mechanical moralities. There can be no doubt that when O'Casey says 'The people are the theatre', he means precisely that.

Because of his faith in people, O'Casey was intensely critical of plays and poems which seemed to him to speak despairingly of humanity. He hit out angrily at what he considered was modern poetry's obsession with futility and despair. With a sort of baffled anger, O'Casey puts a question to modern poets:

> Where is the energy and the humanity in the poetry of our major poets today? Life with them seems to be either rushing to destruction like the Gadarene swine, or running headlong down a hill. 'The dream', as Auden says, 'always leads to the nightmare garden'; or as dull as Mrs Dale's Diary'. As for being 'humane', or even human, full of 'ordinary human feelings', there is not a touch of them in any poem, because they don't seem to know what ordinary human feelings are, or what they are like.[11]

Then, with a quite irrepressible delight, O'Casey proceeds to give a poem of his own, called 'It's No Go', in which he uses the rhythms of Louis MacNeice's 'Bagpipe Music' to express his dislike of art that cannot rise above despair.

> It's no go the gloom or the pessimistic bawl,
> It's no go the death-cry, it's no go at all;
> Life saunters jauntily, life always has her say,
> Plays her games, has a dance, and wears her ribbons gay.

> It's no go the poet's round of ever-present doom,
> For her laughter's heard in London streets and in the Devon coombe.
> It's no go the lesson teaching ev'ry step's a fall,
> For life gets quick up on her feet, so it's no go at all!

> It's no go the chanting of the poet's Doomsday Song,
> That everything that's right becomes just everything that's wrong;
> For life can even sing of life twixt St Peter and St Paul;
> So it's no go thinking differ, it's no go at all(!).[12]

O'Casey declares war on every resolutely pessimistic view of man. The play which best dramatises this war on despair is *Within The Gates*. In this play, O'Casey is campaigning for hope, battling away on behalf of youth and energy and colourful pleasure. He fights against the hopelessness of our age, the grey vague figures who go past in a slow, shuffling march, chanting their miserere. Here is the voice of modern despair:

> We challenge life no more, no more, with our dead faith, and our dead hope;
> We carry furl'd the fainting flag of a dead hope and a dead faith.
> Day sings no song, neither is there room for rest beside night in her sleeping;
> We've but a sigh for a song, and a deep sigh for a drum-beat!
> Oh where shall we go when the day calls?
> Oh where shall we sleep when the night falls?
> We've but a sigh for a song, and deep sigh for a drum-beat! [13]

Against the despairing multitudes, those who 'challenge life no more', O'Casey puts the gaiety of the singer and the dancer. War is one of O'Casey's great themes; the deepest war is the war between life and death, between hope and despair. There is no doubt as to which side O'Casey belongs:

> Sing and dance, dance and sing,
> Brief life should be a joyous thing;
> Theminds that are to troubles wed
> Are fit to host but with the dead!...
> Sling out woe, hug joy instead...[14]

I believe Seán O'Casey thought a great deal about happiness because he had seen so much misery. There is nothing facile or shallow or gaudily optimistic about his conviction that people have the right to be happy. He was not a man to ignore suffering and wretchedness, in whatever form they might appear. It is precisely because he had witnessed despair that his celebration of joy is convincing. Even as he watched his own son die, he praised the life of which that son was once a handsome and vital part. O'Casey never deliberately represses or distorts any feeling; he tends to give all his emotions the fullest expression possible, though he does so, on the whole, without indulgence. One reason why I think his plays will last is because they are, for the most part, emotionally real, emotionally credible. O'Casey himself is always emotionally honest as a writer, even when he is unjust or cock-eyed. He obviously thought a great deal about feeling and was convinced of its primacy and importance in human life. He says:

Feeling, rather than thought or detachment, seems to dominate the world of life. It was not thought but feeling that led the way to human development, for the meaning of the word is based on the word 'to grope', and life, in its first stage of withdrawal from the world's waters, must have felt, groped, its way in to the land. When hands grew handier, we groped our way forward more accurately, and, even today, with all our knowledge and our dependence on mind, the fingers retain an amazingly delicate sense of touch. We usually trust our feelings. How does one feel towards this or that? How often the question is asked! 'I felt sympathy towards him or her; I felt obliged to do that or this; I felt it was time to go; I feel something is bound to happen'; the examples of the use of feeling are a multititude, and there is no escape from them, even in a snarl of a poem or snarl of a play, for cynicism itself is prompted by the feeling that there is little or no hope in humanity.[15]

The more a writer acknowledges the importance of feeling, the more musical his writing will tend to be. The musical potential of language is linked with the heart's capacity to admit emotion. There is a unique music in O'Casey – a music deriving from his determination to think as deeply and fairly as he could, of all those feelings, latent or vividly living within us, sometimes in a bewildering riot of contradiction, and of which we are all victims. The artist is an articulate victim. O'Casey always tried to impart this music of emotional complexity. He didn't always succeed; but he knew what he wanted to do. When he read Shakespeare, he saw it powerfully done. He said:

Bitter, even savage as Shakespeare so often was, he never lost the lovely power of emotional compassion; nor indeed, did the other Elizabethans, though they could be as realistic, as fierce, as dire...as any bitter and cynical writer of today; whose savagery, bitterness and cynicism is always sly, mean and commonplace; with the exception of Beckett who, alongside the greater Elizabethans, never loses the emotion of a great compassion. Ready for tears, as ready for laughter, how bitter Shakespeare can be when he is in the mood!...And Shakespeare looked, saw life, and pronounced it good and lovely...Shakespeare does not stay very long with his sorrows; he sings and dances even in the midst of them.[16]

These are O'Casey's words about Shakespeare; they could be applied, quite as fitly, to O'Casey's own work. How bitter he can be at times! How steeped in sorrows! But he sings and dances even in the midst of them.

A belief in people; a love and understanding of the dramatic portrayal of emotional complexity; a trust in the curative, even redemptive musicality of language; an awareness that even in moments of the most savage cynicism, compassion should be allowed its life; an adamant, agile refusal to dwell too long in sorrow – all these surely point to what is most vital in O'Casey. I mean his comic

genius. Many attempts have been made to define comedy. If we
are to appreciate O'Casey's journey into joy, we must try to define,
or at least describe, what comedy is to this great-hearted artist.
What are the sources of the seemingly inexhaustible energy of
O'Casey's comedy?

It is O'Casey's belief that 'Man's real fight has always been
against sorrow of every kind, a fight to banish it out of sight, out
of feeling, out of the earth altogether; to abolish the weariness of
hard work, the sorrows of insufficient food, the misery of cold
clothing, of misery-making homes, of the pains of illnesses, and,
when possible, the unhappiness of death to life before life is ripe
enough to discard the care of going'.[17] This was O'Casey's wish for
humanity; it is the wish of an idealist; it is impossible. At any rate,
it is impossible in life. Is it impossible in art, in drama? No. In
drama, this ideal is made possible by the recognition and presentation
of men's selfishness, the one emotional commodity of which men
have an inexhaustible supply, and by turning that selfishness into
comedy. We can tolerate, even admire in art, persons, ideas, situations,
feelings and attitudes that, in real life, would infuriate us, or even
drive us mad. O'Casey himself was quick to recognise this. Speaking
of his comic characters, such as Captain Boyle, in *Juno and the
Paycock*, O'Casey says that he loves them, 'so long as I am independent of them, and amn't forced to live with them'. Objectively
for O'Casey, these characters 'are always a nuisance to those who
live with them, at times a menace, despoiling and ruining the lives
of others (as per Captain Boyle), hindering and thwarting sense
and sensibility'.[18]

Now, I think the question we have got to ask is this: why do we,
the audience, get such a laughing, animating kick out of people
who, in O'Casey's own words, are 'a menace, despoiling and ruining
the lives of others'? Further, and this is an even more intriguing
question, why does O'Casey, whose idealistic wish for humanity
smacks of a truly naïve goodness, present with such gusto and
affection those characters who are committed to the destruction of
O'Casey's ideal? If I begin to understand it, I think the answer
lies in the amoral absolution of comedy.

To repeat and amplify the question: why do we *like* men such
as Joxer and the Captain who are so useless, mean, treacherous and
irresponsible? The wages of sin, we are told, are death. I suggest
that the wages of laughter are pardon. Those who are part of the
comic O'Casey scene are not condemned for their vices; they are
appreciated because of them. O'Casey's comedy recognises that

'virtuous' people can be very boring, and that 'wicked' people can
be very entertaining. The comic character, enjoying the insights of
an amoral code of behaviour, knows that the only way to cope with
the problem of hard work is to stop doing it; the best way to banish
the 'sorrows of insufficient food' is to guarantee a plentiful supply
of drink; and the most effective way to avoid the 'unhappiness of
death to life before life is ripe enough to discard the care of going' is
to live as if there were *no* death, by ensuring the endless gratification
of all the senses, by an unfaltering devotion to the gods of comfort,
and by the adamant assertion of the comic ideal itself – personal
survival as a result of total emotional indifference to the sorrows
and troubles of others. What I am describing now is an irresponsible
monster – that monster which comedy drags out into the laughing
light of day. And yet that monster is human; and he has the ability
to spark a strange, sympathetic humanity in us. We are brought
face to face with our own buried capacity for monstrous behaviour,
and in one mesmeric side-splitting moment, we fall in love with
our capacity for sin. The possibility exists that, in one more moment,
we might begin to regret all the sins we have carefully failed to
commit because we were too busy being 'good'. Under O'Casey's
comic spell, we witness our own abhorrent selves in uninhibited
action, and we rejoice in the momentary freedom of those irrespon-
sibles whom we normally keep caged in our hearts, manacled in
cells of respectability, as we work, pay income tax, dutifully remember
to wash our teeth remembering the curious effect of bad breath on
our colleagues, rear the children, and try to get on with or without
the husband or wife.

That is a brief picture of the drab decencies on which comedy
declares hilarious war. Comedy brings us in contact with the frightening possibilities of amoral freedom. Comedy *is* freedom – the
freedom to be selfish and predatory. This contact which we permit
ourselves to establish with the free, amoral, articulate images of
our buried irresponsibility, even criminality, creates laughter of a
very special kind and with a special energy. It is the laughter of
one who has paid his money to be a spectator and then discovers
that he is an accomplice. Tried, and found guilty, he is sentenced
to laugh away his guilt in a place suddenly devoid of gloom, and
electric with gaiety. We are now in the real presence of the comic
figure, the full irresponsibility of whose anarchic being is an insult
to the concept of duty, the idea of work, the notion of altruism,
the chastening, changing power of suffering, the commitment to
familial and social responsibility. The comic figure could not care

less about anything, except his own sensual survival. And he survives because he is a predator. He lives because he feeds and drinks off others. His emotional immunity can be measured in terms of the suffering he causes to others. He endures because his are the resources of irresponsibility – lying, duplicity, cunning, idleness, deception, hypocrisy, treachery and, above all, the strength of selfishness. And yet we find a place for him in our hearts. O'Casey's comedy moves us to laughter and forgiveness. We forgive others. We forgive ourselves. But when we leave the theatre, we return to 'civilised living', and to duty, work, decency and, most likely, to those private, steely attitudes of rational, responsible unforgiveness. In short, we are 'moral' again.

I think it is a real sign of O'Casey's greatness as an artist that his foraging imagination could sympathise with what his humane vision abhorred. What makes his plays of lasting interest to me is this clear-eyed triumph of instinctive creative sympathy over impassioned political conviction. In his weaker plays, this process is reversed.

As a writer, O'Casey has many weaknesses. The worst of these is a kind of intellectual rant, a sort of isolated raving, most obvious in his *Autobiographies* where he is sometimes unjust to others and boring about himself. He is capable of tedium on an epic scale, writing at times like James Joyce parodying James Joyce parodying everybody else. But my overall impression of O'Casey is of a man, an artist who, in his proper medium, the drama, could present a varied, conflicting, credible picture of humanity at once trapped and exultant in a world of suffering, deprivation, sickness, violence and momentarily absolving and salving laughter. It is this great-hearted laughter of the instinctive lover and celebrant of humanity that endures. Near the end of his life, the end of his journey into joy, he was writing as he had always written at his best, writing as a man of hope in a world of sad unbelief. To the end, O'Casey cherished his hope and kept his faith. What more dare we ask of anyone?

> Even here, even now, when the sun had set and the evening star was chastely touching the bosom of the night, there were things to say, things to do. A drink first! What would he drink to – the past, the present, the future? To all of them! He would drink to the life that embraced the three of them! Here, with whitened hair, desires failing, strength ebbing out of him, with the sun gone down, and with only the serenity and the calm warning of the evening star left to him, he drank to Life, to all it had been, to what it was, to what it would be. Hurrah! [19]

James Joyce's Humanism

The kind of humanism I discern in Joyce is possible only to a psyche that is largely unsupported, vigilant in its scrutiny of self-development, consciously experimental. No matter how 'normal' or 'abnormal' a writer's life may seem, all his days are essentially 'an experiment in living'.[1] In the case of Joyce, this experiment was conducted in such a way that his art became his life: he ruthlessly used his life as fodder for his imagination. The choice stated in Yeats' lines –

> The intellect of man is forced to choose
> Perfection of the life, or of the work...
>
> ('The Choice')[2]

– would not have presented a difficulty for Joyce. His despairs, his degradations, most of them conscious, his extraordinary bravery, his unconcealed selfishness, his vicious wilfulness, his blithe exploitation of his brother, his manic toying with language, the bravado of his distortions, the sense that his work is the product of a cosmic solitude, the happy arrogance implied in his natural anarchy, his attitude to drink – all these run with a natural pride in the human river that *is* Joyce. Alessandro Francini Bruni puts the case well about the particular matter of Joyce's drinking:

> One day when he was drunker than usual, I said to him sharply, 'My old Bacchus, have you gone mad?' He answered meekly as an unweened calf, 'No, I am developing myself.'[3]

Allowing always for the possibility of that mockery, both of himself and of others, Joyce's words are 'I am *developing* myself'. He does *not* say:

> 'I am exhausting myself, I am sickening myself, I am creating poison, assailing my body and mind and senses, I am deliberately immersing myself in the most fabulous form of futility that I know'– but – 'I am *developing* myself.'

What frightened others was a source of education for Joyce. He *was* developing himself, as he never ceased to do.

I want to suggest that Joyce did indeed develop himself to the point where he had the detachment of eternity in time – or as close to that detachment as it is possible to get. His experiment in humanness makes one more human to contemplate.

We all know the famous cloud-image of detachment, of indifference, in Joyce. It may seem odd to say that the object of this conscious experiment in self-development is a form of indifference, but how can the ice know it is water until it lets the sun caress it to the point of melting?

What *is* indifference? What does it make possible? Joycean indifference is the opposite of what we may call the popular notion
or idea of indifference, which is simply a couldn't-care-less attitude.
Joycean indifference is different, not only from that sort of indifference, but from its opposite – urgent commitment. Joyce's indifference has to do with his own sense of the complexity of his life,
and therefore of his art. It has to do with what Joyce recognised as
necessity and with how he grappled in art with what he envisioned,
either by choice or compulsion, in life. Simone Weil, a philosopher
whose writings always remind me of Joyce though she writes as a
believer, while Joyce believed in nothing, not even, as has been
said, in the bread he was eating – Simone Weil, out of her *believing* heart, so close in many ways to Joyce's *un*believing heart, has
this to say about necessity (emphasis is mine):

> *Necessity* is an enemy for man as long as he thinks in the first person.
> To tell the truth, he has *with necessity the three sorts of relationship* which
> he has with men. In fantasy, or by the exercise of social power, it seems
> to be his slave. In adversities, privations, grief, sufferings, but above
> all in affliction, it seems an absolute and brutal master. In methodical
> action there is a point of equilibrium where *necessity*, by its conditional
> character, presents man at once with obstacles and with means in relation
> to the partial ends which he pursues and wherein there *is a sort of equality
> between a man's will and universal necessity*...one must try to achieve
> this point of equilibrium as often as possible.
>
> ...The bitterest reproach that men make of this *necessity* is its absolute
> *indifference* to moral values. Righteous men and criminals receive an
> equal share of the benefits of the sun and of the rain; the righteous and
> the criminals equally suffer sunstroke, and drowning in floods. It is
> precisely this *indifference* which the Christ invites us to look upon and
> to imitate as the very expression of the perfection of our heavenly Father.
> To imitate this *indifference* is simply to consent to it, that is, to accept
> the existence of all that exists, including the evil, excepting only that
> portion of evil which we have the possibility, and the obligation, of
> preventing. By this simple work the Christ annexed all Stoic thought,
> and by the same token all of Heraclitus and Plato.
>
> No one could ever prove that such an absurdity as consent to necessity
> could be possible. We can only recognise it. There are in fact souls
> which consent to it.[4]

Necessity is an enemy for man as long as he thinks in the first
person... There is a sort of *equality* between a man's *will* and universal necessity...One must try to achieve this point of equilibrium
as often as possible...The bitterest reproach that men make of this
necessity is its absolute *indifference* to moral values...It is precisely
this *indifference* which the Christ invites us to look upon and to

imitate...To *imitate this indifference* is simply to consent to it, that is, to accept the existence of all that exists, including the evil...

I always find it difficult, even though I recognise it is necessary, as I read Joyce's work, to bear in mind the *quality* of his indifference, and the *quality* of the imaginative *equilibrium* he achieved between necessity and indifference. For, when I do bear this in mind, I seem to understand the *distance* he achieves from human feeling, the high, icy clarity of his perspective on feeling, the better to re-create it in words. Because of this achieved equilibrium between necessity and indifference, he writes like a man who is both a million miles away from the object of his scrutiny and also so close to it that he appears to have a Keatsian capacity for flowing into it, and through it, and out of it again. He presents, therefore, from that cosmic distance and with that felt immediacy, the *reality* of human emotions, that is, not only what people feel, but what they *feel* they feel. The presentation, in 'A Painful Case', of what Mr Duffy *feels* he feels, and therefore feels (for a while) is a case in point. This feeling *of* the feeling of loneliness is the creation of that special indifference:

> She *seemed* to be near him in the darkness. At moments he *seemed* to feel her voice touch his ear, her hand touch his. He stood still to listen. Why had he withheld life from her? Why had he sentenced her to death? He *felt* his moral nature falling to pieces.
>
> When he gained the crest of the Magazine Hill he halted and looked along the river towards Dublin, the lights of which burned redly and hospitably in the cold night. He looked down the slope and, at the base, in the shadow of the wall of the Park, he saw some human figures lying. Those venal and furtive loves filled him with despair. He gnawed the rectitude of his life; he *felt* that he had been outcast from life's feast. One human being had *seemed* to love him and he had denied her life and happiness: he had sentenced her to ignominy, a death of shame. He knew that the prostrate creatures down by the wall were watching him and wished him gone. No one wanted him; he was outcast from life's feast. He turned his eyes to the grey gleaming river, winding along towards Dublin. Beyond the river he saw a goods train winding out of Kingsbridge Station, like a worm with a fiery head winding through the darkness, obstinately and laboriously. It passed slowly out of sight; but still he heard in his ears the laborious drone of the engine reiterating the syllables of her name.
>
> He turned back the way he had come, the rhythm of the engine pounding in his ears. He began to *doubt the reality of what memory told him*. He halted under a tree and allowed the rhythm to die away. He could *not feel* her near him in the darkness nor her voice touch his ear. He waited for some minutes listening. He could hear nothing: the night was *perfectly silent*. He listened again: *perfectly silent. He* felt *that he was alone*.[5] (Emphasis is mine)

Joyce, the narrator, does *not* say, 'his moral nature was falling to pieces' or 'he was outcast from life's feast' or 'he was alone' but 'he felt' these states.

The hallmark of *Dubliners* is the cruel precision with which is revealed the failure of many of the characters to know what they are *not* feeling. In 'A Painful Case', it's as if the narrator were God looking down on this severed monster of a man, a dull compendium of interesting quotations, terrified of connection with a woman, terrified of living, who, because of the way he has diligently *not* lived, the committed rituals of his non-existence, the civilised prowling in the suburbs of self, feels that he feels these things. Viewed in this light, the ending of 'A Painful Case' becomes more bleak and savage and, I would say, more deeply, authentically human.

The problem for me in this essay is to try to get at the roots of Joyce's terrifying ability to get at the true humanity of his characters, his pitiless revelations of their hearts' habitual poverty.

No writer will remain interesting to another human being unless, at the back of his work, there is the sense that he (the writer) is in *contact* with his own humanity. What others call authority is articulate contact with self.

The first thing to say about Joyce is that he was a non-believer (I shall use that term). He was very proud. He had no respect for money and power. He rejected the consolations of belief. He was, as one of his friends said, a genuine negator. He was a hard drinker, practically all the time. He had bad eyes – like Milton, like Homer (we are told), like O'Casey, like Raftery. Joyce was a non-believer. People get upset about this.

A friend of Joyce's, Bruni, is the man who calls Joyce a negator. He then says:

> Joyce...doesn't blaspheme because the Irish don't have our ambition in that exercise. He doesn't destroy and he doesn't rebuild. *He does worse; he denies.* He moves further and further even from Christ the Man. *I feel sorry for him because I love him*, because I would like to see him happy, and because happiness cannot be found in our talents, in the approval of the world, or in the masterpieces that we create. Happiness can be found only in the teachings of Jesus, over whose last words, 'Eli, Eli, lamma sabactani,' I have seen Joyce cry secret tears. (*PAE*, 37-38) (Emphasis mine).

'I felt sorry for him because I love him, because I would like to see him happy.' That is a very decent feeling on the part of Bruni. It is also a complete waste.

Joyce was emptying his heart and mind and soul of the warm friendliness and support of belief. He rejected that warmth, that

especial creative support, and sought instead the loneliness and
mystery and rich potential of language itself, in the beginning was
the Word, and he sought also an *unsupported* perspective on the
casual loneliness of men and women. He wanted *a* way, *a* truth,
and *a* life.

It is this *unsupported* quality in Joyce that some people seem to
find hard to take, even to be afraid of: so, like Bruni, they feel they
should love him. (Yet Joyce was not unsupported, not totally, not
even in his mind: he had Nora; he lived with Nora, he listened to
Nora.)

Yet in so far as it is possible to live the unsupported spiritual
life, the unscaffolded spiritual life, Joyce did live it. It is this quality
of non-belief, of unsupported spirit-life, that drew the following
comment from Professor Curtius, a German critic, in 1929, in *Neue
Schweizer Rundschau*. Bruni is full of intelligent, futile concern.
Curtius, on the other hand, writes out of fear. The fear is as pointless as the concern:

> Joyce's work comes from the revolt of the spirit and leads to the destruc-
> tion of the world. With an inexorable logic there appears in Joyce's
> Walpurgis-night, amid larvae and lemures, the vision of the end of the
> world. A metaphysical nihilism is the substance of Joyce's work. The
> world – 'macro- and microcosmos' – is founded 'upon the void'.
>
> Joyce's intellectual energy has an intensity of which we can speak only
> with the highest admiration. His artistic expression dominates all lin-
> guistic and compositional forms with a free mastery. In the comic story,
> the satire, characterisation, invention, he is the peer of all the masters
> of the literature of the world. His work has the unmistakable sign of
> the great: inexhaustibility.
>
> And yet, in the final analysis, it remains sterile. This entire wealth
> of philosophical and theological knowledge, this power of psychological
> and esthetic analysis, this culture of the mind educated in all the liter-
> atures of the world, this ratiocination which is so far above all positivistic
> platitudes – all this is finally nullified, refutes itself in a world
> conflagration, in a sprinkling of metallically irridescent flames. What
> remains? Odor of ashes, horror of death, apostate melancholy, tortures
> of conscience – Againbite of Inwit.[6]

The fear of 'metaphysical nihilism' underlying that statement is as
futile as the concern, 'I feel sorry for him because I love him',
underlying Bruni's prayer for Joyce. Both men have failed to grasp
the nature of Joyce's indifference – the distance that makes him so
immediate, the immediacy that justifies and clarifies the distance.

Both men are upset by the lonely strength of that indifference
which the faith of one man and the fear of the other cannot tolerate
in the unsupported Joyce.

Also, and most importantly, Joyce was brutally clear in his mind about two things that have a confusing and weakening effect on most of us – money and power.

Joyce's contempt for money is possible only to the prince of mockers. I know this is a complex problem – money is a part of the reality of all our lives, a nagging, hassling, bedevilling part, at times – but Joyce, in that amoral indifference of his, fought off, as far as possible, the claims that money makes. The sad truth is, often, that people do not make money; money makes people. This is terrifying. The question is – how *independent* are we of money? Is the quality of our work dependent (to what extent?) on the nature and extent of that *independence*? The usual justification for selling out, gradually, to money is family – because family is good.

So the indulgence in the traditional decency of the prostitution is justified by the need to support the virtue. As the years wear on, the distinction is blurred – and the prostitution *becomes* the virtue.

As far as I can see, we are all, more or less, guilty of this. Joyce, because of his amoral indifference, is not. On the whole, he is not. I think that God has one thing in common with great writers – he has no morals. Joyce's attitude to power is similar. For example, his attitude to politics – to political conformity – is quite consistent with his attitude to money. 'Material victory is the death of spiritual predominance.'

> As an artist I attach no importance to political conformity. Consider: Renaissance Italy gave us the greatest artists. The Talmud says at one point, 'We Jews are like the olive: we give our best when we are being crushed, when we are collapsing under the burden of our foliage.' Material victory is the death of spiritual predominance. Today we see in the Greeks of antiquity the most cultured nation. Had the Greek state not perished, what would have become of the Greeks? Colonisers and merchants. As an artist I am against every state. Of course I must recognise it, since indeed in all my dealings I come into contact with its institutions. The state is concentric, man is eccentric. Thence arises an eternal struggle. The monk, the bachelor, and the anarchist are in the same category. Naturally I can't approve of the act of the revolutionary who tosses a bomb in a theater to destroy the king and his children. On the other hand, have those states behaved any better which drowned the world in a blood-bath? (*PAE*, 71)

Joycean indifference *has* to result in this attitude to political conformity, to the State. God is a shout in the street; Joyce does not believe in the bread he is eating; he is against every state – what is there room for? What is there left?

A great deal. For a start, there is fascinating human rubbish, mesmeric triviality, a great deal of dirt. Borges says Joyce is 'wondrously paltry' ('Invocation to Joyce'). It is a splendid phrase.

It is possible to see *Ulysses* as an epic of bric-à-brac trivia, a colossal presentation of smallnesses – the evidence available to the non-believing, indifferent mind and eye. To put it another way, and to use one of Joyce's favourite words, it is 'human'. During the war years, Joyce was working in Zurich on *Ulysses*. In the evenings, he liked to sit and talk and drink wine, light gold Fendant, a strong Valois wine. Georges Borach recorded much of Joyce's conversation. In this extract from Borach's notebook, Joyce is talking about the *humanness* of various works of literature:

> The most beautiful, all-embracing theme is that of the *Odyssey*. It is greater, more *human* than that of *Hamlet, Don Quixote*, Dante, *Faust*. The rejuvenation of Old Faust has an unpleasant effect upon me. Dante tires one quickly; it is as if one were to look at the sun. The most beautiful, most human traits are contained in the *Odyssey*. I was twelve years old when we dealt with the Trojan War at school; only the *Odyssey* stuck in my memory. I want to be candid; at twelve I like the mysticism in Ulysses. When I was writing *Dubliners*, I first wished to choose the title *Ulysses in Dublin*, but gave up the idea. In Rome, when I had finished about half of *Portrait*, I realised that the Odyssey had to be the sequel, and I began to write *Ulysses*.
>
> Why was I always returning to this theme?...I find the subject of Odysseus the most *human* in world literature. Odysseus didn't want to go off to Troy; he knew that the official reason for the war, the dissemination of the culture of Hellas, was only a pretext for the Greek merchants, who were seeking new markets. When the recruiting officers arrived, he happened to be plowing. He pretended to be mad. Thereupon they place his little two-year-old in the furrow. In front of the child he halts the plow. Observe the beauty of the motifs: the only man in Hellas who is against the war, and the father. Before Troy the heroes shed their lifeblood in vain. They wish to raise the siege. Odysseus opposes the idea. The strategem of the wooden horse. After Troy there is no further talk of Achilles, Menelaus, Agamemnon. Only one man is not done with; his heroic career has hardly begun: Odysseus. Then the motif of wandering. Scylla and Charybdis – what a splendid parable! Odysseus is also a great musician; he wishes to, and must, listen; he has himself tied to the mast. The motif of the artist, who will lay down his life rather than renounce his interest. Then the delicious humor of Polyphemus... On Naxos the fifty-year-old, perhaps baldheaded, with Ariadne, a girl who is hardly seventeen. What a trait of generosity at the interview with Ajax in the nether world, and many other beautiful touches. I am almost afraid to treat such a theme; it's overwhelming. (*PAE*, 69-70) (Emphasis mine)

The most beautiful, all-embracing, *human* theme.

The first point Joyce makes in relation to his own love of the *humanness* of the Odyssey is this: 'I want to be candid'.

The word 'candid' comes from the Latin *candidus*, meaning 'white' or 'glistening'. I think of that, always, in relation to Joyce – a candid style, a white, glistening style. It is amazingly apt.

'Candid' also means pure, clear, stainless, innocent, free from bias, impartial, just, frank, open, straightforward, sincere in what one says. All that, and more.

'I want to be candid.' This is Joyce's achieved artistic morality, having shed the dead moralities of his youth. This new morality is a morality of candour. The candid heart speaks for itself.

This matter of candour is, and always has been, an extremely complex problem for writers. It is connected with style. How to be candid, spiritually *direct*? 'The poet *never* speaks *directly*,' says Yeats, 'There is *always* a phántasmagoria'[7] (emphasis mine).

Immediately, we are into the paradoxical situation in which candour is made possible through a film, a set of *dramatis personae*, a machinery of *oratio obliqua*, a set of voices mouthing acceptable contradictions, a chorus of complexity.

Yeats, mostly, achieved directness by being indirect. His candour comes to us through masks. He is, nonetheless, in the terms I'm trying to describe, a *candid* poet. But Yeats's candour has, as it were, to be gathered from all the sources, the voices, the personae, the masks.

For Patrick Kavanagh, *in*directness is tedious; almost, in his terms, a lie. Masks are boring. There is no need for masks, Kavanagh would say. He writes:

> The poet has nothing to conceal. There is no skeleton in his cupboard.
> Hence his confidence. The average man, by which I mean the man
> who will not accept his fate and be as God made him, is always afraid
> that he will be found out. He is living a lie. The poet is honest. Poetry
> is honesty.[8]

> The problem that confronts me here
> Is to be eloquent, yet sincere...
>   ('Auditors In')[9]

Of these three writers – Joyce, Yeats, Kavanagh – Yeats, who *may* be the greatest, is the one who most gives the impression of having something to conceal.

Does Joyce achieve total candour? I don't know. Indifference makes possible a savage, disciplined interest. I would say that Joyce's white, glistening style, his impartial, just style, shows a mind that in turn reflects the soul's wish to be candid.

I have not read Brenda Maddox's biography of Nora Barnacle,[10] but there is little doubt in my mind that, in this matter of candour, Nora is the most important single external factor. And from the moment they met, she inspired in Joyce this passion for being candid. There is a book entitled *Nora Barnacle Joyce* by Padraic O'Laoi, which has a lovely description of the evening Joyce and Nora Barnacle went out walking in Dublin, in the direction of Ringsend. This walk with Nora is one of the crucial moments in Joyce's moral-artistic life.

There is something about the man-woman sexual relationship (especially, ironically enough, in marriage) which tends to prevent full candour, and therefore full honesty. Frequently in Joyce, it is marriage (*not* Dublin) which is the centre of the paralysis of the universe, and of the penis. So often, in Joyce, marriage is an intimate abyss, a chasm of familiarity.

Worst of all is the desperation fostered by familiarity. The deepest sadness has to do with the unexpressed aspects of marriage – hence the lies of silence, the anonymous humiliations, little Chandler's 'cheeks suffused with shame',[11] Gabriel Conroy's ludicrous encounter with his own lust and its failure, before the remembered passion of a dead boy. Such attitudes, such moments, such pathetic concealments, seem to me to have appeared to Joyce to be the very *nature* of paralysis, the very opposite of that spiritual, sexual, emotional *fluency* that is the bedrock of his relationship with Nora and the essence of his style as a writer:

> As they strolled towards Ringsend they were very open with each other. Joyce questioned Nora in much detail about her family, her early life and friends in Galway, with particular attention to her boyfriends there and her romances. He was like an explorer discovering some new river. He wended his way step by step back to the source of her life and explored all the tributaries that formed the main stream of her life. On his side Joyce was open and honest with Nora and gave her in much detail the story of his family and life...

> They were both interested in each other's sexuality as their later letters reveal. And soon they engaged in a little love play. In this Nora took a positive role and aroused Joyce without any prompting from him. Later he recalled that encounter at Ringsend as 'a sacrament which left in me a final sense of sorrow' and again 'the recollection of it fills me with amazed joy'...

> ...their love matured over the summer of 1904. Again and again Nora had to listen to a detailed account of his sexual history; his encounters with prostitutes and perverts...

> One quality above all others attracted her to Joyce – it was *his absolute candour*. He opened his soul to her in its entirety and never attempted to hide from her even his most secret thoughts.[12] (Emphasis mine)

Thinking about this situation and its implications, it is possible to appreciate why Joyce's brother, Stanislaus, refers to Joyce as 'a genius of character'. (This is the opposite of the often-heard Irish phrase 'A genius of a character' which is merely a matter of colourful over-simplification). Joyce, in his brother's eyes, is 'a genius of character'. Why? It is interesting that where Padraic O'Laoi talks about Joyce's candour in love, Stanislaus talks about Joyce's candour in hatred – about his extraordinary moral courage – his shocking ability to be scurrilously truthful:

> Jim is a genius of character. When I say 'genius' I say just the least little bit in the world more than I believe; yet remembering his youth and that I sleep with him, I say it. Scientists have been called great scientists because they have measured the distances of the unseen stars and yet scientists who have watched the movements in matter scarcely perceptible to the mechanically aided senses have been esteemed as great; and Jim is, perhaps, a genius though his mind is minutely analytic. He has, above all, a proud wilful vicious selfishness out of which by times now he writes a poem or an epiphany, now commits the meanness of whim and appetite, which was at first protestant egoism, and had perhaps, some desperateness in it, but which is now well-rooted – or developed? – in his nature...He has extraordinary moral courage...His great passion is a fierce scorn of what he calls the 'rabblement' – a tiger-like, insatiable hatred. He has a distinguished appearance and bearing and many graces: musical singing and especially speaking voice (a tenor), a good undeveloped talent in music, and witty conversation. He has a distressing habit of saying quietly to those with whom he is familiar the most shocking things about himself and others, and, moreover, of selecting the most shocking times for saying them, not because they are shocking merely, but because they are true.[13]

To give you a sense of the full nature and impact of this candour, however, let me turn to *Ulysses*. The most obvious choice is Molly's soliloquy. But Joyce's candour is not confined to sex – he brings it to bear on all aspects of human experience, from birth to death. He brings that scientific capacity for minute analysis as well as total sensuous openness to bear on experience. He makes us understand that our own capacity for experiencing practically anything is, in fact, shockingly limited. It's not that we go dream-like or zombie-like through reality – it's just that we half-do, or quarter-do, most things. We half-listen, half-speak, half-taste, half-pay attention, half-reflect, half-remember. When Eliot says ' humankind/Cannot bear very much reality'[14] he is talking, I believe, about the shoddiness, the shadowy cheapness, we enforce on our senses, on our minds, on our hearts, by our lack of candour with ourselves and others. This failure to fully experience normal realities like talking or eating or smelling or brooding or excreting or laughing or good vicious gossiping or using words – is part of that paralysis so ruthlessly scrutinised by Joyce. The unfinished sentences in 'The Sisters' are as much paralysis as the paralysis of the old priest. We are all aware of the paralysis of language in our universities, among our politicians, on radio and television. Near the end of the twentieth century we still have not learned the vital lesson – in, say, literary criticism – of Joyce's candour. Or we don't re-learn it frequently enough.

I want to look at one passage from *Ulysses*. It has to do with eating. On the threshold of the Burton, Mr Bloom halts. Men are eating. He sees men eating. He smells men eating. He studies men eating. They are eating to get strength. They are eating flesh. They are chewing death. Joyce takes us into the mouths, into the busy teeth of these eaters. He makes us think of the casual orgies necessary for everyday life. He hints at eating in Irish history and mythology. He makes us conscious of eating-words in our normal conversation.

(Are you finding it difficult to swallow this discussion? Yes I am yes I am Yes!) He tells us about eating and prayer; do Catholics eat God?; we know that eating and elemental violence are inseparable; we know that, equally, eating and 'good conversation' are said to go together – but in the end, it is the brutality that is most emphasised.

It may well be that we cannot afford to pay too much attention to what we do – do not dwell too long on anything. What is needed is sufficient attention to make us feel we know something, or have experienced it. But no writer I know experiences normal, or so-called normal, reality the way Joyce does. The intensity of his scrutiny of the casual simply stops the mind. Mr Bloom is at the door of the Burton. The Burton is packed with hungry men. We walk straight into a normal orgy, the almost unbearable grotesqueness of this ordinary activity:

> Men, men, men.
>
> Perched on high stools by the bar, hats shoved back, at the tables calling for more bread no charge, swilling, wolfing gobfuls of sloppy food, their eyes bulging, wiping wetted moustaches. A pallid suetfaced young man polished his tumbler knife fork and spoon with his napkin. New set of microbes. A man with an infant's saucestained napkin tucked round him shovelled gurgling soup down his gullet. A man spitting back on his plate: halfmasticated gristle: no teeth to chewchewchew it. Chump chop from the grill. Bolting to get it over. Sad booser's eyes. Bitten off more than he can chew. Am I like that? See ourselves as others see us. Hungry man is an angry man. Working tooth and jaw. Don't! O! A bone! That last pagan king of Ireland Cormac in the schoolpoem choked himself at Sletty southward of the Boyne. Wonder what he was eating. Something galoptious. Saint Patrick converted him to Christianity. Couldn't swallow it all however.
>
> – Roast beef and cabbage.
>
> – One stew.
>
> Smells of men. His gorge rose. Spaton sawdust, sweetish warmish cigarette smoke, reek of plug, spilt beer, men's beery piss, the stale of ferment.

> Couldn't eat a morsel here. Fellow sharpening knife and fork, to eat
> all before him, old chap picking his tootles. Slight spasm, full, chewing
> the cud. Before and after. Grace after meals. Look on this picture then
> on that. Scoffing up stewgravy with sopping sippets of bread. Lick it
> off the plate, man! Get out of this.[15]

That passage is remarkable for it orgiastic detail, the gruesome
precision of its observation, the congested, civilised, ordered gluttony
of the scene. The writing is mercilessly physical.

But even more remarkable is the fact that the entire activity is
filtered through Bloom's consciousness – the man who sees what
is happening before his eyes. He doesn't glimpse it, or half-see it,
or quarter-see it. He stands there at the door of the Burton and
he takes it in; he takes it in and he puts words on it, or Joyce puts
words on it for him. And all the time the entire thing is part of
Bloom's mental life – deliberate, deep, slow, meditative, marginalised,
corrective, discriminating, sensual, fine, oily, sniffy. Bloom sniffs
with his mind.

And his candid mind, inevitable as weather, is the focus and fil-
ter and analytical arena of it all:

> 'Am I like that? See ourselves as others see us. Hungry man is an
> angry man.'
>
> 'Couldn't eat a morsel here.'
>
> 'Get out of this.'
>
> 'Out. I hate dirty eaters.'[16]
>
> 'Eat or be eaten. Kill. Kill.'[17]

For all the implacable physicality of the writing, this is in fact
a mental drama. Joyce creates a consciousness on which all things
impinge, and even enter. Bloom is not made brisk and cocky with
sustained purpose. He is made vulnerable, discriminating and reflective through being endlessly impinged on, entered into. He is
battered by images, smells, impressions. His candid consciousness
makes him a victim of the situation, while his full expression of
that consciousness makes him a quiet master.

> 'Never know whose thought you're chewing.'[18]

My argument is, or has been, that candour in Joyce comes from
getting rid of a certain kind of inherited supportive morality. A
vacuum is created, deepened by the rejection not only of belief,
but of the very notion of belief. (This is impossible: language tells
us that some people believe in nothing – they *do* believe in nothing.)

For the moment, though, I am suggesting that this non-belief creates a spiritual indifference which is the product of necessity. THe mind is rid of the illusion of supportive nobilities and virtues and the way is cleared for the re-creation of the wondrously paltry – the real poetry of men and women – their human smallnesses. Yet the end result is that of a new dignity, coming from the denial of support, coming therefore from the candid heart and mind, the white, glistening style.

Even at a basic stylistic level, this candour brings great rewards. Listen, for example, to the opening words of a few short stories from *Dubliners*. Is there anything more candid than:

> There was no hope for him this time.
>
> ('The Sisters')

> It was Joe Dillon who introduced the Wild West to us.
>
> ('An Encounter')

> She sat at the window watching the evening invade the avenue.
>
> ('Eveline')

> Mrs Mooney was a butcher's daughter.
>
> ('The Boarding House')

> Mr James Duffy lived in Chapelizod because he wished to live as far as possible from the city of which he was a citizen and because he found all the other suburbs of Dublin mean, modern and pretentious.
>
> ('A Painful Case')

> Two gentlemen who were in the lavatory at the time tried to lift him up; but he was quite helpless.
>
> ('Grace')

> Lily, the caretaker's daughter, was literally run off her feet.
>
> ('The Dead')

I have tried to define, or at least to describe, the presence in Joyce's style of a quality, a condition, a customary radiance, which I suggest comes directly from his character (his 'genius of character'), which he consciously developed over the years. That word 'human' which he repeats over and over, like a mantra, is what one has to grapple with. Joyce's humanity is among the bravest of the twentieth century, or indeed in the history of literature. That humanity has been recognised and admired by many, but no one has paid tribute to Joyce's human-ness more beautifully than another blind poet, Jorge Luis Borges, in his poem 'Invocation to Joyce'.

I shall end with that poem:

You, all the while,
in cities of exile,
in that exile that was
your detested and chosen instrument,
the weapon of your craft,
erected your pathless labyrinths,
infinitesimal and infinite,
wondrously paltry,
more populous than history.
We shall die without sighting
the twofold beast or the rose
that are the center of your maze,
but memory holds its talismans,
its echoes of Virgil,
and so in the streets of night
your splendid hells survive,
so many of your cadences and metaphors,
the treasures of your darkness.
What does our cowardice matter if on this earth
there is one brave man,
what does sadness matter if in time past
somebody thought himself happy,
what does my lost generation matter,
that dim mirror,
if your books justify us?
I am the others. I am all those
who have been rescued by your pains and care.
I am those unknown to you and saved by you. [19]

W.B. Yeats: An Experiment in Living

1

Although Yeats claimed that 'the intellect of man is forced to choose/ Perfection of the life or of the work'[1] there's a sense in which his life is so commingled with his poetry as to be almost inseparable from it. Far from diminishing his passionate devotion to his art, this commingling underlines the tenacity with which he explored and developed his language, themes and technique. There is in both Yeats's life and art a sustained blend of vulnerability and control, of risk-taking and mastery, of adventure and caution which helps to account for the impression he gives of being, at one moment, a Victorian uneasily sniffing the challenging air of Modernism and, at another, a daring Modernist bedevilled by Victorian caution and respectability. He is a poet caught, fruitfully, between backward and forward looks.

One can hardly start a paragraph on Yeats without noting how one's writing begins almost immediately to be immersed in two ideas: conflict and opposition. For this we must, I think, look to Blake and Yeats's work on that poet. Blake opened up Yeats's mind and heart, taking him away from a stolid emotional equator to the challenging poles of human thought and experience. When in 'The Fisherman' Yeats talks of writing a poem 'as cold and passionate as the dawn' (167) he is dreaming of a polar art, a poetry bristling between extremes infiltrating and energising each other. There is a very precise sense in which the phrase 'cold and passionate' describes much of Yeats's best poetry: as a poet, he is both a very cold fish indeed, looking on with icy detachment, and an impassioned explorer of emotions, ideas and conflicts, hurtful and confusing, which he suffers even as he explores. The problem is that some readers see only the cold fish and, in response to this, drag in charges of snobbery, fascism, self-obsessed aloofness and, of course, respectability and caution. And indeed all these are to be found, in varying degrees, in the poet's life and work. At times, it's very hard to know what the human heart of his poetry really is. I would say it is a willed constancy co-existing with and inseparable from a state of necessary vacillation. There's a lot of self-dramatisation in the poetry, at once isolated and flamboyant, intrusive and rhetorically seductive. Yeats is at times very impressed by Yeats; he is his own best audience for his own drama. He acclaims and lacerates himself as he sees fit. The rage he writes so much about, especially in his later years, has a quality of almost lunatic isolation, Lear deprived even of the presence of the Fool. And Yeats actually seems to have sought this isolation, to have aspired to a state of severed rage, though he was also an active politician and theatre manager. (I repeat that in talking about Yeats one can hope to be fair or even intelligent only by keeping opposites in mind. It is a difficult and endlessly challenging way of thinking.) The pursuit of isolationism, the conscious removal of himself and his art from 'ordinary' people (even as he struggled to express them) marks his long preoccupation with magic, one of the deepest influences on his poetry. Magic may indeed be the single most profound and pervasive influence on his work. But how many people, or more particularly, how many readers of verse have even the slightest interest in magic? Or apart from a few wispy, vague notions, have the slightest idea of what it's all about? I, for one, know next to nothing about the thing. I've never attended a séance or been a member of any relevant group or society. And how does this non-participation amounting to non-knowledge on my part affect my understanding of a poetry a good deal of which may owe its very existence to magic, and Yeats's experience of it? (He was a member of The Golden Dawn[3] for most of his mature years.) There are those who will poohpooh the notion that a reader should need any knowledge of 'background material' in order to appreciate poetry; I can see why they think like this. Does one have to know about medieval Christianity in order to appreciate Dante? Or the intricacies of science and engineering to get close to the thrilling essence of Hart Crane's poetry, especially his long poem *The Bridge*?[4] No, I suppose. And yet I am always haunted, as I read Yeats, by the feeling that I am missing a lot, that there is much I don't really understand or can't get fully to grips with, because of my ignorance of magic.

Why, then, am I bothering to try to write this essay? Because, in spite of my ignorance, I find Yeats a gritty, gutsy fighter of a poet, a writer with a special courage, who is also in certain respects repellent and impenetrable. For a man who talks so much about beauty, heroism and nobility, there's a forbidding emotional ugliness in his work at times, an arrogant intellectual eccentricity, a chilly hauteur, a crass distancing of himself from others, a stony self-containment, Old Rocky Face himself making a loopy insistence on the universal validity of his own very odd ways of feeling, seeing and saying. Yet nobody was more aware of all this than Yeats; and throughout the years he grappled with his own loneliness, needs, dreams, doubts, nightmares, lusts, rages, craziness, sicknesses of mind and body. He stood for what he called Unity of Being.[5] He wanted to experience it all. He wanted to say it all. He could do this, or hope to do this only by venturing 'into the abyss of himself',[6] by scrutinising the darkness of his own spirit and the spirits of others whom he ruthlessly pursued, examined and analysed. There is in Yeats a fierce predatory energy, an insatiable appetite for inquiry and investigation not only into the muck and squalor of our natural existence but also into the spiritlives of the supernatural world, the other world that is often dismissed by reason, apprehended by imagination, mocked by intelligent disbelief, aggressively promoted by fanatics, experienced in dreams and existing, or not existing, according to the cast of mind and heart as well as the instinctive and educated values of any given individual. Any one of us teachers, writers, journalists, critics, publishers, poets on or off the dole. Otherness is something we usually choose to get involved in. Yeats made a deliberate choice to get involved in the otherworld of spirits and magic. That sense of dramatic interest in chosen otherness is a real, normal presence in his poetry. This is part of his achievement: he normalises in verse what is abnormal in life; his poems are so many bridges between different worlds. Some of them are, in the deepest sense, haunting. They come from beyond the bounds of 'normal' experience; they invite us, even compel us to walk the weird roads of eternity so that afterwards our walking the roads of Kerry or Antrim or Cornwall, or the streets of Dublin or London or Liverpool, is a richer experience, deepened and dramatised by a new awareness of otherness which we then discover, surprisingly, to be, after all, a real if hitherto unexplored part of our 'normal' selves. And this is one of the most valuable abilities of poetry: it extends the reader, sometimes against his or her will. This extension of tolerant awareness can be inspired by poetry that is insulting, outrageous, boorish, deliberately provocative; or by poetry that is serene, reflective, peaceful. What matters is the change, however temporary, in the reader. Quite a number of people read poetry; the more daring among these are read by what they read. My own recurring experience of 'The Cold Heaven' is an example of reading and being read by a poem.

Just as Yeats speaks in 'The Fisherman' of writing a poem 'maybe as cold and passionate as the dawn', so in 'The Cold Heaven' he sees a sky which looks 'as though ice burned' (140). Again the cold. Again the fire. In the mingled extremes, casual thought vanishes, only memories remain to inspire blame which he accepts 'out of all sense and reason' so that he cries and trembles and, 'riddled with light', asks a question about the otherworld and the soul's possible relation to it:

> ...is it sent
> Out naked on the roads, as the books say, and stricken
> By the injustice of the skies for punishment? (140)

Some of Yeats's most striking poems end with a question: 'Leda and the Swan', 'The Second Coming', 'Among School Children', 'John Kinsella's Lament for Mrs Mary Moore' and 'A Model for the Laureate' are examples. These questions are not evasive tactics, climactic cop-outs; they are inevitable and logical and disturbing. 'Naked on the roads' and 'stricken' by the skies' 'injustice' as 'punishment' is a troubling vision posed in the form of a question. And it is a question for which there is no answer. Yeats leaves us looking at the skies, or into the unfathomable abyss. There's no comfort here. The poem ends with, and continues to open on, some cosmic panorama of terror and retribution. The poem reads the reader, leaving him or her with a deeper sense of his or her smallness and insignificance.

Naked. 'A Coat' ends with 'there's more enterprise/In walking naked' (142). Did Yeats ever walk 'naked' in his poetry? Is he too wrapped up in masks, ideas, gestures, postures, theories of history and human personality, consciously dramatic attitudes ever to walk naked, ever to say what he felt in his heart of hearts? There are very touching moments when he seems as vulnerably human as the next man or woman.

> When day begins to break
> I count my good and bad,
> Being wakeful for her sake,
> Remembering what she had,
> What eagle look still shows,
> While up from my heart's root
> So great a sweetness flows
> I shake from head to foot.
>   ('Friends', 139)

> The last stroke of midnight dies.
> All day in the one chair
> From dream to dream and rhyme to rhyme I have ranged
> In rambling talk with an image of air:
> Vague memories, nothing but memories.
>   ('Broken Dreams', 174)

There are other such 'naked' moments, but emotional or spiritual nakedness is not really either Yeats's strength or interest: 'There is always a phantasmagoria' he writes in 'A General Introduction For My Work'.[7] Yeats needed this 'phantasmagoria'. He surrounded himself with characters, ghosts, spirits, creatures of legend and mythology, figures out of history and people, friends and enemies, out of his own experience, all of whom he formed into a private choir, a unique Yeats orchestra, to help him express both the occult and the obvious, the dead and the living, as well as his own ever-deepening personal drama, his intense and systematic exploration of his private darkness. And he did this with a stubborn courage, a tough, lifelong tenacity in a frequently hostile society, an Ireland so convinced of its own pietisms that every energetic alternative was 'heretical', a mauling of a beautiful, delicate, native flower. In Ireland, Yeats continued to maul that flower until a completely new plant took firm root and flourished slowly but surely over the years.

2

Vulnerability and control, risk-taking and mastery, adventure and caution – these are, I suggest, features of Yeats's life and work. It was a rich life, it is a rich poetry, full of passion and violence of private and public kinds, sexual, political, spiritual. Yet, despite its passionate complexity, there's a quality running through it which is the opposite of the haphazard and the accidental and which argues a profoundly *deliberate* approach to experience and to writing, as well as to the mysterious connections between the two. Yeats introduced into Irish poetry the coldly meditative mind, the deliberate, disciplined brooding on internal and external life which helped him to *shape* experience that might otherwise have remained fragmented, dissipated, even chaotic. This deliberateness and this shaping arose in turn from his conviction that a poet's life 'is an experiment in living'.[8] This view of life as conscious, ongoing experiment, changing, failing, succeeding, throwing up new surprises, different approaches, fresh challenges, this view is what I have tried to grasp over the past few decades in my attempt to understand the sharp, internal vacillations, that are not mere contradictions, of this shapely body of poetry. It is like trying to understand the moods of an ever-changing river that remains, in spite of all the tumult, the same river.

   To experiment with living during one's youth is a likely though not an inevitable prospect. As people get older, however, the desire to experiment seems to grow more sluggish and lethargic until a state of 'maturity' has been attained which is in fact another name for dull predictability. There are, of course, exceptions; but in Ireland, at any rate, adult 'maturity' and 'dull predictability' are frequently one and the same. The advantages of this equation are many and too obvious to need comment here. The dangers are perhaps less obvious, particularly if the 'mature' adult happens to be a poet. For Joyce, Dublin was a 'centre of paralysis'.[9] So he simply left the place and fled to Europe, taking with him his own version of Dublin to be brooded on in silence, dissected in exile, reconstructed with cunning. For Yeats, it was

> The daily spite of this unmannerly town,
> Where who has served the most is most defamed,
> The reputation of his lifetime lost
> Between the night and morning.
>
> ('The People', 169)

But Yeats did not flee, and he spent a great deal of his adult working years in Dublin. It's fair to say, I think, that he grew to maturity there.

For reasons best known to themselves, if they are known at all, quite a few poets stop writing, or switch to some other form of writing, when they reach, or are perceived to have reached, this maturity. Yeats, too, had relatively long unproductive periods. But he never lost touch with those forces both within and outside himself which combine to create the conditions that make possible the writing of verse. And when he couldn't produce worthwhile poetry, he was working at the combination of conditions and circumstances which might make possible such production. This is surely the point of that conscious experiment in living which Yeats embarked on at an early age; it means that when the imagination is barren, steps must be taken to make it fertile; it means that when feeling itself seems to have disappeared from life, resources must be drawn on to create new feelings; it means that when belief is stale or dying or even dead, time must be deliberately devoted to its renewal. In short, the conscious experiment in living involves a refusal to allow one's abilities or talents or gifts to wither or shrivel or be frittered away in a whole host of ways from wilful exercises in self-waste or self-diminishing or slow, acceptable forms or rituals of self-destruction to those forms of 'responsibility' that turn many's the stimulating intelligence into a boring 'expert' or a cheerful, amusing individual into a well-dressed, 'successful' lump of complacency and tedium.

This, in short, is the challenge that faces nearly every poet: how does one *not* die even as one continues to breathe? At different times throughout his life Yeats's experiment in living helped him to confront that challenge. He discovered that being alive meant for him, among other things, the defiant refusal to let vital and sparkling aspects of his spiritual, intellectual and emotional life fade and wither away without a word of protest or a step taken to re-animate that fading life. In the matter of the making and re-making of the self, that is, in the business of painful self-resurrection, Yeats became a skilled and dedicated practitioner. The farther Yeats advanced in years, the younger he grew as a poet. Like one of Swedenborgs Angels,[10] eloquently lauded by Yeats himself, he advanced forever towards the dayspring of his youth. Yeats's first long poem, 'The Wanderings of Oisin', finished in his early twenties, is about a poet who goes to, and returns from, the Land of Youth. Yeats's entire life as a poet is an endless aspiration to repeat the first part of that journey. There are those who would say that his poetry made the trip successfully. 'Where does poetry come from?' somebody once asked Michael Longley, the Belfast poet. 'If I knew,' replied Longley, 'I'd go there.'

Can it be that poetry comes from that Land of Youth which is within us all, and which we tend to explain and educate and theorise out of existence? Can it be that we fear what is most splendidly fearless within ourselves ?

Not Yeats. Not silly, arrogant, snobbish, airy-fairy, huffy-puffy Yeats. He had the courage to experiment. He permitted life to live him even as he struggled to master his life. He wanted to go 'walking naked'. He rarely did, but he tried, always. 'Is not all life the struggle of experience, naked, unarmed, timid but immortal, against generalised thought?', he wrote in his *Journal*,[11] in August 1910. He wore mask after mask because he knew in his heart that whoever walks totally naked will always end up crucified by the mob, the public representatives of all our cherished and well protected respectabilities. Hammers and nails have their own style and are at their most impressive and exemplary when penetrating naked flesh. The mob, humanity, ourselves, tend to spectate. Masks are inevitable, for the most part. Even in poetry? Certainly, in Yeats's case. If he couldn't walk naked himself, he might at least imagine someone who could. He could rouse himself into a dramatic awareness of others. Don the mask. Be another. See yourself in a new darkness. Wait for the moment of light.

> If we cannot imagine ourselves as different from what we are, and try to assume that second self, we cannot impose a discipline upon ourselves though we may accept one from others. Active virtue, as distinguished from the passive acceptance of a code, is therefore theatrical, consciously dramatic, the wearing of a mask.
>
> (*Per Amica Silentia Lunae*, 1917)[12]

Yeats's masks are an elaborate mode of self-discipline and, paradoxically, self-revelation. This discipline is a personal exercise, not an external imposition. It extends and deepens Yeats's knowledge of the workings of his own mind and heart. It helps him, as it were, to re-write himself and, in so doing, to clarify himself, to let his own truest rhythms as a human being emerge, to permit himself to sing, criticise and celebrate his own limited, thrilling experience of life. There are moments in Yeats when life and poetry fuse into one. The act of re-writing words on a page is inseparable from the conscious, disciplined re-moulding of the self, that interesting mess which is always capable of being shaped and re-shaped by a vigilant and vigorous imagination. Compare the following lines with the opening lines of 'The Choice' ('The intellect is forced to choose/ Perfection of the life or of the work') and I think it is clear that Yeats is more convincing when he equates the effort to perfect a poem through re-writing with his passion for a more coherent inner life than when he insists on a trite division between living and writing, expression and being.

> The friends that have it I do wrong
> Whenever I rewrite a song
> Should know what issue is at stake:
> It is myself that I re-make. [13]

At one level, Yeats's experiment in living is saying very simply, 'Give imagination a chance. Let it influence your life, your relation-ships, your mind-workings'. As a university teacher, I am some-times appalled at the way imagination is almost completely ousted from the teaching and study of English Literature and, instead, youngsters are expected, even compelled, to stuff their heads with boring, arid theories about poetry, theories often expressed in language that is pedantic and leaden. The actual poetry tends to get buried under all this mechanical clack. Perhaps that's the intention. In any case, it's as if some teachers no longer believe they can *enjoy* poetry. Without such belief, how can joy be communicated, shared?

Belief is a problem, but only if it's seen to be a problem. Belief is not a problem if a person simply dismisses any need for belief; and it is not a problem if a person simply asserts the irrefutable value of belief. For Yeats, belief was a recurring problem. What is belief, for a poet?

The same as for anyone else. The need for belief is an admission of the need to connect with oneself, to try to connect the energies of that self with outside energies, powerful and alien, in such a way that one has a more peaceful, convinced sense of one's own tiny, dignified place in a tumultuous world. Belief can create a sense of the sanity of context. Belief may spring as easily from a deep sense of gratitude as from a desolate, pained sense of incom-pleteness, of growing and alarmingly aimless insufficiency. Believing can be an exercise in apparent folly, a refutation of, even a direct insult to cherished faculties of intellect and reason (the very words 'reason' and 'intellect' may have an intimidating ring of 'true' authority to souls burdened or gifted with belief). The act of believing may, in its turn, involve an unconcealed scorn for the sweet, civilised reassurances of proof. Belief is certainly as much a demonstration of vulnerability as it can be a source of strength. A believer is not afraid to look and sound like a fool; he may exult in that capacity, or incapacity, as you will. This is true, I think, of belief in supernatural forces and beings. At certain moments of any day, such belief may seem ludicrous even to the believer. The act of lifting a cup to one's lips, of listening to children yelp and scream in a street, of considering the ways in which we instinctively and consciously use each other, may quite suddenly and strongly introduce the notion that belief is an act of contemptible cowardice. It would seem that any genuine belief carries within itself the seeds of scepticism and doubt. Belief, in the sense that Yeats wished to experience it, to live it, is not a system of bland certainties, it is rather a further opening up of his increasing appetite for the challenge and stimulation of otherness, his style of encountering and comprehending dreams, his way of coping with that awful blend of chaos and lethargy in the self. When living is an experiment, believing is as attractive a possibility, at least, as the comforts and chills of not believing. For Yeats the experimenter, believing is a dynamic, fragile structure that makes poetry possible. Making poetry possible is why poets are in the world. I want to turn to his essay, 'Magic'. The first two words are 'I believe', repeated in the fifth line. This is Yeats's *Credo*: the *Credo*, it must be remembered, of a great poet of vacillation. Constant, in that.

> I believe in the practice and philosophy of what we have agreed to call magic, in what I must call the evocation of spirits, though I do not know what they are, in the power of creating magical illusions, in the visions of truth in the depths of the mind when the eyes are closed; and I believe in three doctrines which have, as I think, been handed down from early times, and been the foundations of nearly all magical practices.[14]

'I believe in...what we have agreed to call magic'. Who agreed? Where? By what processes? I wasn't at the meeting or meetings. So I don't know .

And Yeats doesn't know what he believes in, either. 'I do not know what they are.' They are spirits. He believes in 'the evocation of spirits'. Evocation is power. He believes in 'the power of creating magical illusions'.

At this point, some readers may say 'Enough, Willie! Spooks! Illusions! Who're you kidding?'

But Yeats believed this. Or he believed he believed it. For how long? And in what circumstances?

I believe he believed in the need to believe in such matters for the sake of his poetry. This is not to say that his view of belief is not rare and beautiful, as well as being a fertile aesthetic stimulant.

> We must not make a false faith by hiding from our thoughts the causes of doubt, for faith is the highest achievement of the human intellect, the only gift man can make to God, and therefore must be offered in sincerity.
>
> (*Per Amica Silentia Lunae*, 1917)[15]

Belief. Faith. The only gift man can make to God. Was Yeats a mystic? Yeats was a joyous wizard of vacillation. For the poet of deliberate vacillation there are no roads not taken. In a letter to John O'Leary in 1892, he wrote:

> The mystical life is the very centre of all that I do and all that I think and all that I write.[16]

In a letter to Ethel Mannin in 1938, he wrote:

> Am I a mystic? – no, I am a practical man. I have seen the raising of Lazarus and the loaves and fishes and have made the usual measurements, plummet line, spirit level, and have taken the temperature by pure mathematic.[17]

Writing to O'Leary, Yeats sounds like Saint John of the Cross. Writing to Ethel Mannin, he is a wise and grizzled Einstein, sipping his favourite whiskey as he mentions some of his achievements. Yeats was a mystic yesterday; today, a practical man. Tomorrow? The experiment continues. The poetry develops, deepens, sings, ever more exultantly, creating its own freedom, wild as a kite, disciplined as a hermit monk would struggle to be in prayer. And very enjoyable. The creation of such joy is impossible without the vulnerability of belief. And is there not some very credible link between the educated notion of belief as absurdity and Yeats's view of it as 'the highest achievement of the human intellect'. Yeats inevitably makes one ask the question: how close are opposites? To experiment with hate may result in a deeper understanding of love. ('I study hatred with great diligence'.)[18] To experiment with gentle love may lead to a deeper understanding of human–animal ferocity. ('Love is like the lion's tooth'.)[19] Cold fish. Warm, vulnerable man. Crafty old magician not always convinced of his magic but writing as if he were: Rhetoric. Writing, too, from a state so immersed in magic, so completely and trustingly at home in it, even as doubt waited mockingly in the wings, he was happy and honoured to be the poet-medium, to let forces from the great mind and the great memory, forces far beyond the merely personal, flow through his imagination into words accurate as any state of grace: Poetry.

'I believe in three doctrines.' If we look at these doctrines we'll see that Yeats's belief in them is like a statement of what he wanted to do in poetry: energise his language; unify his thoughts; evoke reality through symbols. In a similar way, he wished to energise, unify and evoke his life through images, pictures out of mythology, history, pictures of his friends, enemies, panoramic pictures of Irish life, recurring pictures of the love of his life, Maud Gonne, pictures of old age and its 'dull decrepitude',[20] pictures of death, pictures of eternity. If we do not have pictures of our experience, we cannot hope to comprehend it. Out of such pictures come ideas, come philosophy.

Yeats's three doctrines are:

> (1) That the borders of our mind are ever shifting, and that many minds can flow into one another, as it were, and create or reveal a single mind, a single energy.

> (2) That the borders of our memories are as shifting, and that our memories are part of one great memory, the memory of Nature herself.

> (3) That this great mind and great memory can be evoked by symbols.[21]

Preposterous? Magnificent? Both, I would say, depending on the time of night in your mind. In his introductory lines to 'Magic', Yeats spoke of 'the visions of truth in the depths of the mind when the eyes are closed'. Patrick Kavanagh said 'We have to shut our eyes to see our way to Heaven'.[22] The time of night is a source of light in the questing mind. Yeats is driving always towards his goal: Unity of Being. It is impossible. He never gives up. He believes he can do something novel and effective about human fragmentation, loneliness, the sense of being severed, insignificant, a butt of jokes 'where motley is worn',[23] 'a tattered coat upon a stick',[24] a caricature, a victim of 'decrepit age'[25] that is tied to him 'as to a dog's tail'.[26] His answer is: energise, unify, evoke. And he does, up to a point, anyway. In few other poets do we get such a sense of poetry as a kind of courageous failure, an ultimate inability to achieve the dream, in a sustained way. And yet, time and again, the very notion of failure is burned up in poems where his words and rhythms are energised, his thoughts unified (for the moment, that is, forever in a poem), his symbols evoking feelings, dreams, pictures out of the darkness of the soul.

> When a man grows old his joy
> Grows more deep day after day,
> His empty heart is full at length,
> But he has need of all that strength
> Because of the increasing Night
> That opens her mystery and fright.
> *Fifteen apparitions have I seen;*
> *The worst a coat upon a coat-hanger.*
>
> ('The Apparitions', 387)

The very word 'Apparitions' conjures up the picture of visitants from a supernatural world. The sense of such phenomena exists in Yeats; but so does a profoundly ironic sense of the 'worst' apparition he has witnessed: a coat upon a coat-hanger. 'I made my song a coat/Out of old mythologies' he'd written in 'A Coat' (142). Is this new 'worst' apparition of a coat a vision of the ultimate futility of poetry, of words? An old, tattered coat upon a stick. Only a few weeks ago, a dramatist whom I greatly admire, who has written several fine plays, said to me in sadness, 'Words are useless, Brendan. Words are worse than useless.' He said no more. There are moments when I think Yeats's brave experiment ended in an overwhelming sense of loneliness and futility, suffered through a superbly educated consciousness. Then I read a fragile, honest poem like 'Politics', the candid poem of an observant old man, and I thank God and whatever Muses are still knocking about for Yeats's experiment in living.

> How can I, that girl standing there,
> My attention fix
> On Roman or on Russian
> Or on Spanish politics?
> Yet here's a travelled man that knows
> What he talks about,
> And there's a politician
> That has read and thought,
> And maybe what they say is true
> Of war and war's alarms,
> But O that I were young again
> And held her in my arms. (392-93)

I'm not saying that such poems owe their existence to Yeats's belief in magic. I am saying that his belief in magic gave Yeats a new, vital appreciation of the invaluable fragility of human love. He said, 'The only two powers that trouble the deeps are religion and love' (*The Dome*, 1898),[27] and he never ceased to be a love poet just as he never ceased to be a deeply spiritual poet who created generous space in his poems for the body and the body's hungers. Even if one agreed that Yeats's belief in magic is absurd we'd still have to concede that such belief gave him, or helped to give him, a special kind of moral awareness, the sort of nervous awareness that is disturbed by 'a certain evil, a certain ugliness', which does not appear to have an equally disturbing effect on a more conventionally educated kind of consciousness. Yeats is an enraged rebel against ugliness. His belief in magic seems to have given him a clear picture of what ugliness actually is. It also gave him a heightened moral awareness and a razor-sharp power of discrimination, of definition, a visionary insight into what we have lost so completely we no longer even begin to recognise our loss. The evocation through symbols of the hidden content of the one great mind and the one great memory creates the climate in which a disturbing moral awareness, the ability and desire to make acute moral distinctions becomes possible. Yeats sees ugliness for what it is. Therefore, his words make us begin to ask ourselves: what have we lost? He has a suggestion.

> I often think I would put this belief in magic from me if I could, for I have come to see or to imagine, in men and women, in houses, in handicrafts, in nearly all sights and sounds, a certain evil, a certain ugliness, that comes from the slow perishing through the centuries of a quality of mind that made this belief and its evidences common over the world.[28]

How can Yeats possibly know that this belief and its evidences were 'common over the world'? Is this kind of climactic, absolute statement the logical consequence of the momentum of his belief? Belief creates its own laws, logic, visions, absolutes. Belief is dangerous. Belief educates awareness, intensifies consciousness, encourages illuminating connections. Belief is valuable. In 1914, Yeats wrote: 'My father's unbelief had set me thinking about the evidences of religion and I weighed the matter perpetually with great anxiety, for I did not think that I could live without religion' (*Reveries over Childhood and Youth*).[29]

Neither could he. So Yeats created his own religion, his own mode of connection with his own God, his own stylish bridges, his own delicate, firm, probing awareness, his own belief. In his first poem 'The Song of the Happy Shepherd' he writes 'there is no truth/Saving in thine own heart' (8). In his final play, finished on his death-bed, Yeats's hero Cuchulain exclaims 'I make the truth!'[30] First poem and final play say the same thing: look into the abyss of the self, scrutinise that personal darkness, make your truth, create your belief, cherish your constancy, exult in your vacillation, endure your loneliness and pursue your magic with all your heart and mind, with all your scepticism, doubt and sincerity until you achieve those moments of insight which, expressed, renew the tired spirit of man and transfigure the world, if only for a moment, with the poem's light inspired by the heart's darkness. At such moments we know what ugliness is. We begin to remember what we have forgotten.

It's amazing what an old man can do when he believes he believes. Belief in belief is the knowledge that eternity is now. Now is a door opening forever on dangerous, valuable possibilities. Yeats was always ready to open that door.

3

Much of Yeats's prose, including his letters, is concerned with trying to say precisely what he feels about events, people, politics, magic, poetry, drama, love, sex, friendship. This constant attempt to be accurate about what he feels and thinks has to do with the knowledge that any kind of dishonesty in poetry is ruthlessly avenged by language itself. When Ibsen said that 'Poetry is a court of judgement on the soul' [31] I believe he was talking about the merciless retribution exacted by language on moments of sloppiness, lazy imprecision, emotional evasiveness, bombast and rhetorical pomposity. Such moments are in all of us but the writing of poetry tends to emphasise the need to be precise. How do we know what is actually going on in our hearts and minds? Are there not moments when the mind betrays the heart, the heart the mind, in such a way that we may increasingly try to convince ourselves that a manageable emotional fog, a viable confusion, is the least disturbing way to live? The unsettling clarities of poetry are a constant challenge to that way of thinking and feeling (this may be one reason why poetry is not, in fact, widely read). Reading Yeats's prose, one is constantly in touch with his non-stop, urgent need for emotional precision. The question 'How to live?' in Yeats becomes increasingly inseparable from the problem 'How to write?' So when he writes in *The Trembling of the Veil* (1922) that 'We begin to live when we conceive life as tragedy' [32] we realise that this chosen way of thinking about life is also the root of his deepening belief that 'tragic joy' [33] is what he is struggling to achieve in poetry. This chosen way of thinking, dictated by his experience, containing a deep inner logic in itself which is traceable from the first poem in his *Collected Poems* right through to his final poems, is one of the richest fruits of his experiment in living. Yeats is always struggling to find what he believes is the joy of creation, a joy that survives war, famine, horror, evil, death, 'the weasel's twist, the weasel's tooth'.[34] He is not always convincing, and especially when he says things like 'I declare' and 'I, the poet William Yeats' and 'When such as I'.[35] At such moments, he strikes me as a man trying to convince himself of something, to use a thumping rhetoric instead of simply admitting his uncertainty.

At the same time, his ongoing attempt to define emotional realities, to know what he feels, is admirable. An obvious way to realise this is to study his love poetry to Maud Gonne. I would like instead to look at some poems dealing with friendship.

Yeats took friendship very seriously. He thought about his friends, their needs, flaws, strengths. He helped them. He was helped by them. He was fortunate in his friends. Even Maud Gonne becomes a friend in the end. She becomes more and more recognisably human as she gradually ceases to be treated as a goddess in poetry until, in the late poem 'Beautiful Lofty Things', she is referred to simply as Maud Gonne, though Yeats goes on to call her 'Pallas Athene' (348) in the next line. Maud must have been deeply grateful to Yeats for her slow, if incomplete de-Helenisation. Is there, in this persistent deification of a talented, dynamic woman, a refusal to consider her essential character, her complex human qualities? Is it the poet's way of distorting her into an unreal state of elevation? Maud must, at some level, have been somewhat bored by Yeats's ecstatic distortions of her nature. Never once, in all those love-poems, does Yeats refer to her by her own name. I imagine that Maud, reading these poems, must have felt like an acolyte in a temple of goddesses, muttering to herself, 'Willy! Willy! Where am I, and who am I in this luminous company of distinguished divinities?' Women who are pedestalised, who are treated as goddesses, are simply lost sight of. A friend, on the other hand, is a real, undistorted, human presence.

Yeats's best friend was his wife, Georgie. Yet she is uncelebrated in his poetry, even indirectly, as far as I can see. Lady Gregory was a good friend; she made the young Yeats quit his romantic moping and get down to work. 'To a Friend whose Work has come to Nothing' is a splendid poem in her honour. He is close to her, supporting her. He gives her a sense of her own worth, her dignity. She did great work for Ireland, for the Abbey Theatre. She had enemies who flailed her, her achievement. Yeats told her to work at what seemed to him to be the best answer to attacks from her enemies – that exultant self-sufficiency which was always his own aim.

> Be secret and exult,
> Because of all things known
> That is most difficult. (122)

W.B. YEATS: AN EXPERIMENT IN LIVING

Put simply, and perhaps even crudely, Yeats is much more impressive and convincing as a poet of friendship than as a love poet. There is, of course, a great deal of love in these poems on friendship, a love that does not draw attention to itself but is strong, vigilant, concerned, steady. 'In Memory of Eva Gore-Booth and Con Markiewicz', 'In Memory of Major Robert Gregory', 'Friends', 'A Friend's Illness', 'Coole Park, 1929', 'Coole and Ballylee, 1931' and 'Beautiful Lofty Things' are good examples of poems containing this steady, quiet love. But even in these relatively reticent poems Yeats tends to dramatise himself. In 'All Souls' Night', a truly superb dramatic poem, written in Oxford in 1920, in November (in Ireland, the month of the dead), Yeats summons some of his dead friends, William Thomas Horton, Florence Farr Emery and MacGregor Mathers, a student of the occult who translated *The Kabbala Unveiled* (1887).[36] Yeats summons him:

> And I call up MacGregor from the grave,
> For in my first hard springtime we were friends,
> Although of late estranged.
> I thought him half a lunatic, half knave,
> And told him so, but friendship never ends. (258)

Yeats never let go of his friends, even after they died. These friends who are dead 'are not far from us...they cling in some strange way to what is most deep and still within us', he believed. Here, yet again, is another example of Yeats's extraordinary tenacity, his powerfully gripping memory. He did not forget his friends. He simply wouldn't allow himself to. His friends became part of himself; from that self, inseparable in his belief from the 'age-long memoried self'[37] came 'revelation',[38] including the revelation of the meaning of friendship itself, undoubtedly, in Yeats's view, one of the most instructive and valuable experiences in life. In the end, he wished to be judged not only by his work but by the friends he had. Once more, life and art are intertwined. They are, one might say, friends who know the meaning of antagonism. That moving poem of friendship (among other things), 'The Municipal Gallery Revisited' ends:

> You that would judge me, do not judge alone
> This book or that, come to this hallowed place
> Where my friends' portraits hang and look thereon;
> Ireland's history in their lineaments trace;
> Think not where man's glory most begins and ends,
> And say my glory was I had such friends. (370)

These are among the noblest and most humane lines in Yeats. They deepen in truth as the years go by. As a poet of friendship,

Yeats has few equals. Over the decades, friendship, the soul's grittiest expression of its own determination to live close to, and even for, certain people, while actively rejoicing in their difference, their uniqueness, their otherness, came to be for Yeats possibly the sanest aspect of his experiment in living. To live with his poetry is to find a friend.

4

The very notion that a man or a woman should do a job for life must mean that whole interesting areas of their characters and personalities are left undeveloped. Progress creates its own poverties. This neglect of potential has become inseparable from concepts of 'success' and 'achievement'. Some jobs obviously bring more of a person's talent into play than others, but most jobs involve non-development, even non-recognition of what might be interesting or shocking or attractive or inventive in one who 'does a good job'. That's what the world requires of us; and that's what we give the world, or try to. Yeats's concept of 'job' was very different, as I have tried to show. He never succumbed to the lure or the spectre, as you will, of employment. He pursued his experiment in living in such a way that he deepened and extended the whole concept of self in poetry and in life. He invented himself. He experimented with that invention. He never settled for any fixed way of looking at life, or of expressing it. He is at once the most personal and impersonal of poets. He is by turns courageous and stubborn, nervous and lost. He is a loner who created an entire imaginative world populated by fascinating figures. He plays the ring-master, magician, hero, philosopher, rake, mystic, politician, occultist, spiritualist, sensualist, fascist, hater, lover, friend, paternal adviser to succeeding generations of poets ('learn your trade').[39] Yeats has a real go at exploring and discovering the whole self. He produces both poppycock and sublimity in verse, sometimes closely together. He dons masks that some people find boring, others fascinating. He devoted his life to poetry, to the Arts. After forty years, I find I read him, not always with understanding, but with deepening joy.

EDITOR'S NOTE

The essays in this collection have been arranged thematically rather than chronologically. The first section consists of essays on aspects of Irish and Anglo-Irish literature. The second section, on individual Irish writers, begins with Joseph Plunkett and Patrick Kavanagh, two poets with a strong visionary quality seeking lucidity in their detachment and loneliness, leading to Derek Mahon, Louis MacNeice and George Moore, all of whom in their different ways try to deal with the problem of human isolation. These are followed by the first essay on W.B. Yeats, whose works, in this case the Cuchulain plays, are manifestations of his multi-layered and complex personality. Yeats opens a sub-section of writers interested in and frequently writing out of the Gaelic mythology and heritage: Yeats, Austin Clarke, Flann O'Brien and Frank O'Connor. In O'Connor, Kennelly finds a poet, despite the fact that he is most known as a short story writer: 'once a poet, always a poet, practising or otherwise' (189). This notion leads to Liam O'Flaherty, in whom Kennelly finds a related feature, namely that he 'is a poet in prose' (198). What is equally significant, however, is the dominating qualities Kennelly sees in much of O'Flaherty's writing: '...his prose frequently has the intensity and strong momentum of a poetry whose primary impulse is wonder, admiration and praise' (198), an approach to life also taken up and explored in 'Seán O'Casey's Journey into Joy'. 'James Joyce's Humanism' and the second essay on Yeats, 'W.B. Yeats: An Experiment in Living', follow and end the selection as answers to and clear statements of what the writer's search and task are all about, almost closing the circle, yet by their very nature opening up a whole range of issues of the utmost artistic, existential, moral and even political importance. A thematic approach, then, seems to me to be the most appropriate way to present the full scope of Kennelly's artistic and critical stance.

The consistencies of Kennelly's artistic ideals are illustrated by the fact that certain views on life and literature are occasionally repeated between the essays, something which is not possible to avoid in a collection of this kind.

Finally, information concerning the original publication of the essays is given in the notes to each individual essay.

ÅKE PERSSON

NOTES
by Åke Persson

Introduction *(pages 11-22)*

I am indebted to Antoinette Quinn and Britta Olinder for valuable comments on earlier versions of this Introduction.

1. For example, Peter Burnett, 'Seats in the Gallery' [review of *A Kind of Trust*. Dublin: Gallery Books, 1975]. *The Honest Ulsterman*, No.50, Winter 1975, pp.189-90; Ciaran Carson, 'Blarney Stones' [review of *New and Selected Poems*. Dublin: Gallery Books, 1976]. *Hibernia*, No.15, August 1976, p.20.
2. All references are to essays in *Journey into Joy*, unless otherwise indicated. For details of publication history of the essays, see the notes to each individual essay.
3. Unpublished Ph.D. thesis submitted at Trinity College, Dublin, 1966.
4. With this statement, Kennelly echoes Yeats, who poses the question 'Is not one's art made out of the struggle in one's soul?', in his *Journal, Memoirs*, edited by Denis Donoghue (London: Macmillan Papermac, 1988), p.157.
5. W.B. Yeats, from notes for an unpublished lecture on 'Contemporary Poetry' (1910), quoted in Richard Ellmann's *Yeats: The Man and the Masks* (Oxford: Oxford University Press, 1979; first published in 1948), p.6.
6. (Dublin: Profile Press, 1977; reprinted in *Selected Poems*, edited by Kevin Byrne. Dublin: Kerrymount Publications, 1985, and *Breathing Spaces: Early Poems*. Newcastle upon Tyne: Bloodaxe Books, 1992).
7. (Dublin: Gallery Books, 1979; reprinted in *Selected Poems*, 1985, and *Breathing Spaces*, 1992).
8. (Dublin: Beaver Row Press, 1983; Newcastle upon Tyne: Bloodaxe Books, 1987).
9. (Newcastle upon Tyne: Bloodaxe Books, 1991).
10. See note 5; *Yeats: The Man and the Masks*, p.5.
11. Henrik Ibsen, 'Epilogue'. *Lyrical Poems*, selected and translated by R.A. Streatfield (London: Elkin Mathews, 1902), p.38.
12. See *Reader-Response Criticism: From Formalism to Post-Structuralism*, edited by Jane P. Tompkins (Baltimore and London: John Hopkins University Press, 1980), pp.xv-xix.
13. For example, 'Keynote Address', *Culture in Ireland: Division or Diversity? Proceedings of the Cultures of Ireland Group Conference*, edited by Edna Longley (Belfast: Institute of Irish Studies, The Queen's University of Belfast, 1991); also 'Introduction' and involvement in the anthology *Ireland's Women: Writings Past and Present*, edited by Brendan Kennelly, A. Norman Jeffares and Katie Donovan (London: Kyle Cathie and Dublin: Gill & Macmillan, 1994).
14. 'Preface' to *A Time for Voices: Selected Poems 1960-1990* (Newcastle upon Tyne: Bloodaxe Books, 1990), p.11.

Poetry and Violence *(pages 23-45)*

First published in *History and Violence in Anglo-Irish Literature*, edited by Joris Duytschaever and Geert Lernout (Amsterdam: Rodopi, 1988), pp.5-28.

   1. Translated by Brendan Kennelly. Later published in *Love of Ireland: Poems from the Irish* (Cork and Dublin: Mercier Press, 1989), pp.57-64.
   2. 'Ted Hughes and Crow', *London Magazine*, January 1971, pp.5-7.
   3. *The Collected Poems of W.B. Yeats* (London: Macmillan, 1958), p.288. All quotations taken from Yeats's poetry are from this edition. Page numbers will be given in brackets after the quotation.
   4. *Poems 1956-1986* (Dublin: Gallery Press, and Newcastle upon Tyne: Bloodaxe Books, 1986), pp.125-26. The poem appeared in *West Strand Visions* (1974).
   5. *Poems 1963-1983* (Edinburgh: Salamander Press, and Dublin: Gallery Press, 1985), p.86. The poem appeared in *An Exploded View* (1973).
   6. Henrik Ibsen, 'Epilogue'. *Lyrical Poems*, selected and translated by R.A. Streatfield (London: Elkin Mathews, 1902), p.38.
   7. *Twice Round the Black Church: Early Memories of Ireland and England* (London: Routledge and Kegan Paul, 1962), pp.131-32.
   8. *The Collected Poems of Austin Clarke* (Dublin: Dolmen Press, and London: Oxford University Press, 1974), pp.379-80.
   9. 'The Red-Haired Man's Wife' appeared in *Insurrections* (1909).
   10. *Poems 1956-1973* (Mountrath, Co. Laois: Dolmen Press, 1980), p.72. The poem appeared in *Wormwood* (1966).
   11. John Millington Synge, 'Preface' to *The Poems*. For example, *Collected Works, Vol. 1*, edited by Robin Skelton (London: Oxford University Press, 1962), p.xxxvi.

A View of Irish Poetry

I. *Irish Poetry to Yeats* *(pages 46-54)*

First published as 'Introduction' to *The Penguin Book of Irish Verse* (Harmondsworth: Penguin Books, 1970; second edition 1981), pp.26-38.

   1. Translated by Brendan Kennelly, in *A Drinking Cup: Poems from the Irish* (Dublin: Allen Figgis, 1970), p.1. Republished in *Love of Ireland: Poems from the Irish* (Cork and Dublin: Mercier Press, 1989).
   2 .Frank O'Connor, *Kings, Lords, & Commons: An Anthology from the Irish* (New York: Alfred A. Knopf, 1959), p.17. Reprinted by Gill and Macmillan, Dublin, 1991.
   3. Patrick Kavanagh, *Collected Poems* (London: MacGibbon & Kee, 1964), p.38.
   4. Brendan Kennelly, *A Drinking Cup*, p.18. Republished in *Love of Ireland*.
   5. W.B. Yeats, 'An Irish Patriot', review of Lady Ferguson's biography *Sir Samuel Ferguson in the Ireland of His Day*, *The Bookman* 10, May 1896, p.50. Reprinted in *Uncollected Prose of W.B. Yeats, Vol. 1: First Reviews and Articles 1889-1896*, edited by John P. Frayne (London: Macmillan, 1970).
   6. *The Daily Express*, Wednesday, 30 January 1907.
   7. *Sir Samuel Ferguson in the Ireland of His Day, Vol. 2* (London and Edinburgh: William Blackwood and Sons, 1896), p.292.

8. *Poems* (Dublin: William McGee, and London: George Bell and Sons, 1880), p.42.

9. *Autobiography*, edited from the manuscript by James Kilroy (Dublin: Dolmen Press, 1968), p. 9.

10. *Collected Poems* (London: Macmillan, 1958), p.376.

11. W.B. Yeats, 'Nineteen Hundred and Nineteen', p.236.

12. 'Under Ben Bulben', p.400.

13. 'Easter 1916', p.203.

II. *Irish Poetry Since Yeats* *(pages 55-71)*

Previously unpublished; especially written for this volume.

1. *Goodbye Twilight: Songs of the Struggle in Ireland*, edited by Leslie H. Daiken (London: Lawrence & Wishart, 1936).

2. (Dublin: Wolfhound Press, 1993).

3. *Collected Poems* (London: MacGibbon and Kee, 1964), p.185; see also 'Yeats', *The Complete Poems*, edited by Peter Kavanagh (Newbridge: Goldsmith Press, 1984), pp.348-49.

4. For example, 'Signposts', *Collected Pruse* (London: Martin, Brian & O'Keefe, 1973), p.25; also 'Author's Note', *Collected Poems*, p.xiv.

5. W.B. Yeats, 'The Gyres', *Collected Poems* (London: Macmillan, 1958), p.337.

6. Patrick Kavanagh, 'From Monaghan to Grand Canal', *Collected Pruse*, p.228.

7. 'Why Sorrow?', *The Complete Poems*, p.180.

8. 'Shancoduff', *The Complete Poems*, p.13.

9. *The Great Hunger*, *The Complete Poems*, p.88.

10. Denis Devlin, 'Lough Derg', *Collected Poems*, edited by J.C.C. Mays (Dublin: Dedalus Press, 1989); Patrick Kavanagh, 'Lough Derg', *The Complete Poems*; Seamus Heaney, 'Station Island', *Station Island* (London: Faber and Faber, 1984).

11. *Selected Poems*, edited by W.J. McCormack (pseudonym Hugh Maxton) (Harmondsworth: Penguin Books, 1992); first published in 1991, edited by Hugh Maxton (Dublin: Lilliput Press).

12. 'Tiresias', *Selected Poems*, pp.168-88; 'Note', p.267. Poem appeared in 1971.

13. Mary O'Donnell's weekly programme on poetry is entitled *Along the Backwater*; series started on 4 October 1992, and is presently running. Austin Clarke's weekly programme was entitled *Poetry* and broadcast between the late 1940s [1948] and the mid-1960s.

14. *The War Horse* (London: Gollancz, 1975, and Dublin: Arlen House, 1980); *In Her Own Image* (Dublin: Arlen House, 1980); *Night Feed* (Dublin: Arlen House, and London: Marion Boyars, 1982); *The Journey* (Dublin: Gallery Press, 1982); *Outside History* (Manchester: Carcanet, 1990); *In a Time of Violence* (Manchester: Carcanet, 1994).

15. 'Self-Portrait on a Summer Evening', *Selected Poems* (Manchester: Carcanet, 1989), p.73.

16. W.B. Yeats, 'The Spur', *Collected Poems*, p.359.

17. First collected in *Between Innocence and Peace: Favourite Poems of Ireland*, edited by Brendan Kennelly (Cork and Dublin: Mercier Press, 1993), p.205 [Patrick Galvin informed me that the poem first appeared in a limited edition published by the small American hand press Red Hanrahan Press, 1971].

18. *Poems 1956-1986* (Dublin: Gallery Press, and Newcastle upon Tyne: Bloodaxe Books, 1986).

19. 'Wounds', *Poems 1963-1983* (Edinburgh: Salamander Press, and Dublin: Gallery Press, 1985); 'The Ice-Cream Man' appears in *Gorse Fires* (London: Secker & Warburg, 1991).

20. For example, *How's the Poetry Going? Literary Politics & Ireland Today* (Belfast: Lagan Press, 1991), and *A Real Life Elsewhere* (Belfast: Lagan Press, 1993).

21. *The Hungry Grass* (London: Faber and Faber, 1947), p.19.

22. (Dublin: Raven Arts Press, 1985).

23. Edited by Hugh McFadden, introduction by Macdara Woods (Dublin: Dedalus Press, 1991).

24. 'This Houre Her Vigil', *Sandymount, Dublin: New and Selected Poems* (Dublin: Dedalus Press, 1988), p.15. The poem was originally written in 1943.

25. *Hail! Madam Jazz: New and Selected Poems* (Newcastle upon Tyne: Bloodaxe Books, 1992).

26. *The Irish Times*, 10 June, 1993, p.9.

27. W.B. Yeats, 'Remorse for Intemperate Speech', *Collected Poems*, p.288.

28. For example, 'The Last Galway Hooker', 'The Cleggan Disaster', and *The Battle of Aughrim, New Selected Poems* (London: Faber and Faber, 1989), pp. 19-23; 31-41; 45-79.

29. (Newcastle upon Tyne: Bloodaxe Books, 1991).

30. 'Under Ben Bulben', *Collected Poems*, p.400.

A View of Irish Drama *(pages 72-102)*

First published as 'Introduction' to *Landmarks of Irish Drama* (London: Methuen, 1988), pp.vii-xliv. Part of the discussion on Yeats's play *On Baile's Strand* is based on the corresponding part of the chapter on Yeats in Kennelly's Ph.D. thesis *Modern Irish Poets and the Irish Epic* (1966) (see notes to 'The Heroic Ideal in Yeats's Cuchulain Plays' below for further comments).

1. 'The Galway Plains', *Essays and Introductions* (London: Macmillan, 1961), p.214.

2. *John Bull's Other Island* (London: Constable, 1931; reprinted 1964), p.75. All quotations from the play are from this edition. Page numbers will be given in brackets after the quotation.

3. W.B. Yeats, 'Nineteen Hundred and Nineteen', *Collected Poems* (London: Macmillan, 1958), p.236.

4. *The Playboy of the Western World* (Dublin: Maunsel, 1907), p.v. All references to and quotations from the play are from this edition. Page numbers will be given in brackets after the quotation.

5. For example, *Collected Works, Vol. II: Prose*, edited by Alan Price (London: Oxford University Press, 1966), p.3.

6. Walter Pater, 'The School of Giorgione', *The Renaissance: Studies in Art and Poetry* (London: Macmillan, 1910), p.135.

7. 'Preface' to *The Tinker's Wedding* (Dublin: Maunsel, 1907), p.v. (See also *Collected Works, Vol. IV: Plays, Book II*, edited by Ann Saddlemyer (Gerrards Cross, Bucks: Colin Smythe, and Washington, D.C.: Catholic University of America Press, 1982), p.3.)

8. 'Preface' to *The Tinker's Wedding*, p.vi.

9. *Plays in Prose and Verse* (London: Macmillan, 1922), p.vi.

10. *Plays and Controversies* (London: Macmillan, 1923), p.103.

11. *Plays in Prose and Verse*, p.429.

12. *Autobiographies* (London: Macmillan, 1961), p.470.

13. *Plays and Controversies*, p.105.

14. 'The Tragic Theatre', *Essays and Introductions* (London: Macmillan, 1961), p.241.

15. 'The Tragic Theatre', p.239.

16. *The Collected Plays of W.B. Yeats* (London: Macmillan, 1952), p.253. All quotations from the play are from this edition. Page numbers will be given in brackets after the quotation.

17. *Collected Poems*, p.392.

18. *Under a Colored Cap: Articles Merry and Mournful with Comments and a Song* (London: Macmillan, 1963), p.186.

19. 'The Green Crow Caws', *Under a Colored Cap*, p.81.

20. 'The Green Crow Caws', p.80.

21. 'The Green Crow Caws', p.73.

22. 'The Silver Tassie', in *Rose and Crown, Autobiographies, Vol. II* (London: Macmillan, 1981), p.270. *Rose and Crown* first published 1952.

23. 'The SilverTassie', *Rose and Crown*, pp.270-71.

24. *The Silver Tassie: A Tragi-Comedy in Four Acts, Stage Version, Collected Plays, Vol. 2* (London: Macmillan, 1950), p.35. All quotations from the play are from this edition. Page numbers will be given in brackets after the quotation.

25. 'A Note on What Happened', *The Dramatic Works of Denis Johnston, Vol. 1* (Gerrards Cross, Bucks: Colin Smythe, 1977), p.79.

26. 'A Note on What Happened', p.78.

27. 'Opus One' (Preface to *The Old Lady Says 'No!'*), pp.16-17.

28. 'A Note on What Happened', p.76.

29. 'Opus One', p.15.

30. 'A Note on What Happened', p.81.

31. *The Old Lady Says 'No!': A Romantic Play in Two Parts with Choral Interludes*, Part 2, p.74.

32. Alec Reid, *All I Can Manage, More than I Could: An Approach to the Plays of Samuel Beckett* (Dublin: Dolmen Press, 1969), p.10; emphasis Reid's.

33. Alec Reid, p.15.

34. *All That Fall: A Play for Radio* (London: Faber and Faber, 1957), p.8. All quotations from the play are from this edition. Page numbers will be given in brackets after the quotation.

35. 'The End of the Noose', *The Observer*, 27 May 1956, p.11.

36. *The Quare Fellow: A Comedy-Drama* (London: Methuen, 1956), pp.75-76. Quotations from the play are from this edition. Page number will be given in brackets.

The Poetry of Joseph Plunkett *(pages 103-108)*

First published in *The Dublin Magazine: Easter Rising Edition* 5, No.1, Spring 1966, pp.56-62. This essay was included in a special issue of *The Dublin Magazine* to celebrate the 50th anniversary of the Easter Rising in 1916. It was principally a writers' and intellectuals' rebellion, and it was not successful, which resulted in the killing and execution of many of these writers and intellectuals, including Joseph Plunkett.

1. *The 1916 Poets* (Patrick Pearse, Thomas MacDonagh, Joseph Plunkett), edited by Desmond Ryan (Dublin: Allen Figgis, 1963), p.163. (Reprinted by Westport, Connecticut: Greenwood Press, 1979). All quotations from Plunkett's

poetry are from this edition. Page numbers will be given in brackets after the quotations.

2. The title is as above, but the last section consists of Plunkett's collected poems.

3. Namby-Pamby Philips: Ambrose Philips (c. 1675-1749). English poet, contemporary of Pope. Philips achieved some success with a few tragedies, most notably *The Distrest Mother* (1712), which is more or less a translation of Racine's *Andromache*. He also translated Sappho in *Ode to Aphrodite*. Pope and others brought him into ridicule, and his poetry came to be called 'namby-pamby', a name probably first bestowed by Henry Carey.

4. William Blake, 'The Argument', *Marriage of Heaven and Hell* (1793). For example, *The Complete Poems: Second Edition*, edited by W.H. Stevenson (London and New York: Longman, 1989), p.105.

5. Grace Gifford (1888-1955). Irish painter who joined Sinn Féin, and became estranged from her family after converting to Catholicism. Engaged to Plunkett, she took active part in the Republican movement. Just four hours before his execution in Kilmainham Gaol in May 1916, they got married. She has been seen as Plunkett's inspiratory muse during the rebellion, and subsequently, in 1917, she became a member of the Provisional Republican Government; she is represented in the Hugh Lane Municipal Gallery, Dublin.

Patrick Kavanagh's Comic Vision *(pages 109-126)*

First published as 'Patrick Kavanagh' in *Ariel: A Review of International English* 1, No.3, July 1970, pp.7-28. Republished in *Irish Poets in English: The Thomas Davis Lectures on Anglo-Irish Poetry*, edited by Seán Lucy (Cork and Dublin: Mercier Press, 1973), pp.159-84.

1. 'Signposts', *Collected Pruse* (London: MacGibbon and Kee, 1964), p.25. All quotations from Kavanagh's prose are from this edition, which will be referred to as *CPr* after the quotations. Page numbers will be given in brackets.

2. *Collected Poems* (London: MacGibbon and Kee, 1964), p.xiii. All quotations from Kavanagh's poetry in this essay are from this edition. Page numbers will be given in brackets after the quotations.

3. W.B. Yeats, 'The People', *Collected Poems* (London: Macmillan, 1958), p.169.

4. *Arena*, Spring 1965. Revised and later entitled 'Winter in Leeds', *The Complete Poems* (Newbridge: Goldsmith Press, 1984), p.335.

5. *Collected Poems*, pp.391-92.

Derek Mahon's Humane Perspective *(pages 127-135)*

First published in *Tradition and Influence in Anglo-Irish Poetry*, edited by Terence Brown and Nicholas Grene (London: Macmillan, 1989), pp.143-52.

1. *The Collected Poems of Louis MacNeice* (London: Faber and Faber, 1979), pp.193-94.

2. *Poems 1962-1978* (Oxford: Oxford University Press, 1979), p.3. All quotations from Mahon's poetry are from this edition. Page numbers will be given in brackets after the quotations.

3. W.B. Yeats, 'The Tragic Generation, *The Trembling of the Veil: Autobiographies* (London: Macmillan, 1961), p.305; Yeats also used the phrase as the motto for his essay 'The Way of Wisdom', *The Speaker*, 14 April 1900; later entitled 'The Pathway' (without the motto), *Collected Works, Vol. VIII* (Stratford-

upon-Avon: Stratford Head Press, 1908). The phrase is originally from the French writer Villiers de l'Isle-Adam's play *Axel*, first English translation by H.P.R. Finberg (1925), with a preface by Yeats. Later translated by Marilyn Gadelis Rose (Dublin: Dolmen Press, 1970), with Yeats's preface included; quotation on p.170.

4. W.B. Yeats, 'A General Introduction for My Work', *Essays and Introductions* (London: Macmillan, 1961), p.509.

Louis MacNeice: An Irish Outsider *(pages 136-144)*

First published in *Irish Writers and Society at Large: Irish Literary Studies 22*, edited by Masaru Sekine (Gerrards Cross, Bucks: Colin Smythe, and Totowa, New Jersey: Barnes and Noble Books, 1985), pp.96-105.

1. *The Collected Poems of Louis MacNeice* (London: Faber and Faber, 1979), p.69. All quotations from MacNeice's poetry are from this edition. Page numbers will be given in brackets after the quotations.

2. Patrick Kavanagh, 'The Same Again', *Collected Poems* (London: MacGibbon & Kee, 1964), p.191.

3. W.B. Yeats, 'The People', *Collected Poems* (London: Macmillan, 1958), p.169.

4. Patrick Kavanagh, *Collected Pruse* (London: MacGibbon and Kee, 1964), p.14.

5. 'The Personal Factor', *Modern Poetry: A Personal Essay* (London: Oxford University Press, 1938; second edition 1968), pp.88-89.

6. 'Imagery', *Modern Poetry*, p.103.

7. See 'A Change of Attitude', *Modern Poetry*, p.1.

8. *The Poetry of W.B. Yeats* (New York: Oxford University Press, 1941), p.10.

9. *Varieties of Parable* (London: Cambridge University Press, 1965), p.131.

George Moore's Lonely Voices *(pages 145-161)*

First published in *George Moore's Mind and Art*, edited by Graham Owens (Edinburgh: Oliver and Boyd, 1968), pp.144-65.

1. *Celibate Lives*, Ebury Edition (London: Heinemann, 1937), p.viii. All quotations from *Celibate Lives* are from this edition, which will be referred to as *CL* after the quotations. Page numbers will be given in brackets.

2. *The Lonely Voice* (London: Macmillan, 1963), p.19. Pascal's saying in French means: 'The eternal silence of these infinite spaces terrifies me'.

3. James Joyce, 'The Dead', *Dubliners* (Harmondsworth: Penguin Books, 1962), p.220.

4. 'The Dead', p.216-17.

5. *Collected Poems* (London: MacGibbon and Kee, 1964), p.53.

6. Humbert Wolfe, *George Moore*, Modern Writers Series (London: Butterworth, 1931), p.125.

7. *The Untilled Field*, Ebury Edition (London: Heinemann, 1937) (reprint of final version, 1931), pp.217-18. All quotations from *The Untilled Field* are from this edition, which will be referred to as *UF* after the quotations. Page numbers will be given in brackets.

8. James Joyce, *A Portrait of the Artist as a Young Man* (Harmondsworth: Penguin Books, 1960), p.253.

9. *A Story-Teller's Holiday* (London: Heinemann, 1928), I, p.ix. (This was a two-volume revision of the single volume published in 1918.) All quotations from *A Story-Teller's Holiday* are from this edition, which will be referred to as *STH* after the quotations. Page numbers will be given in brackets.

10. James Joyce, 'A Little Cloud', *Dubliners*, p.68.

11. Unpublished essay. MSS in my [Kennelly's] possession.

12. For example, *The Short Stories of Liam O'Flaherty* (London: Four Square Books, 1966).

The Heroic Ideal in Yeats's Cuchulain Plays *(pages 162-169)*

First published as an essay in *Hermathena: A Dublin University Review*, No.CI, Autumn 1965, pp.13-21. This essay is based on the chapter on Yeats in Kennelly's Ph.D. thesis *Modern Irish Poets and the Irish Epic* (1966). Here, Kennelly explores and assesses the creative exploitation of Irish myths by Irish writers: de Vere, Ferguson, Todhunter, Hutton, Yeats, Russell (AE), Stephens, and Clarke. He particularly points to Ferguson's and Yeats's importance and achievement, and is more critical to the attempts of, for example, de Vere and Clarke.

For a further discussion on Kennelly's thesis, and its relation to Kennelly's own poetry, see my chapter 'The Critic: Towards a Literary Credo', in *Dark Fathers into Light: Brendan Kennelly*, Bloodaxe Critical Anthologies 2, edited by Richard Pine (Newcastle upon Tyne: Bloodaxe Books, 1994).

1. Aubrey de Vere, *The Foray of Queen Maeve and Other Legends of Ireland's Heroic Age* (London: Kegan Paul, Trench, & Co., 1882); John Todhunter, *Three Irish Bardic Tales* (London: J.M. Dent and Co., 1896); Sir Samuel Ferguson, *Congal* (Dublin: Edward Ponsonby, and London: Bell and Daldy, 1872), and *Poems* (Dublin: William McGee, and London: George Bell and Sons, 1880).

2. Birgit Bjersby (Bramsbäck), *The Cuchulain Legend in the Works of W.B. Yeats* (Upsala: Upsala Irish Studies, 1950).

3. *Collected Plays* (London: Macmillan, 1952), p.261. All quotations from Yeats's plays, unless otherwise indicated, are from this edition. Page numbers will be given in brackets after the quotations.

4. *Autobiographies* (London: Macmillan, 1961), p.512.

5. *Collected Poems* (London: Macmillan, 1958), p.211.

6. See *Collected Plays*, pp.233, 236, and 239.

7. Ernest Fenollosa and Ezra Pound, *'Noh' or Accomplishment: A Study of the Classical Stage of Japan* (London: Macmillan and Co., 1916).

8. '*Noh*', p.102.

9. '*Noh*', p.6.

10. '*Noh*', p.91.

11. '*Noh*', p.63.

12. '*Noh*', p.119.

13. '*Noh*', p.109.

14. '*Noh*', p.119.

15. '*Noh*', p.121: 'The types of ghosts are shown to us; we see great characters operating under the conditions of the spirit-life; we observe what forces have changed them. Bodhisattva, devas, elementals, animal spirits, hungry spirits or pseta, cunning or malicious or angry devils, dragon kings from the water world, spirits of the moonlight, the souls of flowers and trees, essences

that live in wine and fire, the semi-embodiments of a thought – all these come and move before us in the dramatic types.' It is clear that it was not only the *form* of the Noh that appealed to Yeats, but also the *spiritual* nature of its characteristic themes.

16. '*Noh*', p.120.

17. 'Note on "The Only Jealousy of Emer" ', in *Four Plays for Dancers* (London: Macmillan, 1921), p.105.

18. Preface to Lady Gregory's *Cuchulain of Muirthemne* (London: Murray, 1902), p.xiv.

Austin Clarke and the Epic Poem *(pages 170-181)*

First published as an essay in *Irish University Review: A Journal of Irish Studies: Austin Clarke Special Issue* 4, No.1, Spring 1974, pp.26-40. Apart from a few minor changes, this essay is identical to the chapter on Clarke in Kennelly's Ph.D. thesis *Modern Irish Poets and the Irish Epic* (see comments above).

1. *Twice Round the Black Church: Early Memories of Ireland and England* (London: Routledge and Kegan Paul, 1962), p.169.

2. See *The Irish Digest*, November, 1963, p.88.

3. In a letter to me [Kennelly]; unpublished.

4. *First Visit to England and Other Memories* (Dublin: Bridge Press, Templeogue, 1945), p.33.

5. *First Visit to England*, p.34.

6. Herbert Trench, *Deirdre Wed and Other Poems* (London: Methuen, 1901), p.16.

7. Argument prefixed to *The Vengeance of Fionn* (Dublin & London: Maunsel, 1917), no page number given in book. All quotations from this poem are from this edition, which will be referred to as *VF* after the quotations. Page numbers will be given in brackets.

8. Harold Williams, in his Preface to Trench's *Collected Works* (London: Jonathan Cape, 1924), I, ix, says that Trench's 'preoccupation in later years with the writing of drama was, in some degree, attributable to his association with the theatre. The only completed task of this impulse was that play, finely mingled of chronicle and imagination, *Napoleon*, which was produced by the Incorporated Stage Society in 1919. Whether read in the study or seen on the board, *Napoleon* proved that the poet of the subjective and abstract could command dramatic dialogue written in a vigorous and natural prose, that he could create and sustain characters undoubtedly alive and convincing, as witness Dr Wickham and Anne, his wife; Geoffrey Wickham, the idealist; Elise; and a Napoleon perhaps as real as any in literature.' Trench also produced plays at the Haymarket Theatre, among them *King Lear* and, with notable success, Maeterlinck's *Blue Bird* (Preface, pp.viii ix).

9. *First Visit to England*, p.34.

10.(i) The hero fights a boar, in both poems. See *VF*, p.55, and *Deirdre Wed*, p.38.

(ii) In both poems, the aged, thwarted lover is a curious mixture of senile impotence and sinister treachery. In Clarke's poem:

> Fionn laughed bitterly
> And stared in darkness at the grassy ground
> Unseeing, for his mind groped to his dead love

And towards the past his heart, a hungered hound,
Strained at the leash.
(*VF*, 8)

And in Trench's poem, Connachar:

Consummate lord of fear,
Our never counselled lord, the Forest-odoured,
That kept about his heart a zone full of chill
Smiled, though within the gateway of his fort
A surmise crept, as 'neath a load of rushes
Creeps in the stabber.
(*Deirdre Wed*, 12)

11. *Poetry in Modern Ireland* (Dublin: At the Sign of the Tree Candles, 1951), p.8.

12. *Poetry in Modern Ireland*, p.8.

13. *The Fires of Baal* (Dublin and London: Maunsel & Roberts, 1921), p.31. All quotations from this poem are from this edition, which will be referred to as *FB* after the quotations. Page numbers will be given in brackets.

14. Yeats and AE were interested in Eastern thought and mysticism, but not to such an extent that thought and mysticism dominate their work, or even form an important part of it. Only in the late work of James Stephens can this influence be said to be important; Stephens, under the influence of Madame Blavatsky, turned late in life to the philosophers of India.

15. *The Sword of the West* (Dublin and London: Maunsel & Roberts, 1921), Foreword, no page number given. All quotations from this poem are from this edition, which will be referred to as *SW* after the quotations. Page numbers will be given in brackets.

16. *The Irish Digest*, November 1963, p.88.

17. See, for example, *The Death of Cuchulain*, edited and translated by Whitley Stokes, *Revue Celtique* 3, pp.175-85. This is abridged from the *Book of Leinster*, ff.77, a. 1-78 b. 2.

18. W.B. Yeats, *Collected Plays* (London: Macmillan, 1952), p.278.

19. *The Cattledrive in Connaught and Other Poems* (London: George Allen & Unwin, 1925), p.64. All quotations from this poem are from this edition, which will be referred to as *CC* after the quotations. Page numbers will be given in brackets.

20. See *Táin Bó Cuailgne*, translated by Joseph Dunn (London: David Nutt, 1914).

21. *The Collected Poems of Austin Clarke* (London: George Allen & Unwin, 1936), p.57.

22. Introduction to *Collected Poems*, p.47.

23. *Flight to Africa* (Dublin: Dolmen Press, 1963), p.122.

24. *The Irish Times*, 18 January 1964.

Satire in Flann O'Brien's *The Poor Mouth* (pages 182-188)

First published as 'An Béal Bocht: Myles na gCopaleen (1911-1966)', *The Pleasures of Gaelic Literature*, edited by John Jordan (Cork and Dublin: Mercier Press, and RTE, Dublin, 1977), pp.85-96.

1. The Irish title is *An Béal Bocht* (1941). In Kennelly's original, the quotations are in Irish. However, in this essay the English title and quotations in English will be used.

2. One of the Irish names the writer used was Myles na gCopaleen, but here
his most frequently used English name will be referred to.
3. *The Poor Mouth*, translated by Patrick C. Power (London: Paladin Books,
1989), p.22. All quotations from O'Brien's novel are from this edition. Page
numbers will be given in brackets after the quotations. In Irish, it reads: 'Le
linn m'óige-se, bhíodh drochbholadh sa tigh i gcónaí againn. Uaireanta bhí sé
chomh dona sin gur iarras ar mo mháthair, sula raibh aon tsiúl ceart ionam,
mé chur amach chun na scoile. Daoine a bheadh ag gabháil thar bhráid, ní
dheinidís fuireach ná siúl féin agus iad i ngiorracht ár dtí-ne ach rása reatha
thar bhéal an dorais agus gan aon staonadh ón rith go mbeidís leathmhíle slí
imithe ón mbréantas. Teach eile a bhí dhá chéad slat do bhóthar uainn ghlan
an mhuintir a bhí ann amach as lá amháin nuair bhí an boladh go ró-olc againn,
thug aghaidh ar an Oileán Úr agus níor fhill as ó shin. Bhí sé ráite go ndúradar
le muintir na háite thall gur bhreá an tír í Éire acht go raibh an t-aer go láidir
ann. Faraoir, ní raibh aon aer riamh sa tigh againne.'
4. In Irish: 'B'ait an mhuc é Ambrós agus ní dóigh liom go mbeadh a leithéid
arís ann. Slán go raibh sé más in aon tsaol eile beo inniu dó.'
5. In Irish: ' "A Ghaela," adúirt sé, "cuireann sé gliondar ar mo chroí Gaelach
a bheith anseo inniu ag caint Ghaeilge libhse ar an fheis Ghaelach seo i lár na
Gaeltachta. Ní miste dom a rá gur Gael mise. Táim Gaelach ó m' bhathais
go bonn mo choise – Gaelach thoir, thiar, thuas agus thíos. Tá sibhse go léir
fíorGhaelach mar an gcéanna. Gaeil Ghaelacha de shliocht Ghaelach is ea an
t-iomlán againn. An té atá Gaelach, beidh sé Gaelach feasta. Níor labhair mise
(ach oiread libh féin) aon fhocal ach Gaeilge ón lá rugadh mé agus, rud eile,
is fán nGaeilge amháin a bhí gach abairt dár ndúras riamh. Má táimid fíor-
Ghaelach, ní foláir dúinn bheith ag plé ceist na Gaeilge agus ceist an Ghael-
achais le chéile i gcónaí. Ní haon mhaitheas Gaeilge bheith againn má bhíonn
ár gcomhrá sa teanga sin ar neithe neamhGhaelacha. An té a bhíonn ag caint
Gaeilge ach gan a bheith ag plé ceist na teanga, níl sé fíorGhaelach ina chroí
istigh ní haon tairbhe don Ghaelachas a leithéid sin mar gur ag magadh faoin
Ghaeilge a bhíonn sé agus ag tabhairt masla do Ghaelaibh. Níl aon ní ar an
domhan chomh deas nó chomh deas nó chomh Gaelach le fíorGhaeil fíor-
Ghaelacha a bhíonn ag caint fíorGhaeilge Gaelaí i dtaobh na Gaeilge fíorGhaelaí.
Fógraím an fheis seo anois ar Ghaeloscailt! Na Gaeil abú! Go maire ár nGaeilge
slán!"
'Nuair a shuí an Gael uasal seo síos ar a thóin Ghaelach, d'éirigh clampar
mór agus bualadh bos ar fud an chruinnithe.'
6. In Irish: 'Ní go ró-bhinn a d'éirigh liom más ininste an fhírinne lom.
D'imigh na céadfaithe ar seachrán, is follus. Thit an lug ar an lag orm, thit
lug eile ar an lug sin agus níorbh fhada go raibh na luganna ag titim go tiugh
ar an chéad lag agus orm féin. Ansin thit cith laganna ar na luganna, luganna
troma ar na laganna ina dhiaidh sin agus i ndeireadh báire tháinig lug amháin
mór donn anuas ar mhullach gach ní eile, ag cur múchta ar an solas agus ag
cur stop le réim an tsaoil. Níor mhothaíos aon ní eile go cionn i bhfad, ní
fhaca aon ní agus ní chuala fuaim ar bith. Is i ngan fhios dom a lean an domhan
ag casadh ar a bhealach in aird na formaiminte. Bhí sé seachtain sular bhraith-
eas go raibh bíogadh na beatha fós ionam agus bhí coicís eile ann sula rabhas
lánchinnte go raibh mé beo. Chuaigh leathbhliain thart sula raibh éirithe aniar
ar fad agam as an easláinte a bhronn obair na hoíche sin orm, Dia ag déanamh
grása orainn go léir. An dara lá feise níor airíos.'
7. In Irish: 'Bhí fear ar an mbaile seo uair agus Sitric Ó Sánasa a bhí mar

ainm air go fírinneach. Bhí togha na seilge aige, croí na féile agus gach deá-
thréith eile ar a mbíonn moladh agus urraim le fáil i gcónaí. Ach faraoir, bhí
iomrá eile amuigh air nach raibh maith ná rafar. Bhí scoth an bhochtanais, an
ocrais agus na hanacra aige freisin. Bhí sé fial flaithiúil agus ní raibh an ruidín
ba lua dá raibh riamh aige gan roinnt ar a chomharsana: ina dhiaidh sin, ní
cuimhin liom le m'linn féin aon rud beag dá laghad aige ar a sheilbh féin, fiu
amháin oiread beagphrátaí is bhí riachtanach le hanam agus corp a choimeád
i bhfastó ar a chéile. I gCorca Dorcha, mar a raibh gach sampla daonna beo
bocht, bhí seisean i gcónaí againn mar ábhar déirce agus atrua. Daoine uaisle
a tháinic i mótors ó Bhaile Átha Cliath ag breathnú na mbochtán, mholadar
go hard é as ucht a bhocthanais Ghaelaí agus dúradar nach bhfacadar éinne
riamh ar a raibh dealramh chomh fíorGhaelach. Buidéal beag uisce a bhí ag
Ó Sánasa uair, bhris duine uasal é de bhrí, mar dúirt sé gur *spile* sé an *effect*.
Ní raibh duine beo i nÉirinn inchurtha le Ó Sánasa ar fheabhas a bhochtanais
agus iomad na gorta a bhí breactha ina phearsain. Ní raibh muc ná cupán ná
aon rothaí-tí aige. Is minic a chonnac é sa dubhluachair amuigh ar thaobh an
chnoic ag troid agus ag coraíocht le mada fánach, cnámh caol crua eatarthu
mar dhuais san iomathóireacht, an sranfach agus an tafann conafach céanna
ag teacht uathu araon. Ní raibh aon bhothán aige ach chomh beag, ná taithí
ceart ar fhoscadh ná teas cistine. Bhí poll tochailte aige lena dhá láimh i lár na
tíre agus ar bhéal an phoill chuireadh sé seanshacanna agus craobhacha crainn
nó rud ar bith eile a bheadh úsáideach mar dhíon ar an bhraon a bhíodh anuas
ar an dúiche gach oíche. Daoine iasachta a bheadh ag gabháil thar bhráid,
cheapadh siad gur broc a bhí i dtalamh san am a bhraithidís an t-anáil trom
ag teach ó thóin an phoill, agus féachaint fhiánta ar an áitreabh go hiomlán.'

The Little Monasteries: Frank O'Connor as Poet (pages 189-197)

First published as 'Little Monasteries', *Michael/Frank: Studies on Frank
O'Connor: With a Bibliography of His Writing*, edited by Maurice Sheehy
(Dublin: Gill and Macmillan, 1969), pp.103-13.

   1. Frank O'Connor, *Kings, Lords, & Commons: An Anthology from the Irish*
(New York: Alfred A. Knopf, 1959; republished by Dublin: Gill and Macmillan,
1991), p.141.
   2. *Kings, Lords, & Commons*, pp.144-45.
   3. *The Little Monasteries* (Dublin: Dolmen Press, and London: Oxford
University Press, 1963), p.7. All quotations from O'Connor's poetry are taken
from this edition. Page numbers will be given in brackets after the quotations.
   4. *The Kilkenny Magazine*, Spring 1962.

Liam O'Flaherty: The Unchained Storm *(pages 198-208)*

First published as 'Liam O'Flaherty: The Unchained Storm. A View of His
Short Stories', *The Irish Short Story*, edited by Terence Brown and Patrick
Rafroidi (Gerrards Cross, Bucks: Colin Smythe, and Atlantic Highlands, N.J.:
Humanities Press, 1979), pp.175-87.

   1. *The Stories of Liam O'Flaherty* (New York: Devin-Adair, 1956). All quotations from O'Flaherty's short stories, unless otherwise indicated, are from
this edition, which will be referred to as *SLO* after the quotations. Page
numbers will be given in brackets.

2. *The Irish Statesman*, 18 October 1924, p.171.
3. *Irish Portraits: 14 Stories by Liam O'Flaherty* (London: Sphere Books, 1970). This edition will be referred to as *IP* after the quotations. Page numbers will be given in brackets.
4. *The Pedlar's Revenge and Other Stories* (Dublin: Wolfhound Press, 1976), p.80. This edition will be referred to as *PR* after the quotations. Page numbers will be given in brackets.
5. *A Tourist's Guide to Ireland* (London: Mandrake Press, 1929), pp.55-56.
6. *A Tourist's Guide to Ireland*, pp.99-100.

Sean O'Casey's Journey into Joy *(pages 209-216)*

First published as 'Journey into Joy' in *The O'Casey Enigma: The Thomas Davis Lectures*, edited by Micheál O hAodha (Cork and Dublin: Mercier Press, and RTE, Dublin, 1980), pp.98-111.

1. W.B. Yeats, 'The Gyres', *Collected Poems* (London: Macmillan, 1958), p.337.
2. *Collected Poems*, p.338.
3. Patrick Kavanagh, *Collected Poems* (London: MacGibbon & Kee, 1964), pp.131-32.
4. 'The Green Crow Caws', *Under a Colored Cap: Articles Merry and Mournful with Comments and a Song* (London: Macmillan, 1963), p.89.
5. 'The Green Crow Caws', pp.75-76.
6. 'The Lark in the Clear Air Still Sings', *Under a Colored Cap*, p.134.
7. 'The Lark in the Clear Air Still Sings', p.141.
8. 'The Lark in the Clear Air Still Sings', p.136.
9. 'The Lark in the Clear Air Still Sings', p.140.
10. 'The People and the Theatre', *Under a Colored Cap*, p.213.
11. 'The Green Crow Caws', p.94.
12. 'The Green Crow Caws', p.97.
13. *Within the Gates* (London: Macmillan, 1933), Scene III, p.109. [See also *Collected Plays, Vol. II* (London: Macmillan, 1968)].
14. *Within the Gates*, p.107.
15. 'The Green Crow Caws', p.81.
16. 'The Green Crow Caws', pp.68-71, and 'The Lark in the Clear Air Still Sings', p.137.
17. 'Immanuel', *Under a Colored Cap*, p.186.
18. 'Purple Dust in Their Eyes', *Under a Colored Cap*, p.263.
19. 'And Evening Star', *Sunset and Evening Star*; for example, *Autobiographies, Vol. II* (London: Macmillan, 1981), p.665. *Sunset and Evening Star* first published in 1954.

James Joyce's Humanism *(pages 217-230)*

First published as 'Joyce's Humanism', *The Artist and the Labyrinth: A Critical Re-evaluation*, edited by Augustine Martin (London: Ryan Publishing, 1990), pp.313-32.

1. W.B. Yeats, from notes for an unpublished lecture on 'Contemporary Poetry' (1910), quoted in Richard Ellmann's *Yeats: The Man and the Masks* (Oxford: Oxford University Press, 1979; first published in 1948), p.5.
2. W.B. Yeats, *Collected Poems* (London: Macmillan, 1958), p.278.

3. 'Recollections of Joyce', *Portraits of the Artist in Exile: Recollections of James Joyce by Europeans*, edited by Willard Potts (Dublin: Wolfhound Press, and Seattle: University of Washington Press, 1979), p.40. This volume will be referred to as *PAE* after the quotations. Page numbers will be given in brackets. For publication history of the essays quoted, see Potts's 'Acknowledgements'.

4. Simone Weil, 'The Pythagorean Doctrine', *Intimations of Christianity Among the Ancient Greeks* (London and New York: Ark Paperbacks, 1987), pp.180, 184.

5. 'A Painful Case', *Dubliners* (Harmondsworth: Penguin Books, 1976), p.117.

6. Ernst R. Curtius, 'Technique and Thematic Development of James Joyce', *Neue Schweizer Rundschau*, January, 1929, translated by Eugene Jolas in *transition*, Nos. 16-17, June 1929, pp.310-25. Reprinted in parts in *James Joyce: The Critical Heritage, Vol. II*, edited by Robert H. Deming (London: Routledge & Kegan Paul, 1970), pp.466-70 [p.469].

7. W.B. Yeats, 'A General Introduction for My Work', *Essays and Introductions* (London: Macmillan, 1961), p.509.

8. 'Signposts', *Collected Prose* (London: MacGibbon and Kee, 1964), p.27.

9. Patrick Kavanagh, *Collected Poems* (London: MacGibbon & Kee, 1964), p.123.

10. Brenda Maddox, *Nora: A Biography of Nora Joyce* (London: Hamish Hamilton, 1988).

11. 'A Little Cloud', *Dubliners*, p.85.

12. Padraic O'Laoi, *Nora Barnacle Joyce: A Portrait* (Galway: Kennys Bookshops and Art Galleries, 1982), pp.47-48.

13. Stanislaus Joyce, diary quoted in 'Introduction' to *My Brother's Keeper* (London. Faber and Faber, 1958), pp.xiii-xiv. See also Richard Ellmann, *James Joyce* (New and Revised Edition) (New York: Oxford University Press, 1982), p.137.

14. T. S. Eliot, *Four Quartets, Complete Poems and Plays* (London: Faber and Faber, 1978), p.172.

15. *Ulysses* (Harmondsworth: Penguin Books, 1982) [The Bodley Head Ltd edition from 1960], pp.168-69.

16. *Ulysses*, p.170.

17. *Ulysses*, p.170.

18. *Ulysses*, p.170.

19. *Pomes for James Joyce*, collected by Bernard Bernstock (Naas: Malton Press, no year given), pp.41-42.

W.B. Yeats: An Experiment in Living *(pages 231-247)*

Previously unpublished; written for this volume.

1. 'The Choice', *Collected Poems* (London: Macmillan, 1958), p.278. All quotations from Yeats's poetry are from this edition, unless otherwise indicated. Page numbers will be given in brackets after the quotation.

2. For example, *The Poems of William Blake*, edited by W.B. Yeats (London: Lawrence & Bullen, and New York: Scribner, 1893); see also 'William Blake and the Imagination', and 'William Blake and His Illustrations to the Divine Comedy', both essays in 'Ideas of Good and Evil', *Essays and Introductions* (London: Macmillan, 1961).

3. 'The Hermetic Order of the Golden Dawn' (or 'The Hermetic Students

of the Golden Dawn'). Founded in late 1880s by three occult students, the most enthusiastic of whom was McGregor Mathers. Yeats joined in 1890, and parallel to his writing, the ideals and conduct of the order remained the poet's central interest. For further information, see, for example, George Mills Harper's *Yeats's Golden Dawn* (London: Macmillan, 1974), and Graham Hough's *The Mystery Religion of W.B. Yeats* (Brighton: Harvester Press, and Totowa, N.J.: Barnes & Noble Books, 1984).

4. Hart Crane, *Complete Poems*, edited by Brom Weber (Newcastle upon Tyne: Bloodaxe Books, 1987). *The Bridge* first appeared in 1930.

5 .For example, the poet's comments in 'Ireland after Parnell', and 'The Tragic Generation', *The Trembling of the Veil, Autobiographies* (London: Macmillan, 1966), pp.246-47 and 291.

6. From notes for an unpublished lecture on 'Contemporary Poetry' (1910), quoted in Richard Ellmann's *Yeats: The Man and the Masks* (Oxford: Oxford University Press, 1979; first published in 1948), p.6.

7. *Essays and Introductions*, p.509.

8. See note 6; *The Man and the Masks*, p.5.

9. James Joyce, 'Letter to Grant Richards, 5 May 1906', *Selected Letters of James Joyce*, edited by Richard Ellmann (London: Faber and Faber, 1975), p.83.

10. Emmanuel Swedenborg (1688-1772). Swedish philosopher, scientist, theologian, visionary, who devoted the first part of his life to science, the latter to the study of sacred scriptures and to the exposition of his spirtual communion. For further information on his influence on Yeats, see, for example, Harbans Rai Bachchan's *W.B. Yeats and Occultism* (Delhi: Motilal Banarsidass, 1965).

11. '8 August, 1910', *Reflections by W.B. Yeats*, transcribed and edited by Curtis Bradford from the *Journals* (Dublin: Cuala Press, 1970), p.42.

12. 'Anima Hominis', *Per Amica Silentia Lunae. Mythologies* (London: Macmillan, 1962), p.334.

13. Untitled, *The Poems: A New Edition*, edited by Richard J. Finneran (London: Macmillan, 1983), p.548. The poem first appeared as an epitaph in *Collected Works, Vol. II* (Stratford-upon-Avon: Stratford Head Press, 1908), no page number given.

14. 'Magic', 'Ideas of Good and Evil', *Essays and Introductions*, p.28.

15. 'Anima Hominis', *Per Amica Silentia Lunae*, p.332.

16. *Some Letters from W.B. Yeats to John O'Leary and His Sister*, edited by Allan Wade (New York: New York Public Library, 1953; New York: Macmillan, 1955), p.14.

17. *The Letters of W.B. Yeats*, edited by Allan Wade (London: Rupert Hart-Davis, 1954), p.921.

18. 'Ribh considers Christian Love insufficient', p.330.

19. 'Crazy Jane Grown Old Looks at the Dancers', pp.295-96.

20. 'The Tower', p.224.

21. 'Magic', *Essays and Introductions*, p.28.

22. Patrick Kavanagh, 'Three Favourite Books', *Collected Pruse* (London: MacGibbon and Kee, 1967), p.265.

23. 'Easter, 1916', p.203.

24. 'Sailing to Byzantium', p.217.

25. 'The Tower', p.218.

26. 'The Tower', p.218.

27. 'A Symbolic Artist and the Coming of Symbolic Art', *The Dome*, December 1898. Reprinted in *Uncollected Prose, Vol. 2: Reviews, Articles and*

Other Miscellaneous Prose 1897-1939, edited by John P. Frayne and Colton Johnson (London: Macmillan, 1975); and in *Memoirs*, edited by Denis Donoghue (London: Macmillan Papermac, 1988).

28. 'Magic', *Essays and Introductions*, p.28.

29. *Autobiographies*, pp.25-26.

30. *The Death of Cuchulain* (1939), *Collected Plays* (London: Macmillan, 1952), p.698.

31. Henrik Ibsen, 'Epilogue', *Lyrical Poems*, selected and translated by R.A. Streatfield (London: Elkin Mathews, 1902), p.38.

32. 'Four Years: 1887-1891', *The Trembling of the Veil: Autobiographies*, p.189.

33. 'The Gyres', p.337.

34. 'Nineteen Hundred and Nineteen', p.236.

35. For example, 'To Be Carved on a Stone at Thor Ballylee', p.214, and 'A Crazed Girl', p.349.

36. Mathers translated it from *Kabbala Denudata* (1684) by Knorr von Rosenroth.

37. 'Hodos Chameliontos', *The Trembling of the Veil: Autobiographies*, p.272.

38. 'Hodos Chameliontos', p.272.

39. 'Under Ben Bulben', p.400.

ACKNOWLEDGEMENTS

The author and publisher are grateful for permission to the following for permission to reprint copyright material:

Dardis Clarke: for work by Austin Clarke.
Faber and Faber Ltd: for extracts from *All That Fall* (1957) by Samuel Beckett, and from *Collected Poems* (1966) by Louis MacNeice
Gallery Press: for 'Claudy' by James Simmons from *Poems 1956-1986* (Gallery Press/Bloodaxe Books, 1986); for extracts from *Selected Poems* by Derek Mahon (Gallery Press/Viking, 1991).
HarperCollins: for extracts from *The Poor Mouth* by Flann O'Brien, translated by Patrick C. Power
Estate of Patrick Kavanagh: c/o Peter Fallon, The Gallery Press, Loughcrew, Oldcastle, Co. Meath, for extracts from *Collected Poems* and *Collected Pruse*.
Pan Macmillan: for extracts from *The Silver Tassie* and other work by Seán O'Casey.
Oxford University Press for extracts from *The Little Monasteries* by Frank O'Connor (Dolmen Press/Oxford University Press, 1963).
Peters, Fraser and Dunlop: for work by Liam O'Flaherty; and for 'Wounds' by Michael Longley from *Poems 1963-1983* (Secker & Warburg).
Tessa Sayle Agency: for extracts from *The Quare Fellow* by Brendan Behan (Eyre Methuen, 1957).
Colin Smythe Limited: for extract from *The Old Lady Says 'No!'* by Denis Johnston from *Collected Plays* (Colin Smythe, 1977).
The Society of Authors: as the literary representative of the George Bernard Shaw Estate for extracts from *John Bull's Other Island*; as the literary representative of the Estate of James Stephens for 'The Red-Haired Man's Wife'.

INDEX